THE PENGUIN CLASSICS

FOUNDER EDITOR (1944–64): E. V. RIEU

PRESENT EDITORS
Betty Radice and Robert Baldick

L7

XENOPHON

THE PERSIAN EXPEDITION

TRANSLATED BY
REX WARNER

PENGUIN BOOKS
BALTIMORE · MARYLAND

Penguin Books Ltd, Harmondsworth, Middlesex, England
Penguin Books Inc, 3300 Clipper Mill Road, Baltimore 11, Md, U.S.A.
Penguin Books Pty Ltd, Ringwood, Victoria, Australia

First published 1949
Reprinted 1951, 1952, 1957, 1961, 1965

CONTENTS

CONTENTS

INTRODUCTION

ALTHOUGH Xenophon's story of the march into Persia and the march back again into Greece is intelligible enough as it stands, and interesting enough simply as a record of adventure and military skill and the different characters of men, a reader will enjoy the story more if he has some knowledge of the historical background.

The period is the beginning of the fourth century B.C. Xenophon, a young Athenian, had seen his own city, a city which was still the centre of Greek culture, and had lately been the greatest imperial power in the Mediterranean, totally defeated in war at the hands of Sparta and her allies. The confidence and ease and scope of the days of Pericles had gone for ever. Indeed to many Athenians, including Xenophon himself, the old ideal of total democracy, combined as it had been with imperialism, was discredited utterly. The faults had been too patent, and the next age was to be the age of the individual, the expert and the leader. It was a period full of contradictions. On the one hand there was, partly as a legacy from the long war, an extraordinary confusion of thought. The fundamentals of morality, patriotism and religion were shaken. Yet in this turmoil of disillusion and scepticism were being laid the foundations of European thought by Socrates, Plato and Aristotle. Though the internecine rivalries between the Greek states continued as before, more and more thinkers began to deplore this internal weakness, to advocate the unity of Hellenism and to realise that even complete local autonomy could be paid for at too high a price. They observed that while Athens and Sparta had been wearing themselves out in a death-grapple, Greece as a whole had suffered almost irreparably, and that from such a state of affairs only the great continental empire of Persia stood to gain. Could not the Greeks unite again as they had done in the great days of old when they defeated the might of the East at Marathon, Salamis and Plataea?

Those who, at the beginning of the fourth century, thought along these lines looked inevitably to Sparta for the necessary leadership. Sparta was supreme. Her governors ruled absolutely in states that had formerly been the subjects and allies of Athens. Decisive victory had made her the unchallenged arbiter of Greece. It was a tremendous opportunity, and Sparta failed almost wholly to take advantage of it. The unification of Greece and the great conquest of the east was to be the achievement of the semi-barbarian state of Macedon, under its Kings Philip and Alexander. Yet, in Xenophon's youth, no one could have guessed at so unlikely a future. Xenophon could only see the facts of Athenian collapse and Spartan supremacy. He was a pro-Spartan, as were several others of the Athenians who had come under the influence of Socrates, admiring Spartan discipline and the aristocratic ideal, ambitious himself and knowing that he could not achieve his ambitions in opposition to Sparta. In the end he was exiled from Athens and spent the last years of his life on a country estate given to him by the Spartans, hunting, writing and recalling in his books the great days of the Persian expedition, his ideals of kingliness, as exemplified by Cyrus, his respect for all soldierly qualities and (surprisingly enough) his admiration for Socrates, and not only for Socrates' piety but for his intellectual dexterity. For Xenophon, in spite of his pro-Spartan feelings, was a real Athenian. One has only to read one of his speeches to the army of mercenaries to notice his humour, his delight in an exact analysis of a situation, his sensitive understanding of men – all qualities in which the Spartans were notoriously deficient.

How far he was disappointed by the record of Spartan

oppression in Greek cities and irresolution abroad we do not know. There is no doubt that the average Spartan governor must have fallen far short of Xenophon's ideal ruler, who should be not only powerful but courteous, not only strong but honest. This ideal he found in the character of Cyrus, the pretender to the Persian throne, who certainly seems to have possessed the qualities required to fire the imagination of a young man, a pupil of Socrates, disillusioned with 'politics', an admirer of the heroic, and ambitious for distinction. More-over, the very size of the Persian empire, sprawling from India to Egypt, from the Caucasus to the Persian Gulf, impressed him with a sense of grandeur. Indeed, if he were not an Athenian, one would be tempted to say that his ideas about the Persians were sentimental. Maybe he was blinded by the partiality for hunting which he shared with them. In any case, though he had personal knowledge of the treachery of Tissaphernes and must have known that the recent history of the Persian dynasty had been a record of murder and women's rule behind the scenes, he still emphasised only the Persian sense of honour, Persian loyalty, and the qualities of kingliness. His account of the character of Cyrus sums up his ideals.

Cyrus certainly possessed the ability with which Xenophon credits him. The younger brother of King Artaxerxes, and the favourite son of his mother Parysatis, he was notable for his interest in the Greeks and for his appreciation of the fact that the Greek hoplite (or heavy-armed foot-soldier) was the best infantryman in the world. The peltasts (or light-armed foot-soldiers), acting in co-operation with the line of hop-lites, were a new factor in Greek armies and, as a result of the long war in Greece, had been brought to a high state of efficiency. Cyrus calculated that, with a strong Greek con-tingent in his native army, and by striking quickly and unexpectedly, he stood a good chance of gaining the throne of his brother, whose resources in man power were far greater than anything which Cyrus could bring against him. Cyrus very nearly succeeded. Scholars differ in their estimates of what exactly happened at the battle of Cunaxa, but it is clear, at least, that the Greek army totally defeated the Persian troops opposed to it, and that there was a moment when this local success might have been turned into a victory all along the line. It is clear also that in all the subsequent engagements no infantry could be found capable of standing up in pitched battle with the Greek phalanx. On the other hand, the Greeks, and Cyrus's army generally, were weak in cavalry. This is a weakness which Xenophon recognises, and did his best to amend. But it was not till the days of Alexander that a properly balanced Greek force took the field against Persia. As for Xenophon and Chirisophus, with their ridiculous force of fifty cavalrymen, the perils of a march through Persia were enormous. Their infantry was invincible in pitched battle, but it had to have supplies and it would be harassed and surrounded on the march. Mesopotamia has often seen the rout of splendid infantry armies by more mobile and more numerous assailants. To bring back the ten thousand from Babylon to the Black Sea as an intact fighting force was, in itself, a remarkable military achievement.

Yet the record of this, one of the most famous marches in history, is not the only or the greatest merit of Xenophon's book. Unlike most of classical literature, this is an account or the day-to-day life of ordinary men and soldiers. We see here how Greek theories of government and morality worked out in practice. While danger threatened, they worked out remarkably well. It would appear that the best men were elected to responsible positions, and that the rank and file gave ungrudging obedience to them. With the removal of danger, things usually fell apart. Local rivalries began to make themselves felt and good sense only re-established itself after a defeat or the risk of one. It was an army drawn from all over

Greece, though the majority of its men came from the Peloponnesian states of Arcadia and Achaea, and all through the army persisted not only the consciousness of a common nationality but a strong local patriotism and a fierce feeling for each man's rights as an individual. Of some of these individuals we receive a distinct impression from Xenophon's work, of Agasias, for instance, the Stymphalian captain who risked the anger of a Spartan governor rather than see one of his own men arrested by an officer whom he knew to be a coward; of the tough Spartan soldier Dracontius, exiled a long time ago for an accidental homicide, and of others. With all his admiration for the great, Xenophon has a rare touch in describing and understanding the outlook of lesser men, and it was not for nothing that he was reproached with being 'too fond of the ordinary soldier'. His own fortunes, too, are intensely moving. With what a combination of modesty and pride does he seize the initiative after the murder of his friend Proxenus and the other generals! What brilliant speeches he makes! What skill he shows, and how reluctantly does he decline the supreme command! Perhaps his great dream was to found a city in the Black Sea area, and then, disappointed in this, he suddenly finds himself master of Byzantium, and very sensibly refuses to accept what is thrust upon him. Just before his return he is so poor that he has to sell his horse, and then a quick act of brigandage sets him up for life. Cool, calculating, brilliant and intensely pious, he is one of the most fascinating characters of history, and his account of his own doings is so far from being self-conscious that he seems to us one of the very few Greeks of whose ways and manners we have a really adequate idea. A writer in the *Cambridge Ancient History*, no doubt pursuing the fashionable and dreary task of 'debunking' the great, may, without producing one shred of evidence in support of his views, disparage Xenophon's ability and sneer at his achievements. Yet the very brilliance of what was undoubtedly achieved would seem to demand ability of a high order, and, so far as Xenophon's own narrative goes, it can stand on its own feet.

A word should be said about some points connected with the translation. I have attempted to use as many English words and as few Greek and Persian words as possible; consequently I have, for example, got rid of the 'parasang', so familiar to beginners in Greek, and turned it, rather inaccurately, into miles. The fact is that the distance represented by a parasang differs in accordance with the nature of the country over which one is marching, so it is impossible to give an exact measurement that would not be insupportably cumbrous for each day's march. I have kept the Greek words 'hoplite' and 'peltast' since their sound seems to me so much a part of the narrative. The following is a list of some other words in the text which seem to have no exact English equivalent or whose retention appears justified for other reasons:

Bulimia – the Greek word for what is apparently a state of exhaustion caused by cold and lack of food.

Daric – a Persian gold coin called after Darius (cf. a Louis or a Napoleon) and worth about a guinea.

Ephor – five magistrates at Sparta were called "ephors" or "overseers", and had greater powers even than the kings.

Hoplite – heavy-armed infantryman.

Mina – a sum of money equal to about £4 (pl. *minae*).

Magadis – a sort of pipe with a shrill, strong sound.

Obol – a coin worth about $1\frac{1}{2}$d.

Peltast – lightly-armed infantryman.

Perioikos – a free citizen of a town in Spartan territory.

Stater – a gold coin. The stater of Cyzicus was worth rather over £1.

Talent – a weight of silver equal to about £244.

R. W.

Athens, 1946

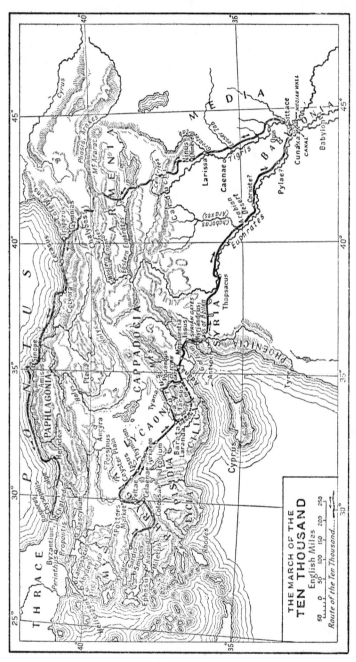

THE MARCH OF THE
TEN THOUSAND
English Miles
50 0 50 100 150 200 250
Route of the Ten Thousand

Reproduced from Bury's *History of Greece* by courtesy of Macmillan & Co. Ltd, London

BOOK

I

THE ATTEMPT
OF CYRUS

Chapter 1

CYRUS BUILDS UP HIS ARMY

DARIUS and Parysatis had two sons. Artaxerxes was the elder of the two and Cyrus was the younger. When Darius was growing feeble and began to suspect that he had not long to live, he wanted both his sons to be at hand. The elder one happened to be there, but he had to send for Cyrus from the province of which he had made him Satrap. (He had also appointed him Commander-in-Chief over all the troops that muster in the plain of Castolus.)

Cyrus, then, travelled up to the capital with Tissaphernes, whom he regarded as a friend, taking with him three hundred Greek hoplites under the command of Xenias of Parrhasia. But, after the death of Darius, when Artaxerxes was established on the throne, Tissaphernes maligned Cyrus to his brother and accused him of plotting against him. Artaxerxes believed the story and arrested Cyrus with the intention of putting him to death; but his mother by her entreaties secured his life and his recall to his province. Still, after the danger and disgrace from which he had escaped, Cyrus took measures to ensure that he should never again be in his brother's power; instead, if he could manage it, he would become king in his brother's place. His mother Parysatis was on his side, as she was fonder of him than of the reigning king, Artaxerxes. And he used his influence on those who came to him from the Court to such effect that, when they returned, they were more friendly to him than to the King. He gave his attention also to the natives in his district, seeing to it that they were in a fit state for a campaign and well-disposed to him. He got together his Greek troops with the utmost secrecy, wishing to take the King as far as possible off his guard.

This was the way in which he collected his army. He sent orders to the commanders of his garrisons in the various cities to enrol troops from the Peloponnese, as many as possible and the best available, ostensibly on the ground that Tissaphernes was contemplating action against the cities. And in point of fact the cities of Ionia had originally belonged to Tissaphernes, since they had been given to him by the King, but at this time they had all gone over to Cyrus, except for Miletus. In Miletus Tissaphernes had got wind of a plot to follow the other states in going over to Cyrus, and he had put to death some of the conspirators and exiled others. Cyrus received the exiles, got together an army, blockaded Miletus by land and sea, and attempted to restore the banished party. He used this as yet another pretext for raising an army, and he sent to the King asking that, as he was his brother, the cities should be handed over to him instead of being governed by Tissaphernes His mother did her part too. As a result the King had no idea of the plot that was on foot against him, but thought that Cyrus was spending his money and raising an army for his war with Tissaphernes, and so, with hostilities going on between these two, he felt no uneasiness, especially as Cyrus regularly sent in to him the tribute from the cities which Tissaphernes used to hold.

Another force was being organised for him in the Chersonese opposite Abydus. This was how it was done. Clearchus the Spartan was an exile. Cyrus met him, was greatly impressed with his abilities and gave him ten thousand darics. Clearchus used the money in raising an army and then, with the Chersonese as his base, made war on the Thracians north of the Hellespont. This was to the advantage of the Greeks, and the result was that more money was contributed to him voluntarily by the cities of the Hellespont for the support of his troops. Here then was another of Cyrus's armies which, maintained in this way, attracted no suspicion.

Then there was Aristippus the Thessalian, a friend of Cyrus, who was in political difficulties at home with the opposing party. He came to Cyrus and asked him for two thousand mercenaries and three months' pay for them, saying that this would enable him to come out on top of his opponents. Cyrus gave him four thousand troops and six months' pay and asked him not to come to any agreement with his opponents without previously consulting him. So in Thessaly another army was being maintained for him without attracting suspicion.

He also sent an order to Proxenus the Boeotian, a friend of his, telling him to come with as many men as possible, as he wished to make an expedition against the Pisidians, who had been causing trouble in his province. And he ordered Sophaenetus the Stymphalian, and Socrates the Achaean, who were also friends of his, to bring as many men as they could, as he was going to make war on Tissaphernes in support of the exiles from Miletus. Sophaenetus and Socrates carried out his instructions.

Chapter 2

THE MARCH FROM SARDIS
TO TARSUS

WHEN he decided that the time had come for the march on
the capital, he pretended that his purpose was to clear out the
Pisidians finally from his district, and, as though they were
his objective, he assembled together both the native and the
Greek contingents of his army. At this point he ordered
Clearchus to report with his whole force, and Aristippus to
come to an agreement with his enemies at home and send
back to him the troops he had. He ordered Xenias the
Arcadian, who had been put in command of his mercenaries
in the cities, to report with all his forces in excess of the
number required to garrison the citadels. He also summoned
those who were besieging Miletus and urged the exiles to join
him in his expedition, promising them that if his campaign
ended in victory he would not rest until he had restored them
to their homes. They agreed cheerfully, for they trusted him,
and they came with their arms to Sardis.

Next Xenias arrived at Sardis with his men from the cities,
about four thousand hoplites; and Proxenus came with about
fifteen hundred hoplites and five hundred light infantry.
Sophaenetus the Stymphalian came with a force of a thousand
hoplites, and Socrates the Achaean with about five hundred
hoplites. Pasion the Megarian had three hundred hoplites and
three hundred peltasts. Socrates and he were from the force
operating against Miletus.

These then reported to Cyrus at Sardis. But when Tissaphernes got to know of it he came to the conclusion that the
force was too large to be designed to fight against the Pisidians,
and he set out to the King as quickly as he could with about

five hundred horsemen. When the King heard from Tissaphernes of Cyrus's army he took measures to meet it.

Cyrus, with those whom I have mentioned, set out from Sardis; and a three days' march through Lydia of sixty-six miles took him to the river Maeander. This is two hundred feet across, and there was a pontoon bridge of seven boats over it. After crossing the river, one day's march of twenty-four miles through Phrygia took him to the large and prosperous inhabited city of Colossae. He stayed there for seven days, and Menon the Thessalian arrived with a thousand hoplites and five hundred peltasts, Dolopes and Ainianes and Olynthians. From there a three days' march of sixty miles took him to Celaenae, a large and prosperous inhabited city in Phrygia. Cyrus had a palace there and a large park full of wild animals which he used to hunt on horseback when he wanted exercise for himself and his horses. The river Maeander runs through the middle of the park, and its springs flow out from the palace. It also flows through the city of Celaenae. The Great King too has a palace at Celaenae in a strong position at the springs of the river Marsyas, underneath the citadel. This river also flows through the city and joins the Maeander. The breadth of the Marsyas is twenty-five feet. Here the story is that Apollo flayed Marsyas, when he had defeated his bid to overcome him in wisdom, and hung the skin up in the cave from which the springs flow out; and so the river is called the Marsyas. Here Xerxes, on his way back from Greece after his defeat, is said to have built both the palace and the citadel of Celaenae.

Cyrus stayed here for thirty days, and Clearchus, the Spartan exile, arrived with a thousand hoplites and eight hundred Thracian peltasts and two hundred Cretan archers. At the same time Sosis the Syracusan appeared with three hundred hoplites, and Sophaenetus the Arcadian with a thousand hoplites. And here Cyrus held a review of the Greeks in his park and took a census of them. The total number came to eleven thousand hoplites, and about two thousand peltasts.

From here a two days' march of thirty miles took him to the inhabited city of Peltae. He stayed there for three days, in the course of which Xenias the Arcadian celebrated the Lycaean festival and organised athletic sports. The prizes were gold crowns, and Cyrus himself watched the sports. From here a two days' march of thirty-six miles took him to Potters' Market, an inhabited city, and the last one before the Mysian border. From here a three days' march of sixty miles took him to Cayster Plain, an inhabited city.

He stayed here for five days, and as more than three months' pay was due to the soldiers, they often went up to his tent and demanded it. He had to keep on putting them off with promises and was obviously upset about it; indeed it was not like Cyrus to hold back pay if he had it. Then Epyaxa, the wife of Syennesis the King of Cilicia, came to visit Cyrus, and it was said that she gave Cyrus a lot of money. In any case it was at this time that Cyrus gave the army four months' pay. The Queen of Cilicia had a bodyguard of Cilicians and Aspendians. It was also said that she and Cyrus slept together.

From here, a two days' march of thirty miles took him to the inhabited city of Thymbrion. By the roadside here there was a fountain which got its name from Midas the King of Phrygia. At this fountain Midas is said to have captured the Satyr by mixing wine with the water. From here a two days' march of thirty miles took him to Tyriaeon, an inhabited city. He stayed there three days, and it is said that the Queen of Cilicia begged him to show her his army. So, as he wanted to provide a show for her, he held a review in the plain of both his Greek and native troops. He ordered the Greeks to fall in and stand in their normal battle order; each officer should see to the order of his own men. So they stood on parade in fours, with Menon and his men on the right wing, Clearchus and his on the left, and the other generals in the centre. Cyrus first of all inspected the native troops, who marched past in bands and also in formation; then he inspected the Greeks, driving in a chariot along their front with the Queen of Cilicia in a covered carriage. They were all wearing bronze helmets, red tunics and greaves, and had their shields uncovered. He rode along the whole parade and then stopped his chariot in front of the centre of the phalanx and sent Pigres, his interpreter, to the Greek generals with the order to make their troops bring their spears to the ready and for the whole phalanx to advance. The generals passed on the order to the soldiers, the trumpet sounded and, with their spears at the ready, they moved forward. Then as the soldiers quickened their pace and shouted, they found that they were actually running towards their tents. All the natives were terrified; the Queen of Cilicia fled in her covered carriage, and the people in the market ran away leaving their stalls behind them, while the Greeks went laughing to their tents. The Queen of Cilicia was amazed when she saw the brilliant show the army made and its discipline; and Cyrus was delighted when he observed the panic which the Greeks caused among the natives.

From here a three days' march of sixty miles took him to Iconium, the last city in Phrygia. He stayed there three days, and then came a five days' march of ninety miles through Lycaonia. This being hostile territory, he handed it over to the Greeks to plunder; and he sent back the Queen of Cilicia from here by the quickest route to her own country, with Menon's soldiers and Menon himself to escort her. Cyrus with the rest advanced through Cappadocia, and a four days' march of seventy-five miles took him to the large and prosperous inhabited city of Dana. He stayed there three days, in the course of which he put to death on the charge of conspiracy a Persian called Megaphernes, who was entitled to wear the

royal purple, and another powerful person among the govern-
ing class.

From here they attempted to cross the frontier into Cilicia.
The pass consisted of a carriage track which was tremendously
steep, impassable for an army if there was any opposition; and
it was reported that Syennesis was guarding the pass from a
position on the heights. Cyrus consequently waited for a day
in the plain. On the next day a messenger arrived with the
news that Syennesis had abandoned the heights after he had
got to know that Menon's army was already across the
mountains in Cilicia, and because he had heard that triremes
under the command of Tamos, some Spartan ships and some
from Cyrus's own fleet, were sailing round the coast from
Ionia towards Cilicia.

In any case Cyrus reached the top of the mountains with
no opposition, and saw the tents where the Cilician garrison
were. He descended from there into a large plain; it was a
beautiful and well-watered place, full of all kinds of trees and
of vines, and produces quantities of sesame and millet and
wheat and barley. High mountains, forming a strong position, and running from sea to sea entirely hem it in. After
coming down the mountains, a four days' march of seventy-
five miles through this plain took him to Tarsus, a large and
prosperous city in Cilicia, in which was the palace of Syennesis,
the King of Cilicia. A river called the Cydnus (two hundred
feet in breadth) runs through the middle of the city. The
inhabitants, apart from the shopkeepers, had abandoned the
city and gone away with Syennesis to a fortified strong position in the mountains. There also remained behind those who
lived by the sea in Soli and Issus.

Epyaxa, the wife of Syennesis, had arrived at Tarsus five
days before Cyrus. Two companies of Menon's army were
lost in crossing the mountains to the plain. According to some
accounts they were cut to pieces by the Cilicians when they

were on a plundering expedition; according to others they had been left in the rear and were unable to find the rest of the army or the right tracks; and so they had wandered about and been destroyed. Whatever the truth, they were a force of a hundred hoplites. When the rest of Menon's troops arrived, they pillaged the city of Tarsus and the royal palace in the city out of anger for the loss of their comrades.

After Cyrus's entry into the city he sent for Syennesis to come to him. Syennesis replied that he had never yet come into the power of anyone stronger than himself, and he maintained his refusal to visit Cyrus on this occasion until his wife persuaded him to go, and he was given a guarantee of safety. Afterwards there was a meeting between them, and Syennesis gave Cyrus a large sum of money for the army, while Cyrus gave him what are considered gifts of honour at the Court – a horse with a golden bit, a golden collar and armlets, a golden scimitar and a Persian robe. He guaranteed that his land should no longer be plundered and promised that his subjects should recover any slaves who had been carried off, if they should come across them anywhere.

Chapter 3

CLEARCHUS DEALS WITH A MUTINY

CYRUS and the army stayed here for twenty days, because the soldiers refused to go any further. They already suspected that they were marching against the King and said that this was not the job for which they had been engaged. At first Clearchus tried to force his own soldiers to go forward, but they threw stones at him and at his baggage animals as soon as they attempted to make a start. Clearchus was very nearly stoned to death on this occasion, but afterwards, having come to the conclusion that he could not get his way by force, he called together a meeting of his own soldiers. First of all he stood still in front of them for a long time, weeping; and they were surprised as they looked on, and kept silent. Then he made the following speech: 'Fellow soldiers, don't be surprised that I am upset by the way things are going. Cyrus became a friend of mine, and when I was in exile from my own land he not only treated me with great respect, but gave me ten thousand darics. When I got the money I did not set it apart for myself, nor did I lay it out on my own pleasures, but I spent it on you. First I made war on the Thracians, and you and I together struck a blow for Greece by driving them out of the Chersonese where they wanted to take away the land from the Greek settlers there. But when Cyrus called for me I set out, taking you with me, with the idea of doing him a good turn, if he wanted my help, in return for all the kindness I have had from him. However, since you are unwilling to march with him I have got to make my choice: I must either throw you over and keep Cyrus's friendship, or else I must break my word to him and go with you. Now whether I am acting rightly or not I do not know, but anyway

I shall choose you and with you I shall endure what has to be. No one shall ever say that I led Greeks into a foreign country and then threw them over and chose to make friends with the natives; no, since you will not obey me, I will follow you and endure what has to be. This is because it is you I think of as being my country and my friends and my allies; when I am with you I think I shall have honour wherever I may be; but apart from you I don't think I shall be able either to do good to a friend or harm to an enemy. So you can make up your minds that I am going to go wherever you go.'

This was what he said, and all the soldiers – not only his own force, but the others as well – applauded him when they heard that he refused to march against the King; and more than two thousand of Xenias's and Pasion's men took their arms and baggage and made their camp near Clearchus. This made Cyrus anxious and unhappy, and he sent for Clearchus. Clearchus would not go, but without the knowledge of the soldiers he sent a messenger to Cyrus and told him to keep up his courage as things would work out all right. He told him to send for him again and then again refused to go. Then he called together his own soldiers and those who had joined him and anyone else who cared to listen, and made the following speech: 'Fellow soldiers, it is obvious that Cyrus's views about us have altered just as ours have about him. For we are no longer his soldiers (how can we be, if we don't march with him?) and he is no longer our employer. However, I know that he thinks that he is being treated wrongly by us, and as a result, even when he sends for me I am unwilling to go to him. This is chiefly from a sense of shame, because I am conscious that I have let him down in every way, but I am also afraid that he may arrest me and punish me for the wrong treatment which he thinks that he has had from me. My view therefore is that this is no time to go to sleep and to neglect our own interests. Instead we must consider

carefully what we ought to do next. Anyway, while we remain here, we must, I think, consider how we can make our
stay as secure as possible; and if it is already decided that we
go away, then we must think how we can go away with the
maximum of security, and how we can get supplies; for without supplies neither a general nor a private is good for anything. The man we have to do with is worth a great deal to
those whom he loves, but he is a most dangerous enemy to
those whom he is against; and the force which he has of
infantry and cavalry and ships is one which every one of us
sees and understands. Indeed in my opinion our camp is none
too far away from him. And so the time has come for people
to say what they think is the best thing to do.'

He paused after saying this, and then some people stood up
of their own accord to say what they thought; but there were
others also who had been put up to it by him, who pointed
out how difficult it was either to stay there or to go away
without Cyrus's consent. One of these made a speech pretending that he was eager to go to Greece as soon as possible.
He told them to elect other generals immediately if Clearchus
would not agree to lead them back, to buy provisions (the
market was in the native camp) and to get together their
luggage; they should go and ask Cyrus for ships so that they
could go away by sea, and if he would not provide the ships
they should ask him for a guide to escort them through
country that was friendly. If he would not even provide a
guide, they should group themselves for battle as quickly as
possible, and also send forward an advance guard to seize the
heights to prevent Cyrus from getting there first, or the
Cilicians, from whom they had seized and still held many
men and large sums of money.

This was the kind of speech he made. Afterwards Clearchus
just said: 'Don't let any of you imagine that I will be your general
in an expedition of this sort. I can see many factors in the

situation which would make this impossible for me. But you can be sure that I shall give the most loyal support to the man you elect to take my place, so that you may know that I can submit to discipline just as well as anybody else.'

Then another man got up and pointed out the absurdity of the speaker who had recommended them to ask Cyrus for ships, as though Cyrus was taking his army back again. 'And how absurd it is,' he said, 'to ask for a guide from the very person who is having his enterprise ruined by us. If we are actually going to trust the guide that Cyrus gives us we might as well ask Cyrus to occupy the heights for us too. I certainly would hesitate to embark on the ships which Cyrus gave us in case he might sink us with his triremes; and I would be afraid of following the guide which he gave us in case he might lead us into a position from which there would be no possibility of escape. If I am to go away against Cyrus's wishes I should like to go away without his knowing of it – which is impossible. But really all this is nonsense. My view is that the right sort of men should go with Clearchus to Cyrus and ask him what he wants to use us for. If the enterprise is more or less of the same kind as other ones in which he has . previously employed mercenaries, then we too ought to go with him and be as brave as those who have served with him in the interior before now. But if it appears that the enterprise is on a bigger scale than previous ones, and will involve more difficulty and danger, then they should ask him that, on a basis of mutual agreement, either he should lead us forward or else should let us go in peace. In this way, if we go with him, we shall go with him on better terms and with greater willingness, and if we leave him, we shall do so safely. Our envoys should report back to us about what he says in reply; and we should take our measures on the basis of what we hear from them.'

This was the course decided upon. They elected delegates

and sent them with Clearchus to put before Cyrus the questions which the army had agreed to ask him. Cyrus replied that he was told that Abrocomas, an enemy of his, was on the Euphrates, twelve days' march away. It was against him, he said, that he wanted to advance. If he was there, then, he said, he wanted to get his revenge on him; if, on the other hand, he should run away, then, he said, ' we must make our plans on the spot to meet the situation.'

On hearing this the delegates reported it back to the soldiers, who, while they suspected that he was leading them against the King, nevertheless decided to go with him. They asked, however, for more pay; and Cyrus promised to give to all half as much again as they had before, three half-darics a month to each soldier instead of one daric. But as to his leading them against the King, no one was told of it even on this occasion, at least not openly.

Chapter 4

THROUGH THE SYRIAN GATES AND ACROSS THE EUPHRATES

FROM here a two days' march of thirty miles took him to the river Psarus, which was three hundred feet in breadth. From here one day's march of fifteen miles took him to the river Pyramus, which was six hundred feet in breadth. From here a two days' march of forty-five miles took him to the large and prosperous inhabited city of Issus. It is the last city in Cilicia and is on the sea.

Cyrus stayed three days here and was joined by the ships from the Peloponnese, thirty-five of them with their admiral Pythagoras, a Spartan. They had been conducted from Ephesus by Tamos the Egyptian, who was in command of twenty-five more of Cyrus's ships, with which he had been blockading Miletus when it was friendly to Tissaphernes. Also on board the ships was the Spartan Chirisophus. He had been sent for by Cyrus and came with seven hundred hoplites which he commanded himself within Cyrus's army. The ships lay at anchor opposite Cyrus's tent. Here too the Greek mercenaries employed by Abrocomas, four hundred hoplites, revolted and came over to Cyrus and joined him in the march against the King.

From here a day's march of fifteen miles took him to the Gates of Cilicia and Syria. There were two fortresses; the inner one, covering Cilicia, was held by Syennesis and a garrison of Cilicians, and the outer one, covering Syria, was said to be held by a garrison of the King's soldiers. A river called the Carsus, a hundred feet in breadth, runs between the two fortresses. The whole space between the fortifications was six hundred yards, and it was out of the question to force a way through, since the pass was narrow and the walls extended to the sea and above them were sheer cliffs. There were gates set in each of the fortifications. It was in order to turn this position that Cyrus had sent for his fleet, the plan being to land hoplites on each side of the gates and to force a way through the enemy if they were manning the Syrian gates, which was what he expected that Abrocomas would do, as he had a considerable force with him. However, Abrocomas did not do so, but, as soon as he heard that Cyrus was in Cilicia, he abandoned Phoenicia and marched to join the King with an army which was reported to consist of three hundred thousand.

From here a day's march through Syria of fifteen miles took Cyrus to Myriandrus, a city on the sea, inhabited by Phoenicians. This place was a centre for trade and there were many merchant ships at anchor there. He stayed here for seven days, during which Xenias the Arcadian and Pasion the Megarian got on board a ship, stowed away their most valuable property and sailed off. Most people thought that they did this out of jealousy because Cyrus had allowed Clearchus to keep under his command the soldiers of theirs who had gone over to him when they had the idea of returning to Greece and not marching against the King. After their disappearance the rumour went round that Cyrus was pursuing them with triremes; and some, calling them cowards, hoped that they would be caught, while others felt sorry for them if they were. Cyrus, however, called together the generals and said: 'Xenias and Pasion have left us, but they can be sure enough that they have not got away out of reach. I know the way they have gone and they have not escaped me, since I have triremes which could overtake their ships. But, by Heaven, I am certainly not going to pursue them. No one shall say that I make use of a man while he is in my service, and then, when he wants to leave, that I arrest him and ill-treat him and take

away his property. No, let them go, with the knowledge that
they have behaved worse to us than we have to them. It is
true that I hold their children and women under guard at
Tralles, but they will not even lose them. No, they will get
them back again in return for the good service they did me
in the past.'

This was what he said. As for the Greeks, even those who
were not very enthusiastic about the journey into the interior,
when they heard how well Cyrus had behaved, they were all
the more happy and keen to march with him.

After this a four days' march of sixty miles took him to the
river Chalus, which was a hundred feet in breadth and full
of large tame fish which the Syrians regarded as gods and
would not allow anyone to harm them. (They think in the
same way about pigeons.) The villages where they pitched
their tents were the property of Parysatis, and had been given
to her for pin-money.

From here a five days' march of ninety miles took him to
the source of the river Dardes, which is a hundred feet in
breadth. Here was the palace of Belesys, the Governor of
Syria, and a very large and beautiful park which had in it all
the plants that can possibly be grown. But Cyrus ravaged the
ground and burned the palace.

From here a three days' march of forty-five miles took him
to the river Euphrates, which was eight hundred yards across.
On its banks was a great and prosperous city called Thapsacus,
where he stayed for five days.

At this point Cyrus sent for the Greek generals and told
them that he was going to march against the Great King
in the direction of Babylon. He asked them to inform the
soldiers of this and to persuade them to go with him. The
generals convened an assembly and gave Cyrus's message.
But the soldiers were in an angry mood. They said that the
generals had known this all along but had kept it back, and

they refused to go further unless they were given extra money, as had been given to those who had gone up before with Cyrus to the capital to Cyrus's father; and on that occasion there had been no question of a battle, but Cyrus's father had simply called him to the Court.

The generals reported all this back to Cyrus and he promised to give each man five minae of silver on their arrival at Babylon together with full pay until he had brought the Greeks back to Ionia again. Most of the Greek army was won over by these terms; but Menon, before it was certain what the rest of the army was going to do, and whether it would follow Cyrus or not, called together his own troops apart from the rest and made the following speech: 'Soldiers, if you take my advice, you will, entirely without risk or hardship, get more consideration from Cyrus than all the rest. And this is what I recommend: Cyrus, at the moment, is begging the Greeks to follow him against the King. I say that you should cross the Euphrates before it is certain what reply the other Greeks will make to Cyrus. For then, if they vote in favour of following him, you, by being the first to cross the river, will get the credit for the decision; Cyrus will be grateful to you as being the most enthusiastic of his supporters, and he will show his gratitude. Believe me, he knows how to. And if the others vote against it, we shall all go back again, but he will look upon you, the only ones to obey his orders, as the most reliable people for garrison duties and promotion from the ranks, and whatever else you want I am sure you will get through Cyrus's friendship.'

After hearing this they took his advice and crossed the river before the others had sent their reply. Cyrus was delighted when he found that they had crossed and he sent Glous to Menon's army with the following message: 'Soldiers, I am pleased with you now. But I shall see to it that you too are pleased with me, or my name is not Cyrus.'

The soldiers on their side, with their great expectations, prayed for his success, and he was said to have sent presents on a very handsome scale to Menon. After this he crossed the river and the whole of the rest of the army followed him. In the crossing no one got wet from the river-water above the nipples. The people of Thapsacus said that this river had never except on this occasion been passable on foot, but could only be crossed in boats; and on this occasion Abrocomas had gone ahead and burned the boats to prevent Cyrus from crossing. It seemed certainly that there was something super-natural about it, and that the river had undoubtedly made way for Cyrus since he was destined to become King.

From here there was a nine days' march of one hundred and fifty miles through Syria until they arrived at the river Araxes. Here there were many villages well supplied with corn and wine. They stayed three days and provided them-selves with food.

Chapter 5

THE ARABIAN DESERT · QUARREL BETWEEN MENON AND CLEARCHUS

FROM here, with the Euphrates on the right, he moved forward through Arabia. It was a five days' march of a hundred and five miles through the desert. In this part of the world the ground was all one level plain, like the sea. Wormwood was plentiful, and all the other shrubs and reeds which grew there smelt as sweetly as perfume. There were no trees, but there was a great variety of animal life. Wild asses were very common and there were many ostriches; also there were bustards and gazelles. The cavalry hunted all these animals on various occasions. In the case of the wild asses, when anyone chased them, they ran ahead and then stopped still; for they ran much faster than the horses. Then again, when the horses got near, they would do the same thing, and it was impossible to catch them except by stationing the horsemen at intervals from each other and hunting in relays. The flesh of those that were caught was very like venison, only more tender. No one succeeded in catching an ostrich. Indeed the horsemen who tried soon gave up the pursuit, as it made them go a very great distance when it ran from them. It used its feet for running and got under way with its wings, just as if it was using a sail. But one can catch bustards if one puts them up quickly, as they only fly a little way, like partridges, and soon get tired. Their flesh was delicious.

Marching through this country, they came to the river Mascas, which is a hundred feet in breadth. Here there was a deserted city of great size called Corsote. The river Mascas curved right round it. They stayed here three days and provided themselves with food. Then came a thirteen days' march of two hundred and seventy miles through the desert, keeping the Euphrates still on the right, till he arrived at a place called The Gates. In this march many of the baggage animals died of hunger, as there was no grass or anything else growing. The ground was completely bare. The inhabitants used to quarry by the river and manufacture stones for grinding corn; they took them to Babylon to sell and lived on the food they bought with the proceeds.

On this march the army ran short of corn, and it was impossible to buy any except in the Lydian market among Cyrus's native troops, where one could get a capithe of wheat flour or pearl barley for four sigli. The siglus is worth seven and a half Attic obols, and the capithe is equal to three pints. So the soldiers lived entirely on meat.

Cyrus made some of these marches extremely long, when it was a case of wanting to reach water or fodder. And there was one occasion on which the road got narrow and muddy and difficult for the waggons, when Cyrus halted with the noblest and richest of his company and ordered Glous and Pigres to take a detachment of native troops and help in getting the waggons out of the mud; and when he thought that they were going slow on it, he looked angry and ordered the most important Persians in his company to give a hand with the waggons. Then certainly one saw a bit of discipline. Wherever they happened to be standing, they threw off their purple cloaks and rushed forward as though it was a race,–down a very steep hill, too, and wearing those expensive tunics which they have, and embroidered trousers. Some also had chains round their necks and bracelets on their wrists. But with all this on they leapt straight down into the mud and got the waggons on to dry ground quicker than anyone would have thought possible.

Generally speaking, it was obvious that Cyrus was pressing on all the way with no pause except when he halted for provisions or some other necessity. He thought that the quicker he arrived the more unprepared would be the King when he engaged him, and the slower he went, the greater would be the army that the King could get together. Indeed, an intelligent observer of the King's empire would form the following estimate: it is strong in respect of extent of territory and number of inhabitants; but it is weak in respect of its lengthened communications and the dispersal of its forces, that is, if one can attack with speed.

On the other side of the river Euphrates, opposite the desert where they were marching, there was a large and prosperous city called Charmande. The soldiers bought what they wanted from here, and crossed the river on rafts in the following way. They stuffed the skins which they used as tent-coverings with dry grass, and then drew them together and stitched them up so that the water would not reach the hay. They crossed the river on these and got provisions, wine made from the fruit of the date-palm and panic corn, of which there was a great abundance in the country.

At this place there was a quarrel about something between the soldiers of Menon and those of Clearchus. Clearchus, judging that Menon's man was in the wrong, ordered a beating for him. When this man got back to his own troops, he told them of it, and the soldiers, after hearing his story, were in an extremely angry and bitter mood against Clearchus. On the same day Clearchus, after visiting the place where they crossed the river and inspecting the market there, was riding back with a few attendants to his own tent by way of Menon's camp. Cyrus was still on the march there and had not yet arrived. One of Menon's soldiers, who was cutting wood, saw Clearchus riding through the camp and threw his axe at him. He missed him with the axe, but another soldier threw a stone and then another and then many more, and there was a general uproar. Clearchus took refuge among his

own troops and immediately gave the call for action. He
ordered the hoplites to stay in position with their shields resting on their knees, while he himself moved against Menon's
men with his Thracians and his cavalry, of whom he had
more than forty (mostly Thracians themselves) in his camp.
The result was that Menon's men (and Menon too) were
terrified and ran to get their arms, though some stood where
they were, unable to cope with the situation. Just at this
moment Proxenus was coming up in the rear leading a column
of hoplites. So he immediately brought his men into position
between the two parties and begged Clearchus not to act as
he was doing. Clearchus, however, was furious that, after he
had been practically stoned to death, Proxenus should speak
without bitterness of what had been done to him, and he told
him to get out of the way. At this point Cyrus also came up
and found out what was happening. He immediately seized
hold of his javelins and rode into the middle of the Greeks
with those of his bodyguard who were at hand, and spoke as
follows:

'Clearchus and Proxenus, and all you other Greeks here,
you do not know what you are doing. If you start fighting
amongst yourselves, you can be sure that I shall be finished
off on the spot, and you not long afterwards. If things between us go wrong, all these natives whom you see will
become more dangerous enemies to us than those on the
King's side are.'

Clearchus came to himself after hearing this. Both sides
relaxed and piled arms in their positions.

Chapter 6

CYRUS DEALS WITH A TRAITOR

As they went on from here, they came across hoof-marks and the droppings of horses. One guessed that the marks were made by about two thousand cavalry. These had gone ahead and burnt up all the fodder and anything else that might be of use.

Orontas, a Persian whose family was related to the King, and who had one of the best military reputations among the Persians, was scheming against Cyrus. He had actually been at war with him before then, but had become reconciled. Now he said to Cyrus that, if he would give him a thousand horsemen, he would either ambush and wipe out the cavalry who were scorching the earth in front of them, or he would take a number of prisoners and so put a stop to the devastation of the ground on their way and prevent them from having any chance of telling the King that they had seen Cyrus's army.

When Cyrus heard the plan he thought it was a good one and told Orontas to take a detachment from each of his commanders. Orontas, feeling sure of getting the cavalry, wrote a letter to the King saying that he would come to him with as many horsemen as he could get hold of, and asking him to instruct his own cavalry to receive him as a friend. He also put in the letter reminders of his former friendship with the King and his loyalty. He gave this letter to a reliable man,- or so he thought. Actually the man took the letter and gave it to Cyrus.

Cyrus, on reading it, put Orontas under arrest and summoned to his own tent the seven most distinguished Persians on his staff. He ordered the Greek generals to bring hoplites and stand on guard around the tent. They carried out his instructions, bringing about three thousand hoplites. Cyrus called Clearchus right into the tent to share in the council, as both he and the other Persians regarded him as the most generally respected of the Greeks. Afterwards, when he left, he told his friends how the trial of Orontas was conducted, as there was no ban on telling of it. He said that Cyrus began the proceedings by making this speech: 'My friends, I have called you together so that I may act with regard to Orontas here in what, after consultation with you, we decide is, from the point of view of gods and men, the right way. This man, in the first place, was appointed by my father to be under my command. Then, on the instructions, as he says, of my brother, he held the citadel of Sardis and made war on me. I fought him and made him decide to stop fighting against me; then I gave him and he gave me the right hand of friendship. Since then, Orontas,' he continued, 'have I injured you in any way?' Orontas replied that he had not. Cyrus then asked another question. 'Is it not true that afterwards, although, as you admit yourself, you had received no injury from me, you went over to the Mysians and did all the harm you could to my territory?' Orontas admitted that he had done so. 'And is it not true,' said Cyrus, 'that, when you had again discovered what your power really was, you came to the altar of Artemis and said that you repented and, as a result of your entreaties, we once again gave and received pledges of friendship?' Orontas agreed that this also was true. 'What injury, then,' said Cyrus, 'have I done you now to account for this third occasion on which you have plainly turned traitor to me?' Orontas replied that he had received no injury, and Cyrus asked him, 'Do you admit, then, that your conduct towards me has been wrong?' 'Indeed,' said Orontas, 'I am forced to admit it.' Cyrus then asked him another question: 'Is it still possible for you to become an enemy of my brother, and a

true friend of mine?' He replied, 'Even if I were to do so
you, Cyrus, could no longer believe in it.'

After this Cyrus spoke to the others there. 'This man's
actions and words are in front of you. Clearchus, will you
give your opinion first, and say what you think?' Clearchus
said: 'My advice is to get the man out of the way as quickly
as possible, so that we shall no longer have to be on our
guard against him, but shall have our hands free, so far as he
is concerned, to do good to the others who really want to
help.'

The others, Clearchus said, agreed with his opinion. Afterwards, he said, they all stood up, even Orontas's kinsmen,
and took hold of Orontas by the girdle, as a sign that he was
condemned to death. Then, those who had been detailed for
the job led him away; and those who had been previously in
the habit of bowing to him, bowed to him even then, although
they knew that he was being taken to his death. He was
brought to the tent of Artapatas, the most trusted of Cyrus's
sceptre-bearers, and after that no one ever saw Orontas alive
or dead, nor could anyone speak with knowledge of how he
died. Various guesses were made, but there was never any
omb of his to be seen.

Chapter 7

CYRUS PREPARES FOR BATTLE, BUT THE KING RETREATS

FROM here he advanced through Babylonia, a three days' march of thirty-six miles. At the end of the third day's march Cyrus held a review of the Greek and native troops in the plain about midnight, as he thought that on the next dawn the King would appear with his army to give battle. He ordered Clearchus to take the right wing and Menon the Thessalian the left, while he himself saw to the disposition of his own troops.

At daybreak, after the review, deserters from the great King came and gave Cyrus information about the King's army. Cyrus called together the generals and captains of the Greeks for a discussion on how he should fight the battle, and then made the following speech himself to spur them on to greater efforts: 'Soldiers of the Greeks, I am not leading you into battle with me because I am short of native troops. No, the reason why I sought your help was that I considered you to be more efficient and formidable than great numbers of natives. I want you, then, to show yourselves worthy of the freedom which you have won and which I think you happy in possessing. You can be sure that I would rather have that freedom than all I possess, and much more. But to give you knowledge also of the type of fighting into which you are going I will tell you about it from my own experience. The enemy's numbers are very great and they attack with a lot of shouting; but if you stand your ground against this, I really feel ashamed to say what sort of people in every other way you will find the men in this country to be. But if you show yourselves men and if my fortunes turn out well, I shall see to it that those of you who want to return home will be envied by their friends when they get there, though I think I shall make many of you prefer what they will get from me here to what they will have at home.'

Then Gaulites, who was at the meeting, spoke. He was an exile from Samos and was in Cyrus's confidence. 'All the same, Cyrus,' he said, 'some people are saying that you are promising a lot now because of being in such a critical position with danger on the way, and, according to them, if things turn out well, you will not remember. And some say that even if you have both the memory and the will, you will not have the power to make good all the promises you have made.'

Cyrus listened to this and said: 'But, soldiers, in front of us lies the empire of my father. It extends southwards to where heat and northwards to where cold make it impossible for men to live. The friends of my brother rule as satraps over all the land between. But if we win, we shall have to make our own friends lords over all this. Consequently I am more afraid of not having enough friends for what I can give than of not having what to give, if things go well, to all my friends. And I shall give an additional present of a golden crown to each one of you Greeks.'

When the Greeks heard this, they became much more enthusiastic themselves and passed on the news to the others. Generals and other Greeks who wanted to know what they would get, if they won, called on Cyrus privately and he satisfied all their expectations before he let them go. All who discussed things with him urged him not to join in the battle personally but to take up a position in their rear. At this time Clearchus asked him some such question as this: 'Do you think, Cyrus, that your brother will come to battle?' 'Certainly,' said Cyrus, 'if he is the son of Darius and Parysatis, and my brother, I shall not gain power without fighting for it.'

A count was taken then of those under arms. In the Greek army there were ten thousand four hundred hoplites and two thousand five hundred peltasts. There were a hundred thousand native troops with Cyrus and about twenty scythed chariots. On the side of the enemy there were said to be one million two hundred thousand men and two hundred scythed chariots; and apart from these there were six thousand cavalry under the command of Artagerses who were placed in position to cover the King's own person. The command of the King's army was in the hands of four generals or leaders, Abrocomas, Tissaphernes, Gobrias and Arbaces. Each had three hundred thousand in his command. Only nine hundred thousand of these, and a hundred and fifty scythed chariots, were engaged in the battle, since Abrocamas, who was marching from Phoenicia, arrived five days late. The deserters from the Great King gave Cyrus this information before the battle, and enemy prisoners taken after the battle told the same story.

Cyrus went a day's march, nine miles, from here with his whole army, Greek and native, in order of battle. He expected that the King would engage him on that day, as about the middle of the day's march there was a deep ditch dug in the ground, five fathoms across and three fathoms deep. The ditch extended inland over the plain as far as the Median wall, but near the Euphrates there was a narrow passage about twenty feet wide between the river and the ditch. The Great King had had the ditch dug as an obstacle when he heard of Cyrus's advance. It was by this passage that Cyrus and the army went and so got beyond the ditch.

On this day, then, the King failed to give battle, but there were many signs to be seen of men and horses in retreat. Cyrus at this time sent for Silanus, the Ambracian soothsayer, and gave him three thousand darics. Eleven days before he had told Cyrus during a sacrifice that the King would not give battle in the next ten days, and Cyrus had said to him:

'Then, if he doesn't fight in that time, he won't fight at all. But if what you say turns out true, I promise you ten talents.' Now the ten days had gone by, and he paid him the money.

As the King had made no attempt at the ditch to stop Cyrus's army crossing over, Cyrus and the rest believed that he had given up the idea of fighting, and, as a result of this belief, on the following day Cyrus went forward with less caution. On the third day he travelled seated in his chariot with only a few regular formations in front of him. Most of his army was marching in no sort of order, and much of the soldiers' equipment was being carried on the waggons and baggage animals.

Chapter 8

THE BATTLE OF CUNAXA AND
DEATH OF CYRUS

IT was already the middle of the morning, and they had nearly reached the place where Cyrus intended to halt, when Pategyas, a Persian and a good friend of Cyrus, came into sight, riding hard, with his horse in a sweat. He immediately began to shout out, in Persian and Greek, to everyone in his way that the King with a great army in order of battle was approaching. There was certainly considerable confusion at this point, for the Greeks and everyone else thought that he would be upon them before they could form up in position. Cyrus leapt down from his chariot, put on his breastplate, mounted his horse and took hold of his javelins. He gave orders for all the rest to arm themselves and to take up their correct positions. This was done readily enough. Clearchus was on the right wing, flanked by the Euphrates, next to him was Proxenus and then the other Greeks, with Menon holding the left wing of the Greek army. As to the native troops, there were about a thousand Paphlagonian cavalry stationed with Clearchus and also the Greek peltasts on the right; Ariaeus, Cyrus's second-in-command, was on the left with the rest of the native army. Cyrus and about six hundred of his personal cavalry in the centre were armed with breast-plates, and armour to cover the thighs. They all wore helmets except for Cyrus, who went into the battle bare-headed. All their horses had armour covering the forehead and breast; and the horsemen also carried Greek sabres.

It was now midday and the enemy had not yet come into sight. But in the early afternoon dust appeared, like a white cloud, and after some time a sort of blackness extending a

long way over the plain. When they got nearer, then suddenly there were flashes of bronze, and the spear points and
the enemy formations became visible. There were cavalry
with white armour on the enemy's left and Tissaphernes was
said to be in command of them. Next to them were soldiers
with wicker shields, and then came hoplites with wooden
shields reaching to the feet. These were said to be Egyptians.
Then there were more cavalry and archers. These all marched
in tribes, each tribe in a dense oblong formation. In front of
them, and at considerable distances apart from each other,
were what they called the scythed chariots. These had thin
scythes extending at an angle from the axles and also under
the driver's seat, turned toward the ground, so as to cut
through everything in their way. The idea was to drive them
into the Greek ranks and cut through them.

But Cyrus was wrong in what he said at the time when he
called together the Greeks and told them to stand their ground
against the shouting of the natives. So far from shouting,
they came on as silently as they could, calmly, in a slow,
steady march.

At this point Cyrus himself with his interpreter Pigres and
three or four others rode up and shouted out to Clearchus,
telling him to lead his army against the enemy's centre,
because that was where the King was. 'And if we win there,'
he said, 'the whole thing is over.' Clearchus saw the troops
in close order in the enemy's centre and he heard too from
Cyrus that the King was beyond the Greek left (so great was
the King's superiority in numbers that he, leading the centre
of his own army, was still beyond Cyrus's left), but in spite
of this he was reluctant, from fear of encirclement, to draw
his right wing away from the river. He replied to Cyrus,
then, that he would see to it that things went well.

While this was going on the Persian army continued to
move steadily forward and the Greeks still remained where

they were, and their ranks filled up from those who were
continually coming up. Cyrus rode by some way in front of
the army and looked along the lines both at the enemy and
at his own troops. Xenophon, an Athenian, saw him from
his position in the Greek line and, going forward to meet him,
asked if he had any orders to give. Cyrus pulled in his horse
and said: 'The omens are good and the sacrifices are good.'
He told him to tell this to everyone, and while he was speaking
he heard a noise going along the ranks and asked what the
noise was. Xenophon told him that it was the watchword
now being passed along the ranks for the second time. Cyrus
wondered who had given the word and asked what it was,
and Xenophon told him it was 'Zeus the Deliverer and
Victory.' On hearing this Cyrus said: 'Then I accept the word.
Let it be so,' and with these words he rode away to his own
position in the field.

By now the two armies were not more than between six
and eight hundred yards apart, and now the Greeks sang the
paean and began to move forward against the enemy. As
they advanced, part of the phalanx surged forward in front of
the rest and the part that was left behind began to advance at
the double. At the same time they all raised a shout like the
shout of 'Eleleu' which people make to the War God, and
then they were all running forward. Some say that to scare
the horses they clashed their shields and spears together. But
the Persians, even before they were in range of the arrows,
wavered and ran away. Then certainly the Greeks pressed on
the pursuit vigorously, but they shouted out to each other
not to run, but to follow up the enemy without breaking
ranks. The chariots rushed about, some going through the
enemy's own ranks, though some, abandoned by their drivers,
did go through the Greeks. When they saw them coming the
Greeks opened out, though one man stood rooted to the
spot, as though he was at a race course, and got run down

However, even he, they said, came to no harm, nor were there any other casualties among the Greeks in this battle, except for one man on the left wing who was said to have been shot with an arrow.

Cyrus was pleased enough when he saw the Greeks winning and driving back the enemy in front of them, and he was already being acclaimed as King by those who were with him; but he was not so carried away as to join in the pursuit. He kept the six hundred cavalry of his personal bodyguard in close order, and watched to see what the King would do, as he was sure that his position was in the Persian centre. Indeed, all Persian commanders are in the centre of their own troops when they go into battle, the idea being that in this way they will be in the safest spot, with their forces on each side of them, and that also if they want to issue any orders, their army will receive them in half the time. The King, too, on this occasion was in the centre of his army, but was all the same beyond Cyrus's left wing. Seeing, then, that no frontal attack was being made either on him or on the troops drawn up to screen him, he wheeled right in an outflanking movement.

Then Cyrus, fearing that the King might get behind the Greeks and cut them up, moved directly towards him. With his six hundred he charged into and broke through the screen of troops in front of the King, routed the six thousand, and is said to have killed their commander, Artagerses, with his own hand. But while they turned to flight, Cyrus's own six hundred lost their cohesion in their eagerness for the pursuit, and there were only a very few left with him, mostly those who were called his 'table-companions'. When left with these few, he caught sight of the King and the closely formed ranks around him. Without a moment's hesitation he cried out, 'I see the man,' charged down on him, and struck him a blow on the breast which wounded him through the breastplate,

as Ctesias the doctor says,—saying also that he dressed the
wound himself. But while he was in the very act of striking
the blow, someone hit him hard under the eye with a javelin.
In the fighting there between Cyrus and the King and their
supporters, Ctesias (who was with the King) tells how many
fell on the King's side. But Cyrus was killed himself, and
eight of the noblest of his company lay dead upon his body.
It is said that when Artapatas, the most trusted servant among
his sceptre-bearers, saw Cyrus fall, he leapt from his horse and
threw himself down on him. Some say that the King ordered
someone to kill him on top of Cyrus, others that he drew
his scimitar and killed himself there. He had a golden scimitar,
and used to wear a chain and bracelets and the other decora-
tions like the noblest of the Persians; for he had been honoured
by Cyrus as a good friend and a faithful servant.

THE CHARACTER OF CYRUS

THIS then, was the end of Cyrus. Of all the Persians who lived after Cyrus the Great, he was the most like a king and the most deserving of an empire, as is admitted by everyone who is known to have been personally acquainted with him. In his early life, when he was still a child being brought up with his brother, and the other children, he was regarded as the best of them all in every way. All the children of Persian nobles are brought up at the Court, and there a child can pick up many lessons in good behaviour while having no chance of seeing or hearing anything bad. The boys see and hear some people being honoured by the King and others being dismissed in disgrace, and so from their childhood they learn how to command and how to obey. Here, at the Court, Cyrus was considered, first, to be the best-behaved of his contemporaries and more willing even than his inferiors to listen to those older than himself; and then he was remarkable for his fondness for horses and being able to manage them extremely well. In the soldierly arts also of archery and javelin-throwing they judged him to be most eager to learn and most willing to practise them. When he got to the age for hunting, he was most enthusiastic about it, and only too ready to take risks in his encounters with wild animals. There was one occasion when a she-bear charged at him and he, showing no fear, got to grips with the animal and was pulled off his horse. The scars from the wounds he got then were still visible on his body, but he killed the animal in the end, and as for the first man who came to help him Cyrus made people think him very lucky indeed.

When he was sent down to the coast by his father as satrap

of Lydia and Great Phrygia and Cappadocia, and had been declared Commander-in-Chief of all who are bound to muster in the plain of Castolus, the first thing he did was to make it clear that in any league or agreement or undertaking that he made he attached the utmost importance to keeping his word. The cities which were in his command trusted him and so did the men. And the enemies he had were confident that once Cyrus had signed a treaty with them nothing would happen to them contrary to the terms of the treaty. Consequently when he was at war with Tissaphernes all the cities, with the exception of the Milesians, chose to follow him rather than Tissaphernes. The Milesians were afraid of him because he refused to give up the cause of the exiled government. Indeed, he made it clear by his actions, and said openly that, once he had become their friend, he would never give them up, not even if their numbers became fewer and their prospects worse than they were.

If anyone did him a good or an evil turn, he evidently aimed at going one better. Some people used to refer to an habitual prayer of his, that he might live long enough to be able to repay with interest both those who had helped him and those who had injured him. It was quite natural then that he was the one man in our times to whom so many people were eager to hand over their money, their cities and their own persons.

No one, however, could say that he allowed criminals and evil-doers to mock his authority. On the contrary, his punishments were exceptionally severe, and along the more frequented roads one often saw people who had been blinded or had had their feet or hands cut off. The result was that in Cyrus's provinces anyone, whether Greek or native, who was doing no harm could travel without fear wherever he liked and could take with him whatever he wanted.

Of course it is well known that he treated with exceptional

distinction all those who showed ability for war. In his first war, which was against the Pisidians and Mysians, he marched into their country himself and made those whom he saw willing to risk their lives governors over the territory which he conquered; and afterwards he gave them other honours and rewards, making it clear that the brave were going to be the most prosperous while the cowards only deserved to be their slaves. Consequently there was never any lack of people who were willing to risk their lives when they thought that Cyrus would get to know of it.

As for justice, he made it his supreme aim to see that those who really wanted to live in accordance with its standards became richer than those who wanted to profit by transgressing them. It followed from this that not only were his affairs in general conducted justly, but he enjoyed the services of an army that really was an army. Generals and captains who crossed the sea to take service under him as mercenaries knew that to do Cyrus good service paid better than any monthly wage. Indeed, whenever anyone carried out effectively a job which he had assigned, he never allowed his good work to go unrewarded. Consequently it was said that Cyrus got the best officers for any kind of job.

When he saw that a man was a capable administrator, acting on just principles, improving the land under his control and making it bring in profit, he never took his post away from him, but always gave him additional responsibility. The result was that his administrators did their work cheerfully and made money confidently. Cyrus was the last person whom they kept in the dark about their possessions, since he showed no envy for those who became rich openly, but, on the contrary, tried to make use of the wealth of people who attempted to conceal what they had.

Everyone agrees that he was absolutely remarkable for doing services to those whom he made friends of and knew to be true to him and considered able to help him in doing whatever job was on hand. He thought that the reason why he needed friends was to have people to help him, and he applied exactly the same principle to others, trying to be of the utmost service to his friends whenever he knew that any of them wanted anything. I suppose that he received more presents than any other single individual, and this for a variety of reasons. But more than anyone else he shared them with his friends, always considering what each individual was like and what, to his knowledge, he needed most. When people sent him fine things to wear, either armour or beautiful dresses, they say that the remark he made about these was that he could not possibly wear all this finery on his own body, but he thought the finest thing for a man was that his friends should be well turned out. There is, no doubt, nothing surprising in the fact that he surpassed his friends in doing them great services, since he had the greater power to do so. What seems to me more admirable than this is the fact that he outdid them in ordinary consideration and in the anxiety to give pleasure. Often, when he had had a particularly good wine, he used to send jars half full of it to his friends with the message: 'Cyrus has not for a long time come across a better wine than this; so he has sent some to you and wants you to finish it up to-day with those whom you love best.' Often too he used to send helpings of goose and halves of loaves and such things, telling the bearer to say when he presented them: 'Cyrus enjoyed this; so he wants you to taste it too.' When there was a scarcity of fodder,–though he himself, because of the number of his servants and his own wise provision, was able to get hold of it,–he used to send round to his friends and tell them to give the fodder he sent to the horses they rode themselves, so that horses which carried his friends should not go hungry.

Whenever he went on an official journey, and was likely

to be seen by great numbers of people, he used to call his friends to him and engage them in serious conversation, so that he might show what men he honoured. My own opinion, therefore, based on what I have heard, is that there has never been anyone, Greek or foreigner, more generally beloved. And an additional proof of this is in the fact that, although Cyrus was a subject, no one deserted him and went over to the King,—except that Orontas tried to do so; but in his case he soon found that the man whom he thought reliable was more of a friend to Cyrus than to him. On the other hand there were many who left the King and came over to Cyrus, when war broke out between the two, and these also were people who had been particularly favoured by the King; but they came to the conclusion that if they did well under Cyrus their services would be better rewarded than they would be by the King. What happened at the time of his death is also a strong proof not only of his own courage but of his ability to pick out accurately people who were reliable, devoted and steadfast. For when he died every one of his friends and table-companions died fighting for him, except Ariaeus, who had been posted on the left wing in command of the cavalry. When Ariaeus heard that Cyrus had fallen, he and the whole army which he led took to flight.

Chapter 10

AFTER THE BATTLE

THEN Cyrus's head and right hand were cut off. The King turned to the pursuit and broke into Cyrus's camp. Ariaeus's men did not stay any longer but fled through their own camp to the place of the last halt, from which they had started. This was said to be twelve miles away.

The King and his men seized, among much other booty, Cyrus's mistress, the Phocaean girl, who was said to be both beautiful and intelligent. His younger mistress, a girl from Miletus, was captured by the King's soldiers, but got away from them half dressed to the Greeks who happened to be there under arms to guard the baggage. They took up position and killed a number of the looters, though some of them were killed too. However, they did not run away. They saved the girl and also all the property,–money and slaves–that was in their quarters.

At this stage the King and the main Greek army were about three miles apart from each other. The Greeks were pursuing the forces in front of them as though they had won a complete victory, and the Persians were busy looting as though their victory also had been a total one. Later, however, the Greeks found out that the King and his army were among their baggage, and the King heard from Tissaphernes that the Greeks had defeated the troops opposed to them and were pressing on forward with the pursuit. He then got his forces together and put them in battle order, while Clearchus summoned Proxenus, who was nearest to him, and discussed with him whether they should send a detachment to relieve the camp or should all march there together.

Meanwhile it became evident that the King, too, was again

moving up to them, as they thought, from the rear. The Greeks then, on the assumption that he was coming from there, turned about and made ready to engage him. The King, however, did not bring up his army from that direction. Just as he had previously gone past the left wing of the Greeks, so now he brought his army back the same way, having picked up on the way both those who had deserted to the Greeks in the course of the battle and also Tissaphernes and the troops under his command.

Tissaphernes had not fled at the first charge, but had driven down on the Greek peltasts along the river and broken through them. However, he did not kill a single man. The Greeks opened their ranks and struck at his men with their swords and shot at them with their javelins. Episthenes of Amphipolis was in command of the peltasts and he was said to have shown great skill.

As for Tissaphernes, when he found that he had had the worse of the exchange, he did not wheel round for another attack, but went on to the Greek camp where he met the King. There they had joined forces and were now marching back in order of battle.

Since they were opposite the Greek left wing the Greeks were afraid that they might attack this wing, encircle it from both sides and cut them to bits. It seemed best then to extend this wing and put the river in their rear. But while they were discussing this manœuvre, the King suddenly changed direction and went past them, bringing up his line facing their front in the same order as he had come out to fight in the first place.

When the Greeks saw them drawn up opposite at close quarters they sang the paean again and charged forward against them with an even more aggressive spirit than before. The natives once more failed to stand up to the attack; indeed they ran away when the Greeks were even further off than last time. The Greeks pursued them until they came to a village, and there they halted because there was a hill above the village, and on this hill the King's men had turned to fight. The infantry, indeed, were still running away, but the hill was covered with cavalry so that it was impossible to see what was going on. They said they saw the King's standard there, a golden eagle on a spear with its wings spread out.

The Greeks were actually advancing on this position when the cavalry, too, left the hill, not in one body, but different contingents going in different directions, so that the hill was gradually stripped of cavalry, until they had all gone. Clearchus did not march up the hill, but halted his army at its foot, sending Lycius the Syracusan and one other to the top with instructions to take a view of the other side and tell him what was going on there. Lycius rode there, made his survey and reported that the enemy were in full retreat.

About the time that this was happening the sun was setting. The Greeks halted where they were, piled arms and rested. At the same time they wondered why Cyrus had not appeared anywhere or why no messenger had come from him. They did not know that he was dead, but imagined that he had either pursued the enemy into the distance or had ridden ahead to occupy some position. They themselves, after discussing whether to remain where they were and bring the baggage there, or to go back to their camp, decided to go back. They got to their tents about supper-time, and that was the end of this day. They found that nearly all their baggage, including the food and drink, had been plundered. There had also been some waggons (four hundred of them, it was said) full of barley and wine, which Cyrus had provided so as to have something to give to the Greeks if there was ever a great shortage of food in the army. These waggons, too, the King's men had plundered, so that most of the Greeks had no supper. Indeed, they had had no midday meal either, as the King had appeared before the army had halted for dinner. And so they passed that night.

BOOK
II
THE GREEKS ARE
ISOLATED

Chapter 1

THE KING'S MESSENGER

AT dawn the generals met and were amazed that Cyrus had neither turned up himself nor sent a messenger to tell them what they were to do. Under the circumstances they decided to pack their belongings and go forward, armed ready for battle, till they could join up with Cyrus. However, just as the sun was rising in the sky and they were on the point or starting, Procles, the Governor of Teuthrania,–a descendant of Damaratus the Spartan,–and Glous, the son of Tamos, arrived with the news that Cyrus was dead and that Ariaeus had taken to flight and was now with the rest of the native troops at the last halting-place from which they had set out the day before. The message from Ariaeus was that he would wait for that day to see if they were going to join him, but on the next day he proposed to set off for Ionia, where he had started from.

When the generals heard this and the other Greeks got to know of it, there was very much despondency. Clearchus spoke as follows: 'I wish that Cyrus was alive. However, as he is dead, you must tell Ariaeus that we have defeated the King and, as you see, there is now no opposition to us. Indeed, if you had not come, we should be marching against him now. We give Ariaeus our word that, if he comes to us, we will put him on the King's throne. Those who win in battle have also the right to supreme power.'

With these words he sent the messengers back and sent Chirisophus the Spartan and Menon the Thessalian with them. Menon was anxious to go on his own account, as he was a friend of Ariaeus and had shared his hospitality.

So they went away and Clearchus stayed behind. The army got food for itself as best it could from the baggage animals by slaughtering the oxen and the asses. They got fuel by going forward a little way from the line to the place where the battle was fought, and using the great quantities of arrows, which the Greeks had made the deserters from the King throw down on the ground, and the wicker shields and the wooden shields of the Egyptians. There were also a number of light shields to be picked up, and chariots abandoned by their drivers. They used all this material for boiling the meat, and so got a meal for that day.

It was already about the middle of the morning when heralds arrived from the King and from Tissaphernes. They were all natives except for one of them, Phalinus by name, a Greek who happened to be in the service of Tissaphernes and was thought a lot of by him, as he professed to be an expert in drill and in infantry tactics. These heralds rode up and asked to speak to the Greek commanders. They said that the King, since he had won the victory and killed Cyrus, commanded the Greeks to surrender their arms, to make an appearance at the Court, and to get for themselves, if they could, the royal favour.

This was what the King's heralds said, and the Greeks were indignant when they heard it. Clearchus, however, merely said: 'It is not for the conquerors to surrender their arms. But,' he went on, 'you other generals must make what seems to you the best and most honourable reply to these men. I shall soon be back again.' This was because one of his officers had called him to inspect the entrails which had been taken out from the victim, as he happened to be in the middle of a sacrificial ceremony.

Then Cleanor the Arcadian, who was the eldest of them, gave his reply, which was that they would die before they surrendered their arms. And Proxenus the Theban said: 'What puzzles me, Phalinus, is whether the King is asking for our arms by right of conquest or as gifts to show our friendship.

If it is by right of conquest, why should he have to ask us for them instead of coming to take them? If he wants to get them as a result of an agreement, then let him say what the soldiers will get if they are prepared to do him this kindness.'

Phalinus replied to this: 'The King considers that, since he has killed Cyrus, the victory is his. Who, in point of fact, is left to contest the empire with him? He thinks that you, too, are in his power, since he has got you in the middle of his territories, surrounded by impassable rivers, and can bring against you such masses of men that you could never kill them all, even if he gave you the chance of doing so.'

Next, Theopompus, an Athenian, spoke, and said 'As you see, Phalinus, the only things of value which we have at present are our arms and our courage. So long as we keep our arms we fancy that we can make good use of our courage; but if we surrender our arms we shall lose our lives as well. So do not imagine that we are going to surrender to you our only valuables. On the contrary, with their aid we shall fight for what you value, too.'

Phalinus smiled when he heard this, and said: 'Quite like a philosopher, young man, and remarkably well expressed! All the same let me inform you that you are crazy if you think that your courage can get the better of the King's power.'

Those who were there said that there were some others who began to lose their resolution and say that, just as they had been faithful to Cyrus so they might be worth a lot to the King, if he wanted to make friends with them; he might, they suggested, amongst other things, like to employ them in an expedition against Egypt, and, if so, they would join him in conquering it.

At this point Clearchus arrived back and asked if they had given their reply yet. Phalinus chipped in and said: 'These men here, Clearchus, have given various answers to me. Now tell us what you say.'

Clearchus said: 'I was very glad, Phalinus, to see you and so, I expect, was everyone else, because you, like all of us whom you see here, are a Greek. And in our present position we want your advice as to what we ought to do about your message. Give us, then, I beg you, the advice which you think is best and most honourable, and the sort which will bring honour to you in the future when people tell of it and say, "Phalinus was once sent by the King to urge the Greeks to surrender their arms. When they asked him for his advice the advice he gave was so-and-so." For you know that the advice you give is bound to be reported in Greece.'

Clearchus threw this out as a hint, with the idea of getting the King's own ambassador to advise them not to surrender their arms, so that the Greeks might gain confidence thereby. Phalinus, however, slipped out of it neatly and spoke in the contrary sense to what Clearchus expected. 'My advice,' he said, 'is not to surrender your arms, if you have one chance in ten thousand of saving yourselves by fighting against the King. But if there is not a single chance of safety in going against the King, then I advise you to take the only steps you can to save yourselves.'

Clearchus replied to this: 'Well, then, so much for your advice. Now you can take back our answer, which is that we consider that, if it is a case of becoming friends with the King, we shall be more valuable friends if we retain our arms than if we surrender them to someone else; and if it is a case of fighting, we shall fight better if we retain our arms than if they are in someone else's possession.'

Phalinus replied: 'Then that is the answer which we will take back. But the King told us to give you this message, too: he assumes that a truce is in existence so long as you remain where you are; but if you move forward or backward it means war. So you must give me an answer to this point as well, whether you will stay here and make a truce or whether I am to tell him from you that you assume a state of war.'

'Tell him,' said Clearchus, 'that on this point we think the same as he does.'

'And what does that mean?' Phalinus asked.

'It means,' Clearchus replied, 'truce if we stay, and war if we go forward or backward.'

Phalinus again enquired. 'Which am I to say, a truce or war?' and Clearchus made the same reply again. 'A truce while we stay here, but, if we go forward or backward, war.' He gave no indication of what course he proposed to take.

Chapter 2

THE GREEKS JOIN ARIAEUS

WHEN Phalinus and those with him had gone, the delegates from Ariaeus returned; at least Procles and Chirisophus did. Menon had stayed on there with Ariaeus. They reported that Ariaeus had said that there were a number of Persians who were in a higher station than he was and would not put up with his becoming King. But, if the Greeks wanted to join him in the journey back, then he urged them to come that night. If not, he would start, he said, early on the next day.

'Well,' said Clearchus, 'that is what we must do. If we come, it will be as you say. If we do not, you must take whatever course you think is most to your advantage.' He did not tell even them what he was going to do.

Afterwards, when it was already sunset, he called together the generals and captains, and made the following speech: 'My friends, when I was sacrificing with a view to marching against the King, the signs were not propitious. This was natural enough; for, as I now understand, between us and the King there is a navigable river, the Tigris. We could not cross this river without boats, and we have no boats. We certainly cannot stay here, because there is no possibility of obtaining supplies. However, when it was a question of making our way to Cyrus's friends, the signs from the sacrifices were extraordinarily favourable. So this is what we ought to do: after leaving the meeting, we must have whatever supper is available. When the normal call on the bugle for turning in is given, then pack up your belongings. On the second bugle call, put them on the baggage animals. On the third call, follow those who are leading you, with the animals next to the river and the hoplites on the outside of them.'

On receiving these instructions the generals and captains went away and carried them out; and from then on Clearchus was in command, and they were his subordinates. This was not the result of an election, but because they realised that he was the one man who had the right sort of mind for a commander, while the rest of them were inexperienced.

Later on, when it became dark, Miltocuthes the Thracian deserted to the King and took with him the forty-odd cavalry which he had, and about three hundred of the Thracian infantry. As for the rest, Clearchus led the way, according to the instructions he had given, and they followed him until they arrived about midnight at the first halting-place, where Ariaeus and his army were. The Greek generals and captains halted their men in battle order, and went to meet Ariaeus. Then the Greeks on their side and Ariaeus and the most important of his officers on the other side swore an oath not to betray each other and to be true allies. The natives also took another oath that they would lead the Greeks back without any deception. These oaths were preceded by the sacrifice over a shield of a bull, a boar and a ram. The Greeks dipped a sword and the natives a spear into the blood.

When these guarantees had been given, Clearchus said: 'Now, then, Ariaeus, since we are both on the same road, tell us what your view is about the way to take. Shall we go back by the same way as we came, or have you any better route in mind?'

Ariaeus replied: 'If we were to go back by the way we came, we should all die of hunger, as we have now no supplies left, and even when we were on our way here we could get nothing from the country in the last seventeen days' march,–or, if there was anything, we have had it already on our way through. Now we propose to go by a route which is certainly longer, but on it we shall not be short of supplies. We must make our first marches as long as we can, so as to put the greatest possible distance between us and the King's army. If we can once get a march of two or three days ahead of him, the King will have no further chance of catching up with us. With a small force he will not risk pursuing us; and if he comes with a large army he will not be able to march fast. Also, perhaps, he will be short of supplies. This,' he said, 'is my view of the position.'

The only possibilities in this strategy were either to get away unnoticed or to outdistance pursuit. Fortune, however, turned out to be a better leader; for, when day came, they marched with the sun on the right hand, calculating that at sunset they would come to villages in the country of Babylon. In this they were not mistaken, but when it was still afternoon they fancied that they could see enemy cavalry. Those of the Greeks who were not marching in formation ran to take up their positions, and Ariaeus, who was travelling in a carriage because he had been wounded, got down from the carriage and put on his breastplate, as did those who were with him. However, while they were arming themselves, the scouts who had been sent forward came back with the news that it was not cavalry but baggage animals grazing. Everyone realised at once that the King's camp must be somewhere near, and, indeed, smoke was visible in the villages not far ahead. But Clearchus did not lead his men forward to attack the enemy, because he knew that the soldiers were tired out and had had no food; it was also late by this time. On the other hand, he took care not to give the impression that he was running away, and so did not alter his course but kept straight ahead and at sunset encamped with the vanguard in the nearest village, where they found that even the woodwork in the houses had been carried off by the King's army.

The vanguard managed all the same to make some sort of a camp; but those who came up later in the darkness camped just as they happened to find themselves, and they made a lot of noise as they called out to each other, so much so that even the enemy could hear them. The result was that those of the enemy who were nearest actually fled from their tents. This became clear on the following day; for there was no longer a single baggage animal in sight, nor was there a camp or smoke anywhere visible in the neighbourhood. The King, too, it appeared, had been terrified at the approach of the Greeks. Indeed, he made this quite plain by what he did on the next day.

Nevertheless the Greeks themselves suffered from a sudden attack of fear in the course of the night, and there was all the commotion and din that one would expect to find when there is a state of panic. Clearchus, however, ordered Tolmides, the Elean, whom he happened to have with him (and he was the best herald of his time), to command silence and then make the proclamation: 'The generals announce that the man who brings information of who it was that let his ass go loose among the arms shall receive a reward of a talent.' Once this proclamation had been made the soldiers realised that their fear was groundless and that the generals were safe. At dawn Clearchus gave the order to the Greeks to fall in in the same formation as that which they had adopted at the time of the battle.

Chapter 3

THE GREEKS SIGN A TREATY
WITH TISSAPHERNES

WHAT I wrote just now, about the King being terrified at the approach of the Greeks, was proved by what happened next. Although on the day before he had sent and ordered the Greeks to surrender their arms, he now sent heralds at sunrise to discuss terms.

These heralds came up to the patrols in front and asked to see the generals. The men in the patrols reported this back, and Clearchus, who happened at the time to be inspecting the detachments, told them to ask the heralds to wait until he had time to spare. Then he drew up the army in formation so that it presented a fine appearance to the eye, a compact phalanx whichever way you looked, with no one visible who was not bearing arms. Clearchus then summoned the messengers, and went forward himself, accompanied by the best looking and best armed of his own troops, and told the other generals to do the same thing. When he came up to the messengers, he asked them what they wanted, and they replied that they had come to discuss terms and that they were persons of sufficient responsibility to communicate the King's wishes to the Greeks, or the Greeks' wishes to the King.

Clearchus answered: 'Then you can communicate this to him, that we shall have to have a battle first. We have nothing for breakfast, and no one shall dare to talk to the Greeks about terms unless he provides breakfast for them.'

On hearing this, the messengers rode away and soon came back again, thus making it clear that either the King or someone else to whom he had entrusted this business was somewhere close at hand. They said that the King regarded what

Clearchus had said as reasonable, and so they had brought guides with them who would, if terms were agreed upon, conduct them to a place where they could get supplies.

Clearchus asked whether the truce would apply just to those who went on their way there and back, or to everyone else as well.

'The truce will apply to everyone,' they said, 'and will be in operation until your message has been communicated to the King.'

Clearchus asked them to withdraw when they had said this, and discussed the question with the others. The general opinion was in favour of making a truce at once and then going off at their ease to get the supplies. Clearchus said: 'That is my own opinion, too; but I won't give an answer immediately. I'll spin out the time until the messengers begin to get frightened that we may decide against a truce. However,' he added, 'I imagine that our own soldiers, too, will feel just as frightened as they do.'

When he thought the right time had come, he replied that he would make a truce, and told them to lead on immediately to the supplies. This they did, but Clearchus, although the truce had been made, marched with the army in battle order and took command of the rear himself. They came upon ditches and canals which were so full of water that they could not be crossed without bridges. However, they made crossings by using palm trees which had fallen and cutting down others.

Here there was a good opportunity of seeing how Clearchus led his men, with his spear in his left hand and a staff in his right. If he thought that any of the men detailed for a job were slacking, he would pick on the right man and beat him. At the same time he went into the mud and lent a hand himself, so that everyone was ashamed not to be working hard with him. The people detailed for the job were those of about thirty years old; but, when they saw Clearchus working hard at it, even the older ones joined in. Clearchus was all the more in a hurry because he had a suspicion that the ditches were not always so full of water, as it was not the right time of the year for irrigating the plain. He suspected that the King had let the water out over the plain with this object in view, that even now the Greeks might get an impression of many dangers waiting for them on their way.

Going forward, then, they arrived at the villages where the guides told them they could get supplies. There was plenty of corn there and date wine, and a sour drink made from boiled dates. As for the dates themselves, the sort which one sees in Greece were set aside for the servants, while the ones reserved for the masters were choice fruit, wonderfully big and good looking. Their colour was just like amber, and they used to dry some of them and keep them as sweets. There was also available a drink which, though sweet, was apt to give one a headache. Here, too, for the first time the soldiers ate the 'cabbage' from the top of the palm tree, and most of them were greatly impressed with its appearance and its peculiarly pleasant taste, though it also was extrmeely apt to cause head-aches. Any palm tree from which the 'cabbage' had been taken out withered away entirely.

They stayed here for three days, and then there arrived, as envoys from the King, Tissaphernes and the King's brother-in-law and three other Persians, with many slaves to attend on them.

The Greek generals went out to meet them and Tissaphernes began the proceedings, speaking as follows through an inter-preter: 'I myself, my Greek friends, live on the frontiers of Greece; and when I saw that you had got into such an extremely awkward position I regarded it as a stroke of luck for me, if I could by any means get the King to grant my request that I should be allowed to bring you back safe to your own country. It would be an act for which, I imagine, both

you and the rest of Greece would be grateful to me. So with
this in mind I made my request to the King and told him that
it would be right and proper for him to do me this favour,
since I was the first to tell him that Cyrus was marching
against him, and when I brought the news I brought troops
with me; also I was the only one of those who faced the Greeks
in the battle who did not run away; on the contrary I broke
right through, and joined up with the King in your camp,
where he had arrived after killing Cyrus; and then, with these
men who are now with me, and are the King's most loyal
friends, I pursued Cyrus's native troops. The King then promised me that he would consider my request. At the same
time he ordered me to go to you and ask you what was your
purpose in marching against him. My advice to you is to give
a reasonable answer, so that it may be easier for me to obtain
for you any advantage I can from him.'

The Greeks then withdrew and discussed what he had said.
They replied, Clearchus being their spokesman, as follows:
'We did not come together in the first place with the purpose
of making war on the King, nor, later on, were we marching
against the King. It was rather the case, as you know perfectly
well, that Cyrus kept on giving us various excuses for the
march, with the idea of catching you off your guard and
getting us to come here. However, when we saw that he had
already run into a dangerous position, we felt ashamed before
the eye of Heaven and in men's eyes to betray him. Now that
Cyrus is dead we are not competing with the King for his
empire, and there is no reason why we should wish to do
harm to his country or want to kill him. What we would like
is to march home, provided that no one molests us. If, however, anyone ill-treats us we shall do our best, with the gods'
help, to drive him off. On the other hand, if there is anyone
who gives us help, we shall certainly do our best to give him
just as much help ourselves.'

That was what Clearchus said. Tissaphernes listened to him and said: 'I will take back your message to the King, and then again bring you his reply. We assume that the truce remains in force until I return, and we will provide you with opportunities for buying food.'

On the following day he did not put in an appearance, with the result that the Greeks began to be worried; but he came on the third day and said that he had arrived after having succeeded in getting the King to give him the job of saving the Greeks,—although there had been very many people who opposed him, saying that it was not right for the King to allow those who had marched against him to escape. Finally he said: 'You are now, therefore, in a position to accept our guarantee. We will promise to give you a safe conduct through our country and bring you back to Greece without treachery, and provide you with opportunities for buying food; when it is impossible to buy food, we will allow you to take your supplies from the country. You on your side must swear an oath to us and promise that you will march as though you were in a friendly country; that, when we fail to provide you with an opportunity for buying provisions, you will take your food and drink without doing damage, and if we do give you an opportunity, you will pay for the supplies you get.'

This was agreed upon. The oaths were sworn, and Tissaphernes and the King's brother-in-law offered their right hands to the Greek generals and captains and took theirs in return. Afterwards Tissaphernes said: 'And now I shall go back to the King. As soon as I have settled the business I have to do, I shall return, fully prepared to escort you back to Greece and to return myself to my own province.'

Chapter 4

THE MARCH BEGINS WITH MUTUAL SUSPICION

AFTERWARDS the Greeks and Ariaeus, camping close to each other, waited for Tissaphernes for more than twenty days. During this time Ariaeus's brothers and other relatives came to see him, and other Persians came to visit his friends. They gave an encouraging account of things and brought to some people guarantees from the King that he bore them no ill will for their having taken service with Cyrus against him nor for anything else in what had happened previously.

After these conversations it became obvious that Ariaeus's people were less interested in the Greeks, and this was an additional reason for most of the Greeks disliking them. Indeed, the soldiers went to Clearchus and the other generals and said: 'What are we waiting for? Is it not clear that the King would do anything to destroy us, so as to make the other Greeks afraid of marching, as we did, against the Great King? At the moment, because his army is dispersed, he is, of set purpose, encouraging us to stay where we are; but as soon as his forces are concentrated again he is quite certain to attack us. Or, perhaps, he is digging trenches or raising fortifications somewhere to make our road impassable. Certainly he won't consent, if he can possibly help it, to us going back to Greece and telling the story of how we, so few of us, conquered the King at his own palace gates and, then, making him a figure of fun, got safe home again.'

Clearchus replied as follows to those who said this: 'I feel exactly the same as you do. On the other hand, I consider that, if we go away now, our action will appear to amount to a declaration of war and an infringement of the truce. The first thing that will happen after this will be that no one will give us an opportunity for buying supplies or any chance of feeding ourselves. Then, there will be no one to show us the way. And, at the same time, if we act as you suggest, Ariaeus will immediately part company with us. The result will be that we shall not have a single friend left. On the contrary, those who were our friends before will become our enemies. Whether we have any more rivers to cross I do not know; but we do know that it is impossible to get across the Euphrates in the face of enemy opposition. Then, we have no cavalry on our side, if it comes to a battle, whereas the enemy's cavalry is the most numerous and the most efficient of his arms. It follows that, if we won a victory, we should hardly be able to kill any of our enemies, while, if we were defeated, none of us could escape. If the King wants to destroy us, I have no idea why he, with all these advantages on his side, should have to take an oath and exchange the right hand of friendship and perjure himself and make his guarantees worthless in the eyes both of Greeks and natives.' This sort of argument Clearchus used frequently.

Meanwhile Tissaphernes with his army arrived with the intention, apparently, of going home. Orontas came, too, with his army, and bringing with him the King's daughter as his wife. They now marched forward from there with Tissaphernes leading the way and providing opportunities for buying provisions. Ariaeus, too, with Cyrus's native army, marched in the company of Tissaphernes and Orontas and camped together with them. The Greeks looked with suspicion on them and kept themselves to themselves on the march, employing their own guides, and the two armies invariably camped with at least three miles between them. Each side watched the other as though each were enemies, and this, of course, produced more suspicion. Sometimes, when they were both collecting firewood from the same place, or bring-

ing in fodder and such things, fights broke out between them,
and this, too, naturally provoked ill feeling.

After a three days' march they came to the Wall of Media,
as it is called, and passed over to the other side of it. This wall
was made of burnt bricks laid in bitumen. It was twenty feet
thick, a hundred feet high, and was said to be sixty miles long.
It is quite close to Babylon.

Then came a two days' march of twenty-four miles in the
course of which they crossed two canals, one of them by a
permanent bridge and the other by a pontoon bridge of seven
boats. The canal water was supplied from the river Tigris,
and from the canals ditches were cut to extend over the
country, big ones at first and then smaller ones, until in the
end they were just little channels like we have in Greece for
the millet fields.

Then they came to the Tigris, near which there was a large
and populous city called Sittace, a mile and a half away from
the river. The Greeks camped by the city near a beautiful
large park thickly planted with all sorts of trees. The native
troops had crossed the Tigris but were nowhere to be seen.

After supper, when Proxenus and Xenophon happened to
be going for a walk in front of the place where the arms were
piled, a man came up and asked the sentries where he could
find Proxenus or Clearchus. He did not enquire for Menon,
though he came from Menon's friend, Ariaeus. Proxenus then
said: 'I am the person you are looking for,' and the man spoke
as follows: 'I have been sent by Ariaeus and Artaozus who are
faithful to Cyrus and friends of yours. They urge you to be
on your guard against attack from the native army during the
night. There is a large force in the park near by. They also
urge you to post a guard on the bridge over the Tigris, as
Tissaphernes plans, if he can, to destroy it during the night so
that you will be unable to get across, and will be stranded
between the river and the canal.'

When Proxenus and Xenophon heard this they took the man to Clearchus and told him what he said. Clearchus was greatly disturbed and alarmed when he heard the story. But there was a young man present who, after a little consideration, said: 'There is an inconsistency in these two plans of making an attack and of destroying the bridge. It is obvious that this attack must be either successful or unsuccessful. If it is successful, what is the point of their destroying the bridge? We would have no chance of escaping to safety even if there were a lot of bridges. Suppose, on the other hand, that it is unsuccessful; then, if the bridge is destroyed, they will have no means of escape. Moreover, if the bridge is destroyed, not one of all their friends on the other side will be able to come to their aid.'

Clearchus listened to this and then asked the messenger how much ground there was between the Tigris and the canal. 'There is a lot,' he replied, 'and there are villages and a number of large cities.'

At this point they made up their minds that the natives had their own object in sending this man. What they were afraid of was that the Greeks might take the bridge to bits and stay on the island, with the Tigris and the canal to form defences on both sides. They could get supplies from the country between the two, which was extensive and rich and contained people to work in it. Finally, their position would become a resort for anyone who wanted to work against the King.

After coming to this conclusion, they turned in for the night. All the same, however, they did post a guard on the bridge, and, as the guard reported, there was no attack from any direction nor did a single enemy come near the bridge.

When it was dawn they crossed the bridge, which was constructed of thirty-seven boats. They took every precaution possible, since some of the Greeks in Tissaphernes' service had reported that the natives were going to attack while the

Greeks were crossing over. This report, however, was untrue, though, while they were going across, Glous and some others put in an appearance to see whether they actually were crossing the river. When he saw that they were, he rode straight off.

A four days' march of sixty miles brought them from the Tigris to the river Physcus, which was a hundred feet in breadth and had a bridge over it. There was a big city here called Opis. Near this city the illegitimate brother of Cyrus and Artaxerxes met with the Greeks. He was leading a large army from Susa and Ecbatana, apparently to fight on the King's side. As the Greeks marched past, he halted his army and watched them. Clearchus led his men forward two abreast, marching and halting them at intervals. When the vanguard halted there was naturally a halt all along the column, with the result that even the Greeks themselves thought that their army was extremely large, while the Persian was absolutely astonished at the sight.

From here a six days' march of ninety miles across the desert through Media brought them to the villages owned by Parysatis, the mother of Cyrus and Artaxerxes. Tissaphernes, by way of an insult to Cyrus, handed these over to the Greeks to take what they liked except for slaves. There was a lot of corn there and sheep and other valuables.

Then came a four days' march of sixty miles through the desert, with the river Tigris on their left. On the first day's march they saw a large and prosperous city called Caenae, built on the other side of the river. The natives from this city brought loaves and cheeses and wine across the river on rafts made of hides.

Chapter 5

TISSAPHERNES' TREACHERY

NEXT, they came to the river Zapatas, which was four hundred feet in breadth. They stayed three days here, and during this time, although suspicion persisted, there was no real evidence of treachery. Clearchus therefore decided to have an interview with Tissaphernes and do his best to put a stop to these suspicions before they ended in open hostility. He sent someone to say that he wanted an interview with him, and Tissaphernes readily invited him to come. When they met, Clearchus spoke as follows: 'I know, Tissaphernes, that we have sworn oaths and exchanged guarantees that we will do no harm to each other; yet I observe that you are watching our moves as though we were enemies, and we, noticing this, are watching yours, too. On looking into things, I am unable to find evidence that you are trying to do us any harm, and I am perfectly sure that, as far as we are concerned, we do not even contemplate such a thing; and so I decided to discuss matters with you, to see if we could put an end to this mutual mistrust. I know, too, of cases that have occurred in the past when people, sometimes as the result of slanderous information and sometimes merely on the strength of suspicion, have become frightened of each other and then, in their anxiety to strike first before anything is done to them, have done irreparable harm to those who neither intended nor even wanted to do them any harm at all. I have come then in the conviction that misunderstandings of this sort can best be ended by personal contact, and I want to make it clear to you that you have no reason to distrust us. The first and most important point is that our oaths to the gods prevent us from being enemies of each other. A man who has his conscience burdened with

neglect of such oaths is not a man whom I would ever congratulate. I do not see how one who is an enemy of the gods
can run fast enough away, nor where he can flee to escape,
nor what darkness could cover him, nor how he could find a
position strong enough for a refuge. For all things in all places
are subject to the gods, and the power of the gods extends
equally over everything.

'This, then, is what I feel about the gods, and about the
oaths we swore, oaths which, for safe keeping, we deposited
in the gods' hands at the time when our friendship was com-
pacted. And now, when it comes to our relations with men, I
think that there you are, at the moment, the greatest advantage
which we have. With your help every road is easy, every
river passable, and there can be no shortage of supplies; but
without your help our entire journey would be in the dark,
since we know nothing about it; every river would be a
difficult obstacle, every collection of people would inspire us
with fear, but most fearful of all would be uninhabited places
in which one is perplexed every way.

'If we were really mad enough to kill you what else would
that amount to except that we should kill our benefactor and
then have to contend with the King, who would be there in
waiting and in full force to avenge you? And as far as I am
concerned, I can tell you of all the great expectations of which
I should be depriving myself if I tried to do you any harm.
The reason why I wanted Cyrus to be my friend was because
I thought that of all his contemporaries he was the best able
to help those he wished to help. But, now, I observe that you
have Cyrus's provinces and Cyrus's power and retain your
own as well; and the King's power, which was opposed to
Cyrus, is on your side. With all these advantages of yours,
who could be such a fool as not to want to be your friend?
I will tell you, too, the reason why I have good hopes that you
also will want to be our friend. First, there are the Mysians,

who, I know, cause you trouble and whom, I feel sure, I could bring to heel with the force I have at present. I know about the Pisidians, too, and I hear that there are a number of equally troublesome peoples, all of whom, I think, I could prevent from constantly interfering with your peace of mind. I am aware that you are particularly angry with the Egyptians, and I do not see how you could get a better force than the one I have now to help you in bringing retribution on them. Yes, and to the states on your borders you could be, if you liked, the most valuable of friends or, if any of them gave you trouble, you could, with us in your service, behave like a dictator, and we would not be serving you merely for the sake of pay, but also because of the proper gratitude which we would feel to you for having saved our lives. When I think of all this, your lack of faith in us seems to me so incredible that I should much like to know the name of the man who can speak so persuasively as to get you to believe that we are intriguing against you.'

This was what Clearchus said. Tissaphernes replied as follows: 'I am really delighted, Clearchus, to hear your sensible speech. With the sentiments which you have, it seems to me that, if you were to contemplate doing me an injury, you would be simultaneously plotting against your own interests. But, now, you must listen in your turn so that you may be convinced that you, too, would be wrong in entertaining any lack of confidence either in the King or in me.

'If we really wanted to destroy you, do you think we are short in numbers of cavalry or infantry or in the right sort of equipment with which to be able to damage you, while incurring no risk of retaliation? Or do you think it likely that we could not find favourable ground on which to attack you? Remember all the flat country which you go through with great difficulty even when the inhabitants are friendly to you. Consider all the mountains you have to cross which we could

occupy first and make impassable for you. Think of all the
rivers where we could cut you into detachments and engage
with as many at a time as we liked. And there are some of
these rivers which you could not get across at all unless we
brought you across. Even supposing we had the worst of it
along all these lines, you can be sure, anyway, that fire is more
powerful than crops, and if we burnt the crops we could bring
famine into the battle against you; and, with all the courage
in the world, you could not fight against that. With all these
means of making war on you at our disposal, and with none
of them entailing any risk on us, how can you imagine that
out of them all we should choose the one method which
involves wickedness in the sight of the gods and shame in the
eyes of men? It is simply and solely among people who are
without means and desperate and without any other way out
(and even then they must be villains) that you will find men
willing to secure their ends by perjury to the gods and faith-
lessness to men. It is not so with us, Clearchus. We are not
such blockheads and simpletons.

'You may ask why, since we have the power to destroy you,
we have not proceeded to do so. Let me tell you that what
is responsible for this is my own desire that I should earn the
confidence of the Greeks and that I should, by doing good to
them, return to the coast with the support of that mercenary
army on which Cyrus, in his journey inland, relied only because
he gave them their pay. As to the ways in which your help
is useful to me, you have mentioned some of them yourself.
The most important of them, though, is one that I know of.
I mean, that it is for the King alone to wear the crown upright
on his head; but, with your help, someone who is not the
King might easily, perhaps, have the crown in his heart.'

Clearchus thought that in this he was speaking sincerely.
'Those people, then,' he said, 'who try by their slanders to
make us enemies, when we have all these reasons for friend-

ship,–do they not deserve the worst that can happen to them?'

'Yes,' said Tissaphernes, 'and if you are prepared, generals and captains, to come to me, I will name openly those who told me that you were in a conspiracy against me and my army.'

'I will bring them all,' said Clearchus, 'and I on my side will let you know where I get my information about you.'

After this conversation Tissaphernes behaved with great affection towards Clearchus, urged him to stay with him for the time being and had him as his guest at supper.

Next day, on his return to camp, Clearchus made it clear that he considered that he was on very good terms with Tissaphernes, and that those Greeks who were proved to have been spreading slanders should be punished as traitors and disaffected to the Greek cause. It was Menon whom he suspected of spreading the slanders, as he knew that he and Ariaeus had had an interview with Tissaphernes, and also that he was secretly forming a party of opposition against him with the idea of getting the whole army on to his side and becoming a friend of Tissaphernes. Clearchus wanted to have the loyalty of the whole army himself and to have grumblers put out of his way.

Some of the soldiers opposed Clearchus, saying that all the captains and generals ought not to go, and that they ought not to trust Tissaphernes; but Clearchus insisted strongly, until in the end he succeeded in getting five generals and twenty captains to go. About two hundred of the other soldiers went with them, too, as though to buy provisions.

When they arrived at the entrance of Tissaphernes' tent, the generals were invited inside. They were Proxenus the Boeotian, Menon the Thessalian, Agias the Arcadian, Clearchus the Spartan and Socrates the Achaean. The captains waited at the entrance. Not long afterwards, at one and the same signal, those who were inside were seized and those who were outside were massacred. After that contingents of native cavalry rode over the plain and killed all the Greeks they could find, slaves and free-men alike. The Greeks saw with surprise these cavalry manœuvres from their camp and were in doubt about what they were doing until Nicarchus the Arcadian escaped and came there with a wound in his stomach and holding his intestines in his hands. He told them everything which had happened,

As a result the Greeks ran to arms. There was general dismay and they expected that the enemy would march immediately on the camp. However, they did not come in full force, only Ariaeus and Artaozus and Mithridates, men who had been most in Cyrus's confidence. The Greek interpreter said that he saw with them, and recognised, Tissaphernes' brother also. Other Persians, about three hundred strong, wearing breastplates, came with them.

When they were near the camp they asked that any Greek general or captain who might be there should come out to them so that they could deliver a message from the King. Then, taking every precaution, the Greek generals Cleanor of Orchomenus and Sophaenetus of Stymphalus went out, and Xenophon the Athenian went with them so as to find out what had happened to Proxenus. Chirisophus happened to be out of camp with a party collecting provisions in some village.

When they had halted within hearing of each other, Ariaeus spoke as follows: 'Greeks, Clearchus has been found guilty of perjury and of breaking the truce. He has got what he deserved, and is dead. But Proxenus and Menon, since they reported his conspiracy, are held in great honour. As for you, the King asks you to surrender your arms. He says that they are his property, as they used to be the property of Cyrus, who was his servant.'

To this the Greeks made their reply, with Cleanor of Orchomenus as their spokesman. 'Ariaeus, you utter villain,' he said, 'and you others who used to be Cyrus's friends, do you feel no shame before the gods and before men? You took an oath that you would have the same friends and enemies as we had, and then you betrayed us with that godless and criminal Tissaphernes. You have killed the very people with whom you swore the oath, and now, after abandoning the rest of us, you come against us with our enemies.'

Ariaeus said: 'The fact is that it was first proved that Clearchus was forming a conspiracy against Tissaphernes and Orontas and all of us who were with them.'

Xenophon replied to this and said: 'Then, so far as Clearchus is concerned, he has got what he deserved, if he did break his oath and contravene the truce. It is right that perjurers should be destroyed. But as for Proxenus and Menon, since they are benefactors of yours and our generals, send them to us. It seems clear that, being friends to both parties, they will try to give the best advice both for your interests and for ours.'

The natives took a long time to discuss this among themselves, and then went away without making any reply to the suggestion.

Chapter 6

CHARACTERS OF THE
FIVE GENERALS

THE generals, who were made prisoners in this way, were taken to the King and beheaded. One of them, Clearchus, was admitted by all who were in a position to speak of him from experience as having been a real soldier and extraordinarily devoted to war. This is clear from the fact that, so long as Sparta was at war with Athens, he remained in Greece, but after the peace he persuaded the home government that the Thracians were acting aggressively towards the Greeks, and, having, up to a point, got his own way with the ephors, he sailed from home to make war on the Thracians north of the Chersonese and Perinthus. After he had set sail, however, the ephors for some reason changed their minds and attempted to make him return from the Isthmus, and at this point he would not obey them any longer, but sailed away for the Hellespont. As a result of this he was condemned to death for insubordination by the Spartan authorities. Then, as an exile, he approached Cyrus, and I have written elsewhere of the arguments he used to gain Cyrus's favour. Cyrus gave him ten thousand darics and, on receiving the money, he did not give himself an easy life, but spent it on raising an army. With this army he made war on the Thracians, defeated them in a pitched battle and from then on plundered and ravaged their land and carried on with the war until Cyrus needed his army. Then he left Thrace with the intention of fighting in another war with Cyrus.

This seems to me to be the record of a man who was devoted to war. He could have lived in peace without incurring any reproaches or any harm, but he chose to make war.

He could have lived a life of ease, but he preferred a hard life with warfare. He could have had money and security, but he chose to make the money he had less, by engaging in war. Indeed, he liked spending money on war just as one might spend it on love affairs or any other pleasure.

All this shows how devoted he was to war. As for his great qualities as a soldier, they appear in the facts that he was fond of adventure, ready to lead an attack on the enemy by day or night, and that, when he was in an awkward position, he kept his head, as everyone agrees who was with him anywhere. It was said that he had all the qualities of leadership which a man of his sort could have. He had an outstanding ability for planning means by which an army could get supplies, and seeing that they appeared; and he was also well able to impress on those who were with him that Clearchus was a man to be obeyed. He achieved this result by his toughness. He had a forbidding appearance and a harsh voice. His punishments were severe ones and were sometimes inflicted in anger, so that there were times when he was sorry himself for what he had done. With him punishment was a matter of principle, for he thought that an army without discipline was good for nothing; indeed, it is reported that he said that a soldier ought to be more frightened of his own commander than of the enemy if he was going to turn out one who could keep a good guard, or abstain from doing harm to his own side, or go into battle without second thoughts. So it happened that in difficult positions the soldiers would give him complete confidence and wished for no one better. On these occasions, they said that his forbidding look seemed positively cheerful, and his toughness appeared as confidence in the face of the enemy, so that it was no longer toughness to them but something to make them feel safe. On the other hand, when the danger was over and there was a chance of going away to take service under someone else, many of them deserted him, since, so far from having anything attractive about him, he was invariably tough and savage, so that the relations between his soldiers and him were like those of boys to a schoolmaster.

Thus it came about that he never had followers who were there because of friendship or good feeling towards him. On the other hand, he exacted complete obedience from all who were put under his command by their cities or who served with him because of poverty or under some other compulsion. Then, once they began to win victories with him, one could see how important were the factors which made his men into good soldiers. They had the advantage of being confident in the face of the enemy, and they were disciplined because they were afraid of his punishments. As a commander, then, this was what he was like; but he was said not to be very fond of serving under anybody's else's command. At the time of his death he was about fifty years old.

Proxenus the Boeotian from his very earliest youth wanted to become a man capable of doing great things, and with this end in view he spent money on being educated by Gorgias of Leontini. After he had been with him for a time, he came to the conclusion that he was now capable both of commanding an army and, if he became friends with the great, of doing them no less good than they did him; so he joined in this adventure of Cyrus's, imagining that he would gain from it a great name, and great power, and plenty of money. Yet, with all these ambitions, he made this point also abundantly plain, that he did not want to get any of these things by unfair means; on the contrary, he thought that he ought to gain them by great and honourable actions or not at all. He was a good commander for people of a gentlemanly type, but he was not capable of impressing his soldiers with a feeling of respect or fear for him. Indeed, he showed more diffidence in front of his soldiers than his subordinates showed in front of him, and it was more obvious that he was afraid of being unpopular with his troops than that his troops were afraid of disobeying his orders. He imagined that to be a good general, and to gain the name of being one, it was enough to give praise to those who did well and to withhold it from those who did badly. The result was that decent people in his entourage liked him, but unprincipled people undermined his position, since they thought he was easily managed. At the time of his death he was about thirty years old.

Menon the Thessalian made it perfectly clear that his dominant ambition was to get rich. He wanted to be a general so that he could earn more pay; he wanted honours so that he could make something extra out of them; his wish to be friends with the most influential people arose from his desire to avoid punishment for his misdeeds. He thought that the shortest cut to the satisfaction of his ambitions was by means of perjury and lying and deceit; consequently he regarded sincerity and truthfulness as equivalent to simple-mindedness. It was obvious that he felt no affection for anyone, but if he said he was anyone's friend, it was pretty clear that he was intriguing against him. He never laughed at his enemies, but in conversation he never took any of his own people seriously. He had no designs on the property of his enemies, as he considered it difficult to get hold of what belonged to people who were on their guard; but as for his friends' property, which was unguarded, he thought he was most remarkable in knowing how easy it was to get his hands on to it. When he saw that a man would break promises and do wrong, he regarded him as well equipped and was frightened of him; but he tried to treat a man who was scrupulous and had regard for truth as though he were a half-wit. In the same way as some people take pride in being god-fearing and truthful and upright, Menon took pride in his ability to deceive, in his fabrications and falsehoods, and in sneering at his friends. He always looked upon a person who had scruples as being only half educated. When he wanted to stand high in anyone's friendship, he thought that the way to achieve this end was by running down those who already occupied the position he wanted. His scheme for ensuring his soldiers' obedience to him was to be a partner in their crimes. He considered that, by making a display both of his great powers and his willingness to misuse them, he was entitled to honours and deference. When anyone left his service, he used to say that it was a kindness on his part to have made use of him and not to have made away with him. With regard to the more obscure passages of his life, one might say what was untrue; but the following facts are general knowledge. When he still had the beauty of a boy, he persuaded Aristippus to give him the command of his mercenaries. Then, he lived on very intimate terms with Ariaeus, though he was a native, because Ariaeus was fond of good-looking young men; and he himself, before he grew a beard, kept Tharypas, who was an adult, as a male friend. His fellow generals were put to death because they had marched with Cyrus against the King; but he, though he had done as they did, did not suffer the same death. After the other generals were put to death he was punished by the King and did not die, as Clearchus and the other generals had died, by beheading (which seemed to be the quickest sort of death), but is said to have finally met his end after having lived for a year under the worst sort of treatment, like a common criminal.

Agias the Arcadian and Socrates the Achaean were also put to death. No one could speak slightingly of their courage in war or accuse them of lacking consideration for their friends. They were both about thirty-five years old.

BOOK

III

THE MARCH TO
KURDESTAN

Chapter 1

XENOPHON TAKES THE INITIATIVE

WITH their generals arrested and the captains and soldiers who had gone with them put to death, the Greeks were in an extremely awkward position. It occurred to them that they were near the King's capital and that around them on all sides were numbers of peoples and cities who were their enemies; no one was likely in the future to provide them with a chance of buying food. They were at least a thousand miles away from Greece; they had no guide to show them the way; they were shut in by impassable rivers which traversed their homeward journey; even the natives who had marched on the capital with Cyrus had turned against them, and they were left by themselves without a single cavalryman in their army, so that it was evident that, if they won a victory, they could not kill any of their enemies, and if they were defeated themselves, none of them would be left alive. With all this to reflect upon they were in a state of deep despondency. Only a few tasted food that evening, and a few lit fires. Many of them did not parade by the arms that night, but took their rest just where each man happened to be, and could not sleep because of their misery and their longing for their home lands and parents and wives and children, which they thought that they would never see again. In this state of mind they all took their rest.

There was an Athenian in the army called Xenophon, who accompanied the expedition neither as a general nor a captain nor an ordinary soldier. Proxenus, who was an old friend of his, had sent for him from his home and promised to make him the friend of Cyrus whom, he said, he valued above his own country. When Xenophon had read Proxenus's letter he consulted Socrates the Athenian about the proposed expedition, and Socrates, suspecting that friendship with Cyrus might involve complaints at Athens (since Cyrus was thought to have been very active in helping the Spartans in their war with Athens), recommended Xenophon to go to Delphi and consult the god on the question of the expedition. Xenophon went there and asked Apollo the following question: 'To what God shall I pray and sacrifice in order that I may best and most honourably go on the journey I have in mind, and return home safe and successful?' Apollo's reply was that he should sacrifice to the appropriate gods, and when Xenophon got back to Athens he told Socrates the oracle's answer. When Socrates heard it he blamed him for not first asking whether it was better for him to go on the expedition or to stay at home; instead of that he had made his own decision that he ought to go, and then enquired how he might best make the journey. 'However', he said, 'since this was the way you put your question, you must do what the god has told you.'

Xenophon then made the sacrifices which the god had ordered and set sail. He found Proxenus and Cyrus at Sardis just on the point of starting on the march into the interior and he was introduced to Cyrus. Proxenus was eager for him to stay with them and Cyrus too joined him in this, saying that as soon as the campaign was over he would send him back home immediately. The expedition was supposed to be against the Pisidians. Xenophon thus joined the army under a false impression, though this was not the fault of Proxenus, since neither he nor anyone else among the Greeks, except for Clearchus, knew that the expedition was marching against the King. However, when they got to Cilicia, it already seemed obvious to everyone that it was against the King that they were marching. All the same, though unwillingly and with apprehensions about the journey, most people continued on the march, not wanting to lose face in each other's eyes, and in the eyes of Cyrus. Xenophon was no different from the rest, and

now in their difficult position he was as miserable as anyone
else and could not get to sleep. However, he got a little sleep
in the end and had a dream. He dreamed that there was a
thunderstorm and that a thunderbolt fell on his father's house
and then the whole house was on fire. He woke up immediately, feeling very frightened, and considered that in some
respects the dream was a good one, because in the midst of his
difficulties and dangers he had dreamed of a great light from
Zeus; but in other respects he was alarmed by it, because the
dream seemed to him to have come from Zeus in his character
of the King and the fire had seemed to blaze all round him
and this might mean that he would not be able to leave the
King's country but would be shut in on all sides by one difficulty or another. But what is really meant by having a dream
like this can be seen from what happened after the dream.

This is what did happen. As soon as he woke up the first
thing that came into his head was this: 'What am I lying here
for? The night is passing and at dawn the enemy will probably be here. If we fall into the King's hands, there is nothing
to prevent us from seeing the most terrible things happening,
from suffering all kinds of tortures and from being put to
death in ignominy. Yet so far from anybody bothering to
take any steps for our defence, we are lying here as though we
had a chance of enjoying a quiet time. What city, then, do I
expect will produce the general to take the right steps? Am
I waiting until I become a little older? I shall never be any
older at all if I hand myself over to the enemy to-day.'

Then he stood up and first of all called together Proxenus's
captains. When they had come together, he said: 'I personally,
captains, cannot sleep any more than, I expect, you can, and
I can no longer lie still when I think of the position we are in.
For there is no doubt that the enemy only made open war on
us when they thought that their plans were complete, but on
our side there is now nobody who is thinking out counter

measures whereby we can put up as good a fight as possible. Yet if we relax and fall into the King's power, what sort of treatment can we expect from him? He is the man who cut off and fixed to a stake the head and hand of his own brother, his own mother's son, even when he was dead. So what sort of treatment can we expect, we who have no blood relation to take our side, and who marched against him with the intention of deposing him and making him a subject, and killing him if we could? Will he not go to all possible lengths in trying to inflict on us every conceivable misery and so make all men afraid of ever marching against him again? No, it is surely clear that we must do everything in our power to avoid falling into his hands.

'Now, personally, while the truce was in force, I could never stop feeling sorry for us and looking with envy on the King and those on his side. I considered what a large and splendid country they had, what inexhaustible supplies, what quantities of servants, of cattle and gold and clothing material; and then I thought on the other hand of our men's prospects –that we could only get a share of all these good things by paying for it (and I knew that there were not many left who had the money to do so), and that the oaths we had sworn prevented us from acquiring supplies in any other way except by paying for them. When I reckoned all this up, I sometimes used to feel more misgivings about the truce than I now do about the war. Now, however, they have put an end to the truce, and I think that the period of their arrogance and of our uneasy feelings is also ended. For now these good things lie in front of us as prizes for whichever side shows itself to be the better men; the gods are judges of the contest, and they will naturally be on our side, since it was our enemies who took their names in vain, while we, with many good things before our eyes, resolutely kept our hands off them because of the oaths we had sworn to the gods. So it seems to me that we can enter the contest with much more confidence than they can. Then we are physically better able than they are to endure cold and heat and hardship; our morale is, with the gods on our side, better than theirs; and if the gods grant us victory, as they did before, our enemies are easier to wound and kill than we are.

'Quite likely there are others who feel the same as I do. Well then, in heaven's name, let us not wait for other people to come to us and call upon us to do great deeds. Let us instead be the first to summon the rest to the path of honour. Show yourselves to be the bravest of all the captains, with more of a right to leadership than those who are our leaders at present. As for me, if you are willing to take the initiative like this, I am prepared to follow you, and if you appoint me to be your leader I am making no excuses about my age. Indeed I think I am already sufficiently grown up to act in my own defence.'

This was what Xenophon said, and, after listening to him, all the captains urged him to be their leader–all except for a man there called Apollonides, who had a Boeotian accent. This Apollonides declared that it was nonsense to say that there was any chance of safety except by getting, if it was possible, the King's goodwill, and at the same time he started talking about all their difficulties. Xenophon, however, cut him short and spoke as follows: 'My dear good man, you are the sort of person who neither understands what he sees nor remembers what he hears. Yet you were there with all the rest when the King, after Cyrus's death and in his pride because of it, sent and demanded that we should surrender our arms; and then, when we, so far from surrendering them, made ready for battle and went and encamped by his army, he left no stone unturned–sending people to negotiate, begging for a truce, providing us with supplies–until he got his truce. But when our generals and captains went into a conference, just as you are recommending, and left their arms behind, relying on the truce, what happened? Are they not at this moment being beaten and tortured and insulted, and are not even able, poor devils, to die, though death, I imagine, is what they are longing for? With all this knowledge in your possession, do you actually maintain that those who recommend self-defence are talking nonsense, and tell us to go and make another attempt at getting the King's goodwill? Soldiers, my view is that we should not suffer this fellow in our society; we should take away his captaincy, put the baggage on his back and use him as an animal. Being a Greek, and being what he is, he brings shame not only on his own native place but on the whole of Greece.'

Then Agasias the Stymphalian broke in and said: 'This fellow has got nothing to do either with Boeotia or with Greece. I have observed that he has holes in both his ears, just like a Lydian.' This was actually the case, and so they drove him out.

The others went round the various detachments and where there was a general still alive they called for him, or, in cases where he was missing, for his deputy commander; where there was a captain still alive, they called for the captain. When they had all assembled they sat down in front of the place where the arms were kept. The generals and captains assembled there were about a hundred all together, and the meeting took place at about midnight. Hieronymus of Elis, the oldest of Proxenus's captains, then began the proceedings and spoke as follows: 'Generals and captains, in view of our present position we decided to meet together ourselves and to invite you to join us, so that, if possible, we might come to some useful decision. I now call upon Xenophon to speak as he has already spoken to us.'

Xenophon accordingly spoke as follows: 'Here is one thing which we all know, namely, that the King and Tissaphernes have made prisoners of all those of us whom they could and are obviously planning, if they can manage it, to destroy the rest of us. Our part, as I see it, is to do everything possible to prevent our ever coming into the power of the natives–indeed to see rather that they are in our power. I should like to assure you of this point–that you who have assembled here in your present numbers are placed in an extraordinarily responsible position. All these soldiers of ours have their eyes on you, and if they see that you are downhearted they will all become cowards, while if you are yourselves clearly prepared to meet the enemy and if you call on the rest to do their part, you can be sure that they will follow you and try to be like you. It is right, too, I think, that you should show some superiority over them. After all you are generals, you are officers and captains. In peace time you got more pay and more respect than they did. Now, in war time, you ought to hold yourselves to be braver than the general mass of men, and to take decisions for the rest, and, if necessary, to be the first to do the hard work. I think that first of all you could do a great service to the army by appointing generals and captains as quickly as possible to take the places of those whom we have lost. For where there is no one in control nothing useful or distinguished can ever get done. This is roughly true of all departments of life, and entirely true where soldiering is concerned. Here it is discipline that makes one feel safe, while lack of discipline has destroyed many people before now.

'Then I think that, after you have appointed the required number of officers, if you were to call a meeting of the rest of the soldiers and put some heart into them, that would be just what the occasion demands. At the moment I expect you realise, just as I do, how dispirited they were in handing in their arms for the night and in going on guard. In that condition I cannot see how any use can be made of them, whether by night or by day. But there will be a great rise in their spirits if one can change the way they think, so that instead of having in their heads the one idea of "what is going to happen to me?" they may think "what action am I going to take?"

'You are well aware that it is not numbers or strength that bring the victories in war. No, it is when one side goes against the enemy with the gods' gift of a stronger morale that their adversaries, as a rule, cannot withstand them. I have noticed this point too, my friends, that in soldiering the people whose one aim is to keep alive usually find a wretched and dishonourable death, while the people who, realising that death is the common lot of all men, make it their endeavour to die with honour, somehow seem more often to reach old age and to have a happier life when they are alive. These are facts which you too should realise (our situation demands it) and should show that you yourselves are brave men and should call on the rest to do likewise.'

So he ended his speech. Chirisophus spoke after him and said: 'Up to now, Xenophon, the only thing I knew about you was that I had heard you were an Athenian. Now I congratulate you on your speech and your actions, and I should like to see here as many people of your sort as possible. Then we should have the right spirit all through the army. And now,' he went on, 'let us not waste time, my friends. Let us go away, and let those who are short of officers choose new ones. When you have chosen them, come to the centre of the camp and bring along those whom you have elected. Then we will muster the rest of the soldiers there. Tolmides the herald had better come with us.'

With these words he got to his feet so as to show that there should be no delay, that what was necessary should be done at once. Afterwards the following were chosen as officers: Timasion, a Dardanian, to take the place of Clearchus, Xanthicles, an Achaean, to take Socrates' place, Cleanor, an Arcadian, to take Agias's place, Philesius, an Arcadian, to take that of Menon, and Xenophon, an Athenian, in the place of Proxenus.

Chapter 2

THE COUNCIL OF WAR

DAWN was just breaking when the new officers were chosen, and they came to the centre of the camp and decided to post sentries and call the soldiers to a meeting. When the rest of the army were assembled, Chirisophus stood up first and spoke as follows: 'Soldiers, our position is undoubtedly difficult. We have lost some very able generals and captains and soldiers, and in addition to that even Ariaeus's men, who used to be on our side, have turned traitor to us. All the same what we have to do is to surmount our difficulties like brave men, not to give in, but to try, if we can, to win honour and safety by victory. And if that is beyond us, then at least let us die with honour, and never, so long as we live, come into the power of our enemies. For if we do, we shall have to suffer, I imagine, the sort of fate which I pray the gods will bring upon our opponents.'

Next Cleanor of Orchomenus stood up and spoke as follows: 'You can see with your own eyes, soldiers, how perjured and godless the King is. You can see the treachery of Tissaphernes. He it was who said that he was a neighbour of Greece, and that he would attach the greatest importance to saving our lives. On this understanding he swore an oath to us in person, he in person gave us his right hand, and in person he deceived our generals and made prisoners of them, showing so little respect for Zeus, the guardian of hospitality, that he actually shared a meal with Clearchus and then used this very fact to entrap and destroy our officers. Then there is Ariaeus, whom we were prepared to make King, and with whom we exchanged guarantees that neither would betray the other: he too, showing no fear of the gods or respect for the memory of the dead Cyrus, though he was treated with the utmost distinction by Cyrus when he was alive, has now left us and joined with Cyrus's bitterest enemies, with whom he is attempting to injure us, who were Cyrus's friends. Well, I pray that the gods will give these men what they deserve. As for us, who see all this, we must never again be deceived by them, but must fight as hard as we can, and bear whatever is the will of heaven.'

After him Xenophon stood up. He had put on the best-looking uniform that he could, thinking that, if the gods granted victory, victory deserved the best-looking armour, or if he was to die, then it was right for him to put on his best clothes and be wearing them when he met his death. He began his speech as follows: 'Cleanor has spoken of the natives' perjury and treachery, and I feel sure that you agree with what he has said. If, then, we want to make friends with them again, we shall have to be very downhearted indeed, when we consider what happened to our generals, who, because they trusted in their good faith, put themselves into their hands. But if our purpose is to take our arms in our hands and to make them pay for what they have done and for the future to fight total war against them, then, with the help of heaven, we have many glorious hopes of safety.'

Just as he was saying this, someone sneezed, and, when the soldiers heard it, they all with one accord fell on their knees and worshipped the god who had given this sign. Xenophon went on: 'I think, soldiers, that, since an omen from Zeus the Saviour appeared just when we were speaking about safety, we ought to make a vow that we will give thank-offerings to the god for our safety in the place where we first reach friendly soil, and we should also vow to offer sacrifices to the other gods to the best of our ability. Whoever agrees with this, put up his hand.'

Then they all raised their hands, and afterwards they made

their vows and sang the paean.

The claims of religion having been thus satisfied, Xenophon started again and spoke as follows: 'I was just saying that we had many glorious hopes of safety. First of all, we have kept our oaths to the gods, while our enemies have broken theirs, and in addition to this perjured themselves in transgressing the truce. This being so, it is reasonable to suppose that the gods will be against our enemies, but will fight on our side; and they are capable of quickly making even the strong weak, and of saving the weak easily, when such is their will, even if they are in the midst of danger. And next I shall remind you of the dangers which our fathers also have been through, so that you may realise that it is right for you to be brave men and that, with the help of the gods, the brave find safety even from the worst of difficulties. Remember how the Persians and their friends came with an enormous army, thinking that they would wipe Athens off the face of the earth; but the Athenians had the courage to stand up to them by themselves, and they defeated them. On that occasion they had made a vow to Artemis that they would sacrifice to her a goat for every one of their enemies whom they killed, but, since they could not get hold of enough goats, they decided to sacrifice five hundred every year, and they are still sacrificing them to-day. Then, when Xerxes later on collected his innumerable army and came against Greece, there was another occasion when your fathers defeated the fathers of these people both on land and on sea. You can find proof of all this in the trophies we have, but the greatest piece of evidence of all is the freedom of the cities in which you have been born and brought up. For you worship no man as a master, but only the gods. These were the men whose sons you are; and I shall certainly not say that you dishonour your fathers. Not many days ago you were in battle order against the children of our old enemies, and, though they were many times your number, you, with the help of the gods, defeated them. And on that occasion you showed yourselves brave men in order to get Cyrus a kingdom; but now the fight is on for your own safety, and therefore I am sure it is right to expect from you much greater courage and a much greater will to victory. Then, too, you ought also to feel much greater confidence against the enemy. On the last occasion you had had no experience of them and you could see their prodigious numbers, but all the same in the spirit of your fathers you had the courage to set about them. Now, however, when you know from experience that, even if they are many times your number, they are not anxious to face you, what reason have you to be afraid of them any longer? Do not imagine that we are any the worse off because the native troops who were previously in our ranks have now left us. They are even greater cowards than the natives whom we have beaten, and they made this clear by deserting us and fleeing to the other side. It is far better to see people who want to be the first to run away standing in one's enemy's army than in one's own ranks.

'If any of you feel disheartened because of the fact that we have no cavalry, while the enemy have great numbers of them, you must remember that ten thousand cavalry only amount to ten thousand men. No one has ever died in battle through being bitten or kicked by a horse; it is men who do whatever gets done in battle. And then we are on a much more solid foundation than cavalrymen, who are up in the air on horseback, and afraid not only of us but of falling off their horses: we, on the other hand, with our feet planted on the earth, can give much harder blows to those who attack us and are much more likely to hit what we aim at. There is only one way in which cavalry have an advantage over us, and that is that it is safer for them to run away than it is for us.

'You may, of course, be quite confident about the fighting, but upset by the fact that Tissaphernes will no longer show you the way, nor will the King provide opportunities of buying food. If this is so, then consider whether it is better to have Tissaphernes to guide us, a man who is quite clearly working against us, or to have prisoners whom we shall order to show us the way and who will know that, if they make any mistakes which affect us, they will be mistakes that will also effect their own persons and their own lives. And on the question of supplies, it is better to buy in the markets which they provide, where we have to pay a lot to buy a little (and we have no longer even got the money), or is it better to beat them in battle and then take our supplies for ourselves, each man taking the quantity he feels like having?

'You may realise that these alternatives are the better ones, but still think that the rivers are an insuperable obstacle and regard yourselves as having been led properly into a trap by crossing them. If so, then I will ask you to consider whether the natives have not done here a very stupid thing. For all rivers, however impassable they may be at a distance from their springs, can be forded, and without so much as getting one's knees wet, if one follows them up towards their sources. And even if we cannot get across the rivers, even if no one comes forward to show us the way, even then we have no reason to get downhearted. We would not call the Mysians better men than we are, yet we know that they hold many large and prosperous cities in the King's country and against the King's will. We know that the same is true of the Pisidians, and we saw with our own eyes how the Lycaonians have seized the fortified positions in the plains and enjoy the profit of the land that belongs to these natives. Now in our case I should say that we ought not to make it obvious that we are setting off home, but we should make our dispositions as though we had the idea of settling here. I am certain that the King would offer the Mysians all the guides they wanted, and would give them numbers of hostages to guarantee his good faith in sending them out of the country, and would actually build roads for them, even though they wanted to go away in four-horse chariots. And I am certain that he would be three times as pleased to do all this for us, if he saw that we were planning to stay here. No, what I am really afraid of is that, if we once learn to live a life of ease and luxury, enjoying the company of these fine great women, the wives and daughters of the Medes and Persians, we might be like the Lotus eaters and forget about our road home. So I think that it is right and reasonable for us to make it our first endeavour to reach our own folk in Greece and to demonstrate to the Greeks that their poverty is of their own choosing, since they might see people who have a wretched life in their own countries grow rich by coming out here. Soldiers, I need not elaborate the point. It is obvious that all these goods thing come to the conquerors.

'I must, however, deal with these questions–how we can make our march as free from danger as possible, and how, if we have to fight, we can fight to the best advantage. The first suggestion I shall make to you is to set fire to all the waggons we have, so that we may not be led by our animals but may be able to march wherever the interest of the army dictates. Then we should set fire to our tents as well: they too cause difficulties in transport, and are no use either for fighting or for getting provisions. Then let us get rid of all inessentials in the rest of our equipment, only keeping what we have for the purpose of fighting and eating or drinking, so that as many of us as possible may carry arms and as few as possible carry baggage. When people are defeated, as you know, all their property changes hands; and if we win, we must look upon our enemies as if they were carrying baggage for us.

'It remains for me to mention what I think is the most important point of all. You can see what our enemies thought about it. They did not dare to make war on us until they had made prisoners of our generals, and this was because they thought that, so long as we had commanders and we were obedient to them, we were capable of coming out on top in the fighting; but once they had seized our commanders they thought that we would collapse through lack of control and lack of discipline. It is therefore necessary that the generals we have now should take much greater care than those we had before, and that those in the ranks should be much better disciplined and much more ready to obey their officers now than they were before. In cases of disobedience, we ought to vote that whichever of you happens to be on the spot should join with the officers in enforcing punishment. That would be the bitterest disappointment to our enemies; for, on the day that this is voted, they will see not one Clearchus but ten thousand, each one intolerant of any unsoldierly action.

'But it is time for me to make an end. It may be that the enemy will be upon us at once. If you agree with the suggestions I have made, then let us have them passed officially as soon as possible, so that they may be put into practice. If anyone knows a better way of going about things than the one I have outlined, then let him have the courage to tell us of it, even if he is only a common soldier. The safety which we are looking for is everyone's concern.'

Afterwards Chirisophus spoke. 'If we want,' he said, 'to pass any other measure in addition to those which Xenophon suggests, we can do so in a moment or two. I propose that, with no delay, we should vote that what he has just suggested is the best course to pursue. Will those who agree put up their hands?'

They all put their hands up, and Xenophon got up again and spoke as follows: 'Soldiers, listen to the additional proposals which I have to make. Obviously we must march somewhere where we can get provisions, and I gather that there are some fine villages not more than two miles away from here. But I should not be surprised if the enemy, like cowardly dogs that run after and try to bite anyone who goes past them, but run away from anyone who chases them – I should not be surprised if they too follow in our tracks as we go away. Perhaps then it would be safer for us to march with the hoplites forming a hollow square, so that the baggage and the general crowd may be more secure inside. If, then, we were told now who should be in the front of the square and organise the leading detachments, and who should be on the two flanks, and who should be responsible for the rear, we should not have to plan all this when the enemy are approaching us, but could immediately make use of those who have been specially detailed for the job. If anyone has a better suggestion to make, let us adopt it. If not, then I propose that Chirisophus should lead the square: he has the additional advantage of being a Spartan. Two generals, the oldest ones, should look after the two flanks; and the youngest of us, that is Timasion and myself, should be responsible for the rear. I suggest this as a temporary measure. Later on we shall have tried out this order of march, and we can decide on what seems best as different circumstances arise. If anyone has a better suggestion to make, I should like him to put it forward.'

Then, as nobody raised any objections, Xenophon said. 'Will those who agree with this put up their hands?' And the proposal was carried.

'Now then,' he continued, 'we must leave the meeting and put into operation what we have decided. Whoever wants to see his own people again must remember to be a brave soldier: that is the only way of doing it. Whoever wants to keep alive must aim at victory. It is the winners who do the killing and the losers who get killed. And those who want money must try to win battles. The winners can not only keep what they have themselves, but can take what belongs to the losers.'

Chapter 3

THE GREEKS SUFFER FROM
SLINGS AND ARROWS

AT the conclusion of this speech they stood up and went away to set fire to their waggons and their tents. If anyone wanted any of the extra equipment, they shared it out among themselves and threw all the rest into the fire. When this was done, they had breakfast, and, while they were in the middle of it, Mithridates arrived with about thirty horsemen. He asked the generals to come within hearing and then spoke as follows: 'I, my Greek friends, was, as you know, faithful to Cyrus, and I am still a friend of yours. Also I find my present position here very alarming. If, then, I found that you were thinking of any safe way out, I should like to join you and bring all my followers with me. Tell me, then, what you propose to do, and consider me as a friend who is on your side and who would like to join you in your march.'

After a discussion the generals decided to give him the following reply. Chirisophus was the spokesman. 'What we have decided,' he said, 'is this: if we are allowed to make our way home, we shall go through the country doing as little damage as possible; but if anyone tries to stop us on our way, we shall fight our way out as hard as we can.'

Mithridates then made an attempt at proving that it was impossible to get to safety against the King's will, and at this point he was recognised as having been sent with a hidden object in view. Indeed there was actually one of Tissaphernes's men in his company to ensure his reliability.

After this incident the generals decided that it would be better to make a resolution that, so long as they were in enemy country, the war should be conducted without any negotiations with the enemy, since ambassadors from the other side tended to seduce the soldiers' allegiance. They actually did seduce one of the captains, Nicarchus the Arcadian, who deserted in the night with about twenty men.

Next, after having had a meal, they crossed the river Zapatas and marched in battle order, with the baggage animals and the camp followers inside the square. Before they had gone far Mithridates again put in an appearance with about two hundred cavalry and about four hundred archers and slingers. These were lightly armed and very quick on their feet.

Mithridates approached the Greeks as though he was on friendly terms with them, but, as soon as they got close together, his men, both cavalry and foot, suddenly shot their arrows, while the others slung stones and caused some casualties. The Greek rearguard suffered badly, but were unable to retaliate, since their Cretan archers could not shoot so far as the Persians and also, being light troops, had taken refuge in the centre of the square; as for the javelin-throwers, their range was not great enough to reach the Persian slingers.

Xenophon then came to the conclusion that they should drive the enemy back, and this was done by the hoplites and peltasts who were with him in the rearguard. In the pursuit, however, they failed to catch a single one of the enemy. This was because the Greeks had no cavalry, and their infantry could not, over a short distance, catch up with the enemy infantry, who ran away when they were still some way off. It was naturally impossible to press the pursuit over a long distance from the rest of the army. The native cavalry, however, by shooting backwards from on horseback, managed to inflict wounds even when they were in flight; and when the Greeks had pursued them for a certain distance, they had to fall back again over the same distance, fighting all the way. The result was that in the whole day they covered no more

than two and a half miles. However, they reached the villages
in the afternoon.

Here again there was much despondency. Chirisophus and
the oldest of the generals blamed Xenophon for carrying on a
pursuit away from the main body, and, in spite of the risks he
ran, not being able to do any damage to the enemy. Xenophon listened to their criticism and admitted that they were
right in blaming him, and had the facts on their side to prove
their case. 'Nevertheless,' he said, 'I had to drive them back,
when I saw that we were suffering badly by staying where we
were and that we could do nothing in retaliation. Once we
started driving them back, what you say is true. We were no
better able to do them any damage, and we had the greatest
difficulty in getting back ourselves. We should be grateful to
the gods, then, that they did not come with a large force, but
only in small numbers, with the result that, without doing us
very great harm, they have shown us where we are deficient.
At present the enemy archers can shoot further than our
Cretans can shoot in reply, and their slingers can operate out
of range of our javelin-throwers. When we drive them back,
it is not possible for us to pursue them over much of a distance
from the main army, and in a short distance no infantryman,
however fast he runs, can catch up with another infantryman
who has a bow-shot's start of him. Therefore, if we are going
to prevent them from having the power to harm us on the
march, we must get hold of slingers and cavalry as soon as we
can. There are some Rhodians, I hear, in our army, and they
say that most of them know how to use a sling. Their weapon,
too, has actually twice the range of the Persian sling. Persian
slings do not carry far because they use stones as big as one's
fist for throwing; but the Rhodians know how to use leaden
bullets as well. If, then, we find out who has a sling in his
possession, and pay for any there are, and pay more money to
anyone who volunteers to make more slings, and think of some

extra privilege we can give to anyone who volunteres to serve as a slinger in the ranks, then perhaps enough will come forward to be of use to us. I have noticed, too, that we have horses in the army: some are mine, others are part of Clearchus's property which he has left,. and there are many more which we have captured and now use for carrying baggage. If, then, we sort them out, putting baggage animals in the place of some, and equipping horses for the use of cavalrymen, they too, perhaps, will give the enemy trouble when he runs away.'

This was agreed upon, and about two hundred slingers came forward that night. On the next day about fifty horses and cavalrymen were passed fit for service. They were provided with leather jerkins and breastplates, and Lycius the son of Polystratus, an Athenian, was given the command of the cavalry.

Chapter 4

TISSAPHERNES STILL IN PURSUIT

THEY halted for that day and went forward on the next, rising earlier than usual, as they had a watercourse to cross and were afraid that the enemy might attack them while they were crossing it. They had got across this before Mithridates again put in an appearance, this time with a thousand cavalry and about four thousand archers and slingers. He had asked and obtained this number of troops from Tissaphernes and had promised that if he got them, he would hand the Greeks over to him as prisoners. His low opinion of the Greeks was based on the fact that in the earlier attack he had come to no harm, in spite of his small numbers, and thought that he had inflicted severe losses on the Greeks.

When the Greeks were nearly a mile away from their crossing of the watercourse, Mithridates with his whole force moved over too. Orders had been issued to the necessary numbers of peltasts and hoplites to drive the enemy back, and the cavalry had been told to press the pursuit confidently, as adequate forces would be there to support them. When Mithridates caught them up and the sling stones and arrows began to arrive, a trumpet was sounded, and immediately those who had been ordered to do so ran forward in a body and the cavalry made their charge. The enemy did not wait for them, but fled back to the watercourse. Many of the native infantry were killed in this pursuit and about eighteen of their cavalry were taken alive in the watercourse. The Greeks, acting on their own initiative, mutilated the corpses, so that the sight of them might cause as much fear as possible among the enemy.

After suffering this defeat the enemy retired, and the Greeks marched on safely for the rest of the day and reached the river Tigris. There was a large deserted city there called Larissa, which in the old days used to be inhabited by the Medes. It had walls twenty-five feet broad and a hundred feet high, with a perimeter of six miles. It was built of bricks made of clay, with a stone base of twenty feet underneath. At the time when the Persians seized the empire from the Medes, the King of the Persians laid siege to this city but was quite unable to take it. A cloud, however, covered up the sun and hid it from sight until the inhabitants deserted the place, and so the city was taken. Near the city there was a pyramid of stone, a hundred feet broad, and two hundred feet high. Many of the natives from the neighbouring villages had run away and taken refuge on it.

From here a day's march of eighteen miles brought them to a large undefended fortification near a city called Mescila, which was once inhabited by the Medes. The base of this fortification was made of polished stone in which there were many shells. It was fifty feet broad and fifty feet high. On top of it was built a brick wall fifty feet in breadth and a hundred feet high. The perimeter of the fortification was eighteen miles. Medea, the King's wife, is supposed to have taken refuge here at the time when the Medes lost their empire to the Persians, and the King of the Persians, when he besieged the city, could not take it either by the passing of time or by assault. Zeus, however, drove the inhabitants out of their wits with a thunderstorm, and so the city was taken.

Next came a day's march of twelve miles in the course of which Tissaphernes made his appearance. He had with him not only his own cavalry, but also the force which Orontas (the man who had married the King's daughter) commanded, the native troops which Cyrus had commanded on his march inland, the troops with which the King's brother had come to reinforce the King, and, in addition, all the troops which the

King had given him; so that his army appeared enormous. On coming close, he brought up some of his companies to the rear of the Greeks, and led others round on the flanks, but did not dare to make a direct assault or show any willingness to take a risk. Instead he ordered his men to use their slings and bows. Then the Rhodians, who were posted at intervals in the Greek ranks, used their slings, and the archers shot their arrows, and no one failed to hit a man (indeed one could hardly miss if one tried to), and Tissaphernes got out of range with alacrity, as did the rest of his army.

For the remainder of the day the Greeks marched on, with the Persians following them. The natives did no further damage by their old methods of long-range fighting since the Rhodians could sling further than the Persian slingers and further even than most of their archers. The Persians use large bows, and so all the arrows of theirs which were picked up came in useful to the Cretans, who constantly used the enemy's arrows and practised long-range shooting with a high trajectory. A number of bow-strings were found in the villages, and some lead also which could be used for the slings.

On that day, then, after the Greeks had come to some villages and encamped, the natives retired, having had the worst of the long-range fighting. Next day the Greeks stayed where they were and provided themselves with food, of which there was a good supply in the villages. On the day after that they continued their march over the plain, with Tissaphernes following them and shooting at them from a distance. On this march the Greeks came to the conclusion that the square was a bad formation to adopt when the enemy were in the rear. When the two flanks of the square are compressed, because of the road becoming narrower, or in going through a pass in the mountains or in crossing a bridge, what is bound to happen is that the hoplites get pushed out of position and make heavy going of it, crowded together as they are, and confused; and the result is that, when they are in this disordered state, one can make no use of them. Then, when the flanks diverge again, those who were previously pushed out of position are bound to get dispersed, and the space between the two flanks is not filled up, and, when this happens to the men they get dispirited with the enemy at their heels. So whenever they had to make any sort of crossing, over a bridge or anything else, each man struggled to be the first across, and that gave the enemy an excellent chance of attacking them.

The generals took note of this situation, and formed six companies of a hundred men each. They appointed captains for the companies and other commanders for each fifty men and for each twenty-five men. Whenever the two flanks were pushed in on each other on the march, these six companies waited behind, so as not to cause any disorder in the flanks: afterwards they came up again on the left and right of the flanks. And when the sides of the square opened out, they would fill up the centre, marching into the opening, if it was a small one by companies with six men in front, or if it was larger with twelve men in front, or if it was very large indeed with twenty-five men in front, so that the centre of the square was always full. When they had to make any crossing, by a bridge or otherwise, they preserved their order, the captains leading their companies across in turn. They were also ready for action if there was any demand for it in any part of the main body.

In this formation they went forward for four days. In the course of the fifth day's march they noticed a kind of palace with a number of villages in its neighbourhood, and saw that the road to the place went across high ground which formed the foothills of the mountain beneath which the village was. The Greeks were pleased to see the hills, as was natural enough considering that their enemy's force was of cavalry; but when they had marched on and, after ascending the first hill, had just gone down into the valley to ascend the next, the natives made an attack on them. Whipped on to it under the lash, they hurled their javelins and sling-stones and arrows from their high ground down on to the ground below, inflicting a number of wounds. They got the upper hand of the Greek light troops and kept them penned up inside the square of hoplites, so that for that day both the slingers and the archers, being mixed up with the general crowd, were of no use at all. When the Greeks tried to escape from their difficulties by driving the enemy back, they, being hoplites, found it hard going to get to the top of the hill, while the enemy darted away from them quickly. Again, when they made their way back to the rest of the army, they suffered just as before, and the same thing happened on the second hill. They therefore decided not to allow the soldiers to move from the third hill until they had led up into the mountain a force of peltasts from the right flank of the square. When these peltasts got on to higher ground than the enemy who were coming after, the enemy gave up attacking the troops on their descent, since they were frightened of being cut off and having enemies on both sides of them. They marched in this way for the rest of the day, some by the road over the hills and others keeping pace with them along the mountain, until they came to the villages. They then appointed eight doctors, as there were a number of wounded.

They stayed here for three days, partly for the sake of the wounded, and partly because they could get plenty of food–wheat-flour and wine and a lot of barley that had been stored there for horses. All this had been collected for the man who was satrap of the country.

On the fourth day they went down to the plain; but when Tissaphernes and his force caught them up, they took the lesson of hard facts which was to encamp at the first place where they saw a village and not to go on marching and fighting at the same time. This was because they had many men out of action, both the wounded and those who were bearing them, and those who took over the arms of the bearers. However, when they had encamped and the natives advanced on the village in an attempt to engage in long-range fighting, the Greeks had very much the better of it. There was a great difference between starting from one's own ground to repel the enemy, and fighting while on the march with the enemy at one's heels.

In the middle of the afternoon came the time for the enemy to retire, as the natives (fearing that the Greeks might make a night attack) always encamped at least six miles away from the Greek army. A Persian army is useless at night, since their horses are tethered and usually tied by the feet as well, so that they cannot run away if they are loosed. If, then, there is a disturbance, the horses have to be caparisoned for their Persian riders, and bridled, and then the rider has to put on his armour and mount – all of which is difficult to do by night and in the middle of an uproar. This was the reason why they camped a great distance away from the Greeks.

Now, when the Greeks became aware that the enemy wanted to retire and indeed were passing round the order to do so, they issued, in the enemy's hearing, an order to their own troops that they should get their baggage together. The natives then put off their departure for a time, but when it got late they went off, not thinking it desirable to march and come into camp by night.

The Greeks, seeing that they were now undoubtedly retiring, broke camp themselves and marched away, doing as much as six miles. This put such a distance between the two armies that there was no sign of the enemy either on the next day or on the day after that. On the fourth day the natives, who had gone forward during the night, occupied a commanding position on the right of the road by which the Greeks intended to march. This was one of the heights of a mountain which overlooked the way down into the plain. When Chirisophus saw that this height had been occupied in advance of them he summoned Xenophon from the rear and asked him to bring his peltasts and come to the front. Xenophon, however, observed Tissaphernes and his whole force coming into sight and so he did not lead the peltasts forward. Instead he rode up himself to Chirisophus and asked him, 'Why are you calling for me?'

Chirisophus replied: 'You can see for yourself. The hill that overlooks our way down has been occupied in advance of us. We cannot get past unless we drive them off it. But why didn't you bring the peltasts?'

Xenophon replied that he did not think it was wise to leave the rear unguarded while the enemy were in sight. 'However,' he said, 'the time has certainly come to decide how one can dislodge those people from the hill.'

At this point Xenophon noticed that the summit of the mountain was higher than the ground on which their own army was and that there was a possible approach from it to the hill where the enemy were. So he said: 'The best thing to do, Chirisophus, is for us to advance on the summit as fast as we can. If we can occupy it, those who are commanding our road will not be able to maintain their position. If you like, you stay here with the main body. I will volunteer to go ahead. Of, if you prefer it, you march on the mountain and I will stay here.'

'I will give you the choice,' said Chirisophus, 'of doing whichever you like.'

Xenophon, pointing out that he was the younger man, chose to make the advance on the mountain, but asked Chirisophus to let him have some men from the front to go with him, as it would take time to bring up men from the rear. Chirisophus let him have the peltasts who were at the front and took those who were in the middle of the square. He also ordered the three hundred, all picked men, whom he had under his personal command at the front of the square to go with Xenophon.

They then marched away as quickly as they could, but when the enemy on the hill saw that the Greeks were making their way to the summit, they too started off immediately to contest the position. Then there was a lot of shouting, from the Greek army cheering on its men on the one side and from Tissaphernes's people cheering on their men on the other side. Xenophon rode along the ranks on horseback, urging them on. 'Soldiers,' he said, 'consider that it is for Greece you are fighting now, that now you are fighting your way to your children and your wives, and that with a little hard work now, we shall go on the rest of our way unopposed.'

Soteridas, a man from Sicyon, said: 'We are not on a level, Xenophon. You are riding on horseback, while I am wearing myself out with a shield to carry.'

When Xenophon heard this, he jumped down from his horse, pushed Soteridas out of the ranks, took his shield away from him and went forward on foot as fast as he could, carrying the shield. He happened to be wearing a cavalry breastplate as well, so that it was heavy going for him. He kept on encouraging those in front to keep going and those behind to join up with them, though struggling along behind them himself. The other soldiers, however, struck Soteridas and threw stones at him and cursed him until they forced him to take back his shield and continue marching. Xenophon then remounted and, so long as the going was good, led the way on horseback. When it became impossible to ride, he left his horse behind and hurried ahead on foot. And so they got to the summit before the enemy.

Chapter 5

BETWEEN THE TIGRIS AND
THE MOUNTAINS

THE natives thereupon turned tail and fled in all directions, and the Greeks held the summit. The army with Tissaphernes and Ariaeus turned aside, and went off by another way, and Chirisophus's men descended into the plain and camped in a village that was full of good things. In this plain beside the Tigris there were a number of other villages too, equally well provided.

However, in the late afternoon the enemy suddenly appeared in the plain and cut off some of the Greeks who were scattered about there and were engaged in plunder, as several herds of cattle had been caught as they were being taken across to the other side of the river. Tissaphernes and his men then tried to set fire to the villages, and there were some of the Greeks who became very downhearted about this, since they got the idea that, if they burned the villages, they would have nowhere to get supplies from.

Chirisophus and his men had just returned from rescuing those in the plain, and Xenophon, who was met by the rescue party when he came down from the hill, rode along their ranks and said: 'Do you see, Greeks, that they are admitting that we are now the owners of their land? When they were arranging the truce they made a great point of this, that there should be no burning of the King's land; and now they are burning it themselves as though it wasn't his. But if they have any food for themselves anywhere, they will see us marching there too. Really, Chirisophus, I think we ought to consider this property our own and stop them burning it.'

Chirisophus said: 'I don't think so. But we might help them in the job, and then they will stop all the sooner.'

When they got back to their quarters the generals and captains had a meeting, while the rest were occupied with the provisions. They were now in a very difficult position. On one side there were mountains of a very great height and on the other side was the river, which was so deep that when they tested the depth, not even the spears stood out above the water. While the generals were uncertain what to do, a man from Rhodes came forward and said: 'I will undertake to bring you across in parties of four thousand hoplites at a time, if you will supply me with what I need and give me a talent by way of payment.'

When they asked him what he needed, he said: 'I shall need two thousand bags made of hide, and I can see that there are numbers of sheep and goats and oxen and asses about. When we have skinned them and inflated their hides they will give us an easy means of getting across. I shall also need the ropes which you use for the baggage animals. With these ropes I shall tie the bags together and keep each bag in its place by fastening stones to it and letting them down into the water like anchors. Then I shall string the bags across the river and fasten them to both banks; then put wood on top of them and cover the wood with earth. I can make it clear to you in a moment that there is no risk of sinking. Each bag will keep two men from sinking; and the wood and earth will stop them slipping off.'

The generals listened to him, but thought that, though it was a nice idea, it was impossible to put into practice, as there were great numbers of cavalry on the further bank to stop them getting over, and they would immediately have prevented the first people across from doing their jobs.

Next day they went back again over their former route to the villages that had not been burnt. They set fire to the villages from which they started, so that the enemy did not come close to them, but watched them from a distance, wondering, apparently, where the Greeks would go next and what their intentions were. The generals then held another meeting, while the rest of the army was occupied with provisions. They brought in the prisoners and questioned them in detail about the country all round them. The replies were to the effect that the country to the south was on the road to Babylon and Media, the way, indeed, by which they had come; the way eastward led to Susa and Ecbatana, which was said to be the King's summer residence; if one crossed the river and went westward, the way went to Lydia and Ionia; and the road going north over the mountains led to the Carduchi. These people, they said, lived in the mountains and were very warlike and not subject to the King. Indeed a royal army of a hundred and twenty thousand had once invaded their country, and no a man of them had got back, because of the terrible conditions of the ground they had to go through. However, on occasions when they made a treaty with the satrap who controlled the plain there was mutual intercourse between the Carduchi and them.

The generals listened to these reports and separated out those who said they knew the road in each direction, not giving any indication of which one they were going to take. They thought, however, that they would have to invade the country of the Carduchi across the mountains, since, according to the prisoners, once they had got through these people, they would arrive in Armenia, a big rich country governed by Orontas; and from there, the prisoners said, it was easy going in whatever direction one wished to march.

They held sacrifices to bless this project, so that they could start the march when they thought the right time had come. As it was, they feared that the pass over the mountains might be occupied in advance of them. Then they issued orders that, after supper, everyone should pack up his belongings and rest: they should be ready to follow their officers at the word of command.

BOOK

IV

THE MARCH TO
THE SEA

Chapter 1

THE ENTRY INTO KURDESTAN

AT about the last watch, with enough of the night remaining for them to be able to cross the plain under cover of darkness, they got up when the signal was given and marched toward the mountain, which they reached at dawn. Chirisophus then took the lead with his own troops and also all the light troops; Xenophon brought up the rear with the hoplites of the rear-guard, but with no light troops at all, as there seemed to be no danger of any attack being made on them from the rear while they were on the ascent.

Chirisophus reached the summit before any of the enemy realised what was happening. He then went steadily forward, and as the various contingents of the army crossed the pass they followed him into the villages which lay in the folds and recesses of the mountains. The Carduchi immediately aban-doned their houses and fled into the mountains with their women and children. Plenty of food remained for the Greeks to take, and there were a lot of brazen utensils in the furni-ture of the houses too. The Greeks did not take any of these, or pursue the people. They wished to behave leniently on the chance that the Carduchi, since they were enemies of the King, might be willing for them to go through their country peace-ably. Food, however, was a matter of necessity, and they took whatever they came across. The Carduchi paid no attention when they called out to them, and indeed gave no signs at all of friendly feeling.

It was already dark when the last of the Greeks had come down from the summit to the villages, since, owing to the narrowness of the road, the ascent and descent had taken up the whole day. At this point some of the Carduchi got together in a body and made an attack on the last of the Greeks. They killed some and wounded others with stones and arrows, though they were not in great numbers, as the Greek army had come upon them unexpectedly. Indeed, if more of them had got together on this occasion, a large part of the army might possibly have been wiped out.

So for that night they encamped as they were in the villages, and the Carduchi lit a number of beacons on the mountains all round them as signals to each other. At dawn it was decided at a meeting of the Greek generals and captains to take on the march only the strongest and most essential of the baggage animals, and to leave the rest behind; also to let go all the slaves in the army that had been captured recently. This was because the great numbers of baggage animals and slaves slowed up the march, and there were numbers of men who were in charge of these and so were out of action; and with so many people on the march, they had to provide and transport double the necessary quantity of supplies. After having made this decision, they gave orders by herald that it was to be carried into effect.

When they had had breakfast and started on their way, the generals stationed themselves in a narrow part of the road and took away from the soldiers any of the proscribed articles which they found had not been left behind. The men did as they were told, though there were some cases of people getting away with things, cases when a soldier was in love with a particularly good-looking boy or woman. For that day, then, they went ahead, having a certain amount of fighting to do and resting from time to time.

On the next day there was a great storm, but they had to go forward as there were not sufficient supplies. Chirisophus was leading the march and Xenophon was with the rearguard. The enemy made violent attacks and in the narrow passes came to close range with their bows and slings with the result that they had to travel slowly, as they were constantly chasing the enemy off and then returning again. Xenophon had often to order a halt when the enemy launched his violent attacks; and on these occasions Chirisophus, when the word was passed forward, halted his men too; but on one occasion he did not stop, but led on fast, passing back the word to follow him. It was obvious that something was the matter, but there was no time to go forward and see what was the cause of this haste. The result was that for the rearguard the march almost turned into a full retreat. Here a gallant Spartan soldier, called Leonymus, was killed by an arrow which went into the side of his body through the shield and the jerkin, and Basias the Arcadian was also killed, shot clean through the head.

When they reached the place where they were to camp, Xenophon went just as he was to Chirisophus and blamed him for not waiting, the result of which had been that the soldiers had had to fight at the same time as they were retreating. 'And now,' he said, 'two most gallant fellows have been killed, and we could not recover their bodies or bury them.'

Chirisophus replied: 'Look at the mountains. See how impassable they are in every direction. This one road, which you see, is a steep one, and you can see that there are men on it, a great crowd, who have occupied the pass and are on guard there. That is why I was in a hurry and so did not wait for you. I thought there was a chance of being able to get there first, before the pass was seized. The guides we have say that there is no other road.'

Xenophon said: 'I have got two men. When the enemy were giving us trouble, we set an ambush–which also gave us a chance of getting our breath back–and we killed some of them, and made up our minds to take a few alive just for this very reason, to have the services of guides who know the country.'

At once they brought the two men and questioned them

separately, to see if they knew of any other road apart from
the obvious one. One of the two, although he was threatened
in every kind of way, said that he did not know of any other
road. Since he said nothing that was of any help he was killed,
with the other man looking on. The survivor then said that
the reason why the other man had denied knowledge of
another road was that he happened to have a daughter who
had been married to somebody in that direction. He declared
that he would lead them by a road that was a possible one for
animals as well as men. He was then asked whether there was
any part of the road which was difficult to get past, and he replied that there was one height which it would be impossible to
pass, unless it was occupied in advance. It was then decided
to call a meeting of the captains, peltasts and hoplites as well,
to give them an account of the situation, and ask who was
willing to do a good job and come forward as a volunteer
for the expedition. The hoplites who came forward were
Aristonymus the Methydrian and Agasias the Stymphalian,
and Callimachus of Parrhasia put forward a separate claim for
himself, saying that he was willing to go, if he could take with
him volunteers from the whole army. 'Personally,' he said, 'I
am sure that a lot of the young men will follow if I am their
leader.' Then they asked if any of the officers of the light-
armed troops would volunteer to join with the others.
Aristeas of Chios came forward, a man who, on many occasions of this sort, was worth a lot to the army.

Chapter 2

FIGHTING IN THE MOUNTAINS

IT was now afternoon, and they told the volunteers to have their food and then start. They bound the guide and handed him over to them, and made arrangements that, if they took the height, they should guard the position for the night and give a trumpet signal at dawn: those on the height should then make an attack on the Carduchi holding the regular way out of the valley, while the rest of them should proceed as quickly as they could and join up with them.

After agreeing on this plan, the volunteers set out, a force of about two thousand. There was a lot of rain at the time. Xenophon, with the rearguard, led on towards the regular exit from the valley, in order that the enemy might give their attention to this part of the road and that the party which was making a detour might, as far as possible, escape detection. However, when the rearguard got to a watercourse which they had to cross to make their way up to the higher ground, the natives at this point rolled down boulders big enough to fill a waggon, some bigger, some smaller, which came crashing down against the rocks and ricocheted off, so that it was absolutely impossible even to get near the pass. Some of the captains, finding things impossible in one direction, tried somewhere else, and continued their efforts until it became dark. Then, when they thought that their retreat would be unobserved, they went back for supper. Those of them who had been in the rearguard had not had any breakfast either. The enemy, however, went on rolling down stones all through the night, as was evident from the noise.

Meanwhile the men who had taken the guide went round in a detour and came upon the guards sitting round their camp fire. They killed some of them and drove the others down-hill, and then stayed there under the impression that they were occupying the height. This, however, was not the case. Above them there was a small hill, past which ran the narrow road where the guard had been stationed. Nevertheless there was a way from this position to where the enemy was stationed on the regular road.

They passed the night where they were, and, at the first sign of dawn, formed up and marched in silence against the enemy. As there was a mist they got close up to them without being noticed. Then, as soon as they came into sight of each other, the trumpet sounded, and they raised their war-cry and charged down on the men, who did not wait for them, but abandoned the road and fled. Only a few were killed, as they were quick on their feet.

Meanwhile Chirisophus's men, on hearing the trumpet, immediately attacked uphill along the regular road; and some of the generals advanced along little-used paths, just where they happened to find themselves, climbing up as best they could and pulling each other up with their spears. These were the first ones to join up with the party that had previously occupied the position.

Xenophon, with half the rearguard, went by the same way as those who had the guide, as it was the easiest going for the baggage animals. He had placed the other half of his men in the rear of the animals. As they went forward they came to a ridge commanding the road and found it occupied by the enemy. They had either to dislodge them or else be cut off from the rest of the Greeks. They themselves might have gone by the same road as the others, but this was the only possible route for the baggage animals. Then they shouted out words of encouragement to each other and made an assault on the ridge with the companies in column. They did not attack from every direction but left the enemy a way of escape, if he wanted to run away. So long as they were climbing up, each man by the best route he could find, the natives shot arrows at them and hurled down stones; but they made no attack when it came to close quarters, and, in the end, abandoned the position and fled.

The Greeks had no sooner got past this hill when they saw in front of them another hill, also occupied by the enemy. They decided to make an assault on this hill too, but Xenophon realised that, if they left the hill which they had just taken unguarded, the enemy might reoccupy it and make an attack on the baggage animals as they were going past. (The baggage train extended a long way, as it was going along a narrow road.) He therefore left on the hill the captains Cephisodorus the son of Cephisophon, an Athenian, and Archagoras, an exile from Argos, while he himself advanced with the rest upon the second hill and took it too by the same methods as before.

There was still a third hill left to deal with, and much the steepest of the three. It was the one that overlooked the guard who had been surprised at their fire during the night by the volunteers. However, when the Greeks got close to it, the natives gave up this hill without putting up a fight, a thing which surprised everyone and made them think that they had abandoned the hill through fear of being cut off and surrounded. Actually they had seen from the top what had happened further down the road and had all gone off to attack the rearguard.

Xenophon climbed to the summit with the youngest of his men, and ordered the rest to lead on slowly, so that the companies in the rear could join up with them, and he told them to halt under arms on level ground when they had gone a little way along the road. At this point Archagoras of Argos came running with the news that his men had been driven off the hill and that Cephisodorus and Amphicrates had been killed together with all the rest who had not managed to jump down from the rock and reach the rearguard. After achieving this success, the natives appeared on a ridge opposite the third hill. Xenophon spoke to them through an interpreter. He suggested a truce and asked them to hand over the dead. They replied that they would give back the bodies on condition that the Greeks did not burn their houses, and Xenophon agreed to this. However, while this conversation was going on and the rest of the army was going forward, all the natives in the district had rushed up: and when the Greeks began to come down from the hill and make their way towards the rest where they were standing by their arms, then, in great numbers and with terrific shouting, the enemy launched an attack. On reaching the summit of the hill from which Xenophon was descending, they began to roll down rocks. They broke one man's leg, and the man who was carrying Xenophon's shield ran away, taking the shield with him. Eurylochus of Lusia, however, a hoplite, ran up and held his shield in front of both of them during the retreat. The rest rejoined their comrades who were already in battle order.

The whole Greek army was now together again. They camped where they were and found a number of comfortable houses and plenty of food. There was a lot of wine, so much so that the people stored it in cellars which were plastered over the top. Xenophon and Chirisophus came to an arrangement with the enemy by which they got back the dead bodies and gave up their guide. For the dead they did, to the best of their ability, everything that is usually done at the burial of brave men. On the next day they set out without a guide, and the enemy fought back at them, and tried to stop their march by occupying any narrow passes there might be ahead of them. Whenever they got in the way of the vanguard, Xenophon led his men up into the mountains from the rear and made the road-block in front of the vanguard ineffectual by trying to get on to higher ground than those who were manning it; and whenever they made an attack on the rearguard, Chirisophus rendered this attempt to block the march ineffectual by altering direction and trying to get on to higher ground than those who were attempting it. So they were continually coming to each other's help and giving each other the most valuable support. There were times, too, when the natives gave a lot of trouble to the parties who had climbed up to higher ground, when they were on their way down again. The natives were quick on their feet, and so could get away even when they did not start running until we were right on top of them. Their only arms were bows and slings, and as bowmen they were very good. The bows they had were between four and five feet long and their arrows were of more than three feet. When they shot they put out the left foot and rested the bottom of the bow against it as they drew back the string. Their arrows went through shields and breastplates. When the Greeks got hold of any, they fitted them with straps and used them as javelins. In this type of country the Cretans were extremely useful. Stratocles, a Cretan himself, was their commander.

Chapter 3

THE CROSSING INTO ARMENIA

THEY camped for this day in the villages overlooking the plain of the river Centrites, which is about two hundred feet across, and forms the boundary between Armenia and the country of the Carduchi. The Greeks rested here and were glad to see the plain. The river was more than half a mile distant from the Carduchian mountains. They felt very pleased, then, as they camped here, with plenty of provisions, and often talked over the hardships they had been through; for they had been fighting continually through all the seven days during which they had been going through the country of the Carduchi, and had suffered more than they had suffered in all their engagements with the King and with Tissaphernes. Consequently the thought that they had escaped from all this made them sleep well.

At dawn, however, they saw that on the other side of the river there were cavalry, ready for action, and prepared to prevent them crossing over: on the high ground above the cavalry were infantry formations to stop them getting into Armenia. These were Armenian, Mardian and Chaldaean mercenaries in the service of Orontas and Artouchas. The Chaldaeans were said to be a free nation and good fighting men. They were armed with long wicker shields and spears. The high ground, on which the infantry was formed up, was three or four hundred feet away from the river. The only visible road led uphill and looked as though it had been specially built.

It was at this point that the Greeks attempted to cross; but, on making the attempt, they found that the water rose above their breasts, and the river-bed was uneven, covered with large slippery boulders. It was impossible for them to hold their arms in the water and, if they tried, the river swept them off their feet, while, if one held one's arms above one's head, one was left with no defence against the arrows and other missiles. They therefore withdrew and camped where they were on the bank of the river. They then saw that great numbers of the Carduchi had got together under arms and were occupying the position on the mountain where they had been themselves on the previous night. At this point the Greeks certainly felt very downhearted: they saw how difficult the river was to cross, and they saw also the troops ready to stop them crossing, and now the Carduchi waiting to set upon them from the rear if they attempted it. So for that day and the following night they stayed where they were, not knowing what to do.

Xenophon had a dream. He dreamed that he was bound in fetters, but the fetters fell off of their own accord, so that he was free and recovered the complete use of his limbs. Just before dawn he went to Chirisophus and told him that he felt confident that things would be all right, and he related his dream. Chirisophus was delighted, and at the first sign of dawn all the generals assembled and offered a sacrifice. The appearance of the victims was favourable from the very first. Then the generals and captains left the sacrifice and passed round the word to the troops to have their breakfast.

While Xenophon was having breakfast two young men came running up to him. Everyone knew that it was permissible to come to him whether he was in the middle of breakfast or supper, or to wake him from his sleep and talk to him, if they had anything to say which had a bearing on the fighting. These young men now told him that they had been collecting kindling for their fire, and had then seen on the other side of the river, on the rocks that went right down to the water, an old man and a woman and some girls storing away what looked like bundles of clothing in a hollow rock.

On seeing this, they had come to the conclusion that this was a safe place to get across, as the ground there was inaccessible to the enemy's cavalry. So they had undressed and taken their daggers and gone across naked, expecting that they would have to swim. However, they went ahead and got to the other side without the water ever reaching up to the crutch. Once on the other side they made off with the clothing and came back again.

Xenophon at once poured a libation and gave directions for the young men to join in it and pray to the gods who had sent the dream and revealed the ford, that they should bring what remained to a happy fulfilment. As soon as he had made the libation he took the young men to Chirisophus and they told their story to him. Chirisophus, after hearing it, also made a libation, and, when the libations were over, they gave instructions for the soldiers to pack their belongings, while they themselves called a meeting of the generals and discussed the question of how to make the crossing as efficient as possible, and how they could defeat the enemy in front and at the same time suffer no losses from those in the rear. They decided that Chirisophus should go first with half the army, while the other half stayed behind with Xenophon, and that the baggage animals and the general crowd should go across between the two.

When things were in order, they set off, and the two young men led the way, keeping the river on their left. The way to the ford was a distance of less than half a mile and, as they marched, the enemy's cavalry formations on the other bank kept pace with them. On reaching the bank of the river where the ford was, they grounded arms, and then Chirisophus himself first put a ceremonial wreath on his head, threw aside his cloak and took up his arms, telling the rest to follow his example. He ordered the captains to lead their companies across in columns, some on the left and others on the right of him. The soothsayers then cut the throats of the animals over the river, and meanwhile the enemy were shooting arrows and slinging. However, they were still out of range. The appearance of the victims was pronounced favourable, and then all the soldiers sang the paean and raised the battle-cry, and all the women joined in the cry; for a number of the soldiers had their mistresses with them in the army.

Chirisophus and his men then went into the river. Xenophon, with those of the rearguard who were quickest on their feet, ran back at full speed to the ford opposite the road into the Armenian mountains. He was trying to give the impression that he intended to make a crossing there and so cut off the cavalry on the river-bank. When the enemy saw that Chirisophus's men were getting across the river easily and that Xenophon's men were running back on their tracks, they became frightened of being cut off and fled at full speed in the direction, apparently, of the river crossing further up. However, on reaching the road, they turned uphill into the mountains. Lycius, who was in command of the cavalry formation, and Aeschines, who was in command of the formation of peltasts that accompanied Chirisophus, gave pursuit as soon as they saw the enemy in full retreat, and the soldiers shouted out to each other not to stay behind but to go on after them into the mountains. However, when Chirisophus had got across he did not pursue the cavalry, but immediately went up on to the high ground that went down to the river to attack the enemy who were up there. They, seeing their own cavalry in flight and hoplites moving up to attack them, abandoned the heights overlooking the river.

When Xenophon saw that things were going well on the other side, he made his way back as quickly as he could to that part of the army which had crossed, for there were also the Carduchi to think of, and they were evidently coming down into the plain with the intention of making an attack on the rear. Chirisophus was now holding the high ground, and Lycus, who with a few men had made an attempt at a pursuit, had captured some of their baggage animals, which they had abandoned, and some fine clothing and some drinking cups as well. The Greek baggage train and the general crowd was actually engaged in crossing. Xenophon then brought his men round and halted them in battle order, facing the Carduchi. He ordered the captains to split up their companies into sections of twenty-five men and bring each section round into line on the left: the captains and the section commanders were then to advance towards the Carduchi while those in the rear were to halt facing the river.

As soon as the Carduchi saw that the troops in the rear of the general crowd were thinning out and that there appeared now to be only a few of them, they began to come on faster, chanting their songs as they came. Chirisophus, however, when his own position was secure, sent Xenophon the peltasts and slingers and archers, and told them to do what they were ordered. Xenophon saw them coming across, and sent a messenger to tell them not to cross, but to stay on the further bank: when his own men started to cross over, they were to go into the river on each side of them as though they intended to cross to the other side, the javelin-throwers with their weapons at the ready, and the archers with arrows fitted to their bowstrings; but they were not to go far into the river. The orders he gave to his own men were that, when they were within range of the enemy slingers and could hear the stones rattling on the shields, they were to sing the paean and charge: when the enemy ran away and the trumpeter sounded the attack from the river, the men in the rear were to wheel right and go first, and then they were all to run to the river and get across as fast as they could, each at the point opposite his own position, so as not to get in each other's way: the best man would be the one who got to the other side first.

The Carduchi saw that there were now not many left in the baggage train; for a number even of those who had been detailed to remain behind had gone over to see what was happening either to the animals or to their kit or to their mistresses. Consequently the Carduchi came on with confidence and began to sling stones and shoot arrows. The Greeks then sang the paean and advanced on them at the double. The natives could not stand up to them, since, though they were armed well enough for quick attacks and retreats in the mountains, when it came to standing up to close fighting they were insufficiently armed. At this point the trumpeter sounded the attack, and the enemy ran away all the faster, while the Greeks turned about and escaped across the river as quickly as they could. Some of the enemy saw what they were doing and ran back again to the river where they wounded a few men with their arrows; but the majority of them were obviously still running away even when the Greeks had got to the other side. The relieving party, in their desire to show off their courage, had gone into the water further than they should, and came back across the river after Xenophon's party. A few of these men too were wounded.

Chapter 4

THEY SACK THE CAMP
OF TIRIBAZUS

AFTER crossing the river they formed up in order about mid-day and marched at least fifteen miles through Armenia, over country that was entirely flat, with gently sloping hills. Be-cause of the wars between the Armenians and the Carduchi there were no villages near the river; but the one which they reached at the end of their march was a big one, containing a palace belonging to the satrap; most of the houses were built like fortresses and there were plenty of provisions. Then a two days' march of thirty miles took them past the sources of the river Tigris, and from here a three days' march of forty-five miles brought them to the Teleboas, a beautiful river, but not a large one. There were a number of villages near the river, and all this part is called Western Armenia. Its governor was Tiribazus who was a personal friend of the King, and when he was present no one else had the right to assist the King in mounting his horse. He now rode up to the Greeks with a cavalry escort and sent forward an interpreter to say that he would like to speak with their commanders. The generals thought it best to hear what he had to say and, going forward till they were within hearing distance, asked him what he wanted. He replied that he would like to come to terms by which he would undertake to do the Greeks no harm and they would undertake not to burn the houses, though they could take any supplies which they needed. The generals agreed to this and made a treaty on these terms.

After this came a three days' march of forty-five miles over level ground. Tiribazus with his force kept pace with them, with about a mile between the armies. In the course of the

march they came to a palace with a number of villages, full
of all kinds of supplies, in the vicinity. There was a heavy
fall of snow in the night, while they were in camp here, and
at dawn it was decided that troops with their officers should
take up quarters separately in the villages. There were no
enemies in sight, and it seemed a safe thing to do because of
the quantity of snow that had fallen. In these quarters they
had all kinds of good food,—meat, corn, old wines with a
delicious bouquet, raisins, and all sorts of vegetables. However, some of the soldiers who had wandered off some way
from the camp reported that at night they had clearly seen a
number of camp fires. The generals then decided that it was
not safe for the troops to be in separate quarters, and that the
whole army should be brought together again. Consequently
they camped all together; and it looked also as though the
weather was clearing up. However, while they were spending
the night here, there was a tremendous fall of snow, so much
of it that it covered over both the arms and the men lying on
the ground. The baggage animals too were embedded in the
snow. The soldiers felt very reluctant to get to their feet, as,
when they were lying down, the snow which fell on them and
did not slip off kept them warm. But when Xenophon was
tough enough to get up and, without putting his clothes on,
to start splitting logs, someone else soon got up too and took
over the job of splitting the wood from him. Then others also
got up and lit fires and rubbed themselves down with ointment. A lot of ointment was found in this place and they used
it instead of olive oil. It was made of hog's lard, sesame, bitter
almonds and turpentine. A perfumed oil, too, made from the
same ingredients, was found here.

After the snowstorm it was decided to take up separate
quarters again under cover, and the soldiers went back with
a lot of shouting and jubilation to the houses and the stores of
food. The ones who, when they had left the houses, had acted

like hooligans and burned them down, now had to pay for it by having uncomfortable quarters. The generals gave a detachment of men to Democrates of Temenus, and sent him out from here by night to the mountains where those who had been out of camp had said they had seen the fires. They chose him because he had already on previous occasions won the reputation for bringing in accurate information on subjects like this. When he said something was there, it was there; and when he said it wasn't, it wasn't. He now went out to the mountains and said that he had not seen any fires, but he returned with a prisoner who was armed with a Persian bow and quiver and a battle-axe like those which the Amazons carry. This prisoner was questioned as to where he came from, and said that he was a Persian and was going from Tiribazus's army to get provisions. They then asked him what was the size of the army and what was the purpose for which it had been mobilised. He replied that Tiribazus had under him his own force together with mercenary troops from the Chalybes and Taochi: his plan was to attack the Greeks, as they crossed the mountain, in a narrow pass through which went their only possible road.

When they heard this the generals decided to bring the army together again. They left a guard, with Sophaenetus the Stymphalian in command of those who stayed behind, and immediately set out, with the man who had been captured to show them the way. After they had crossed the mountains, the peltasts went forward, and, coming in sight of the enemy's camp, raised a shout and charged down on it without waiting for the hoplites. When the natives heard the noise, they did not stand their ground, but took to flight. In spite of this, some of them were killed and about twenty horses were captured, as was Tiribazus's own tent which contained some couches with silver legs and some drinking vessels; also some men who said that they were his bakers and cup-bearers.

As soon as the generals of the hoplites found out what had occurred, they decided to return to their camp as quickly as possible, in case an attack might be made on those who had been left behind. So they sounded the trumpet to call the men back, set off and got back to their camp on the same day.

Chapter 5

MARCHING THROUGH THE SNOW

NEXT day they decided that they ought to get away as fast as they could, before the native army could reassemble and occupy the pass. They packed their belongings at once and, taking a number of guides with them, set off through deep snow. On the same day they passed the height where Tiribazus had intended to attack them, and then pitched camp. From here a three days' march of forty-five miles through desert country brought them to the river Euphrates, which they crossed without getting wet beyond the navel. The source of the river was said to be not far from here.

Next came a three days' march of forty-five miles over level ground and through deep snow. The third day's march was a hard one, with a north wind blowing into their faces, cutting into absolutely everything like a knife and freezing people stiff. One of the soothsayers then proposed making a sacrifice to the wind and his suggestion was carried out. It was agreed by all that there was then a distinct falling off in the violence of the wind. The snow was six feet deep and many of the animals and the slaves perished in it, as did about thirty of the soldiers. They kept their fires going all night, as there was plenty of wood in the place where they camped, though those who came up late got no wood. The ones who had arrived before and had lit the fires would not let the latecomers approach their fire unless they gave them a share of their corn or any other foodstuff they had. So each shared with the other party what he had. When the fires were made, great pits were formed reaching down to the ground as the snow melted. This gave one a chance of measuring the depth of the snow.

The whole of the next day's march from here was through the snow, and a number of the soldiers suffered from bulimia. Xenophon, who, as he commanded the rearguard, came upon men who had collapsed, did not know what the disease was. However, someone who had had experience of it told him that it was a clear case of bulimia, and that if they had something to eat they would be able to stand up. So he went through the baggage train and distributed to the sufferers any edibles that he could find there, and also sent round those who were able to run with more supplies to them. As soon as they had had something to eat they stood up and went on marching.

On this march Chirisophus came to a village about night-fall, and found by the well some women and girls, who had come out of the village in front of the fortification to get water. They asked the Greeks who they were, and the inter-preter replied in Persian and said they were on their way from the King to the satrap. The women answered that he was not there, and said that he was about three miles away. Since it was late, they went inside the fortification with the water-carriers to see the head-man of the village. So Chirisophus and as many of the troops as could camped there, but as for the rest of the soldiers, those who were unable to finish the march spent the night without food and without fires, and some died in the course of it. Some of the enemy too had formed themselves into bands and seized upon any baggage animals that could not make the journey, fighting among themselves for the animals. Soldiers who had lost the use of their eyes through snow-blindness or whose toes had dropped off from frostbite were left behind.

It was a relief to the eyes against snow-blindness if one held something black in front of the eyes while marching; and it was a help to the feet if one kept on the move and never stopped still, and took off one's shoes at night. If one slept with one's shoes on, the straps sank into the flesh and the soles of the shoes froze to the feet. This was the more likely to happen since, when their old shoes were worn out, they had made themselves shoes of undressed leather from the skins of oxen that had just been flayed. Some soldiers who were suffering from these kinds of complaints were left behind. They had seen a piece of ground that looked black because the snow had gone from it, and they imagined that the snow there had melted–as it actually had done–this being the effect of a fountain which was sending up vapour in a wooded hollow near by. The soldiers turned aside here, sat down, and refused to go any further.

As soon as Xenophon, who was with the rearguard, heard of this, he begged them, using every argument he could think of, not to get left behind. He told them that there were large numbers of the enemy, formed into bands, who were coming up in the rear, and in the end he got angry. They told him to kill them on the spot, for they could not possibly go on. Under the circumstances the best thing to do seemed to be to scare, if possible, the enemy who were coming up and so prevent them from falling upon the soldiers in their exhausted condition. By this time it was already dark, and the enemy were making a lot of noise as they advanced, quarrelling over the plunder which they had. Then the rearguard, since they had the use of their limbs, jumped up and charged the enemy at the double, while the sick men shouted as hard as they could and clashed their shields against their spears. The enemy were panic-stricken and threw themselves down through the snow into the wooded hollows, and not a sound was heard from them afterwards. Xenophon and his troops told the sick men that a detachment would come to help them on the next day, and he then proceeded with the march. However, before they had gone half a mile they came across some more soldiers resting by the road in the snow, all covered up, with no guard posted. Xenophon's men roused them up, but they said that the troops in front were not going forward. Xenophon then went past them and sent on the most able-bodied of the peltasts to find out what was holding them up. They reported back that the whole army was resting in this way; so Xenophon's men posted what guards they could, and also spent the night there, without a fire and without supper. When it was near daybreak Xenophon sent the youngest of his men back to the sick with instructions to make them get up and force them to march on. At this point Chirisophus sent a detachment from his troops in the village to see what was happening to the troops in the rear. Xenophon's men were glad to see them and handed over the sick to them to escort to the camp. They then went on themselves and, before they had marched two miles got to the village where Chirisophus was camping. Now that they had joined forces again, it seemed safe for the troops to take up their quarters in the villages. Chirisophus stayed where he was, and the other officers drew lots for the villages which were in sight, and each went with his men to the one he got.

On this occasion Polycrates, an Athenian captain, asked leave to go on independently and, taking with him the men who were quickest on their feet, ran to the village which had been allotted to Xenophon and surprised all the villagers, with their head-man, inside the walls, together with seventeen colts which were kept there for tribute to the King, and the head-man's daughter, who had only been married nine days ago. Her husband had gone out to hunt hares and was not captured in the village.

The houses here were built underground; the entrances were like wells, but they broadened out lower down. There were tunnels dug in the ground for the animals, while the men went down by ladder. Inside the houses there were goats, sheep, cows and poultry with their young. All these animals were fed on food that was kept inside the houses. There was also wheat, barley, beans and barley-wine in great bowls. The actual grains of barley floated on top of the bowls, level with the brim, and in the bowls there were reeds of various sizes and without joints in them. When one was thirsty, one was meant to take a reed and suck the wine into one's mouth. It was a very strong wine, unless one mixed it with water, and, when one got used to it, it was a very pleasant drink.

Xenophon invited the chief of the village to have supper with him, and told him to be of good heart, as he was not going to be deprived of his children, and that, if he showed himself capable of doing the army a good turn until they reached another tribe, they would restock his house with provisions when they went away. He promised to co-operate and, to show his good intentions, told them of where some wine was buried. So for that night all the soldiers were quartered in the villages and slept there with all sorts of food around them, setting a guard over the head-man of the village and keeping a watchful eye on his children too.

On the next day Xenophon visited Chirisophus and took the head-man with him. Whenever he went past a village he turned into it to see those who were quartered there. Everywhere he found them feasting and merry-making, and they would invariably refuse to let him go before they had given him something for breakfast. In every single case they would have on the same table lamb, kid, pork, veal and chicken, and a number of loaves, both wheat and barley. When anyone wanted, as a gesture of friendship, to drink to a friend's health, he would drag him to a huge bowl, over which he would have to lean, sucking up the drink like an ox. They invited the head-man too to take what he liked, but he refused their invitations, only, if he caught sight of any of his relatives, he would take them along with him.

When they came to Chirisophus, they found his men also feasting, with wreaths of hay round their heads, and with

Armenian boys in native dress waiting on them. They showed the boys what to do by signs, as though they were deaf mutes. After greeting each other, Chirisophus and Xenophon together interrogated the head-man through the interpreter who spoke Persian, and asked him what country this was. He replied that it was Armenia. Then they asked him for whom the horses were being kept, and he said that they were a tribute paid to the King. The next country, he said, was the land of the Chalybes, and he told them the way there.

Xenophon then went away and took the head-man back to his own people. He gave him back the horse (rather an old one) which he had taken, and told him to fatten it up and sacrifice it. This was because he had heard that it was sacred to the Sun and he was afraid that it might die, as the journey had done it no good. He took some of the colts himself, and gave one colt to each of the generals and captains. The horses in this part of the world were smaller than the Persian horses, but much more finely bred. The head-man told the Greeks to tie small bags round the feet of the horses and baggage animals whenever they made them go through snow, as, without these bags, they sank in up to their bellies.

Chapter 6

THEY CAPTURE A PASS
BY A MANŒUVRE

WHEN the eighth day came, Xenophon handed over the head-man of the village to Chirisophus for a guide. He left behind all his family for him in the village, except for his son, who was just growing up. He gave the young man to Plisthenes of Amphipolis to look after, with the idea that, if the father was a reliable guide, he could take back his son too when he left them. They brought all the provisions they could into the head-man's house, and then packed their belongings and set out.

The head-man was not put under any restraint and led them on through the snow. When they had already marched for three days Chirisophus got angry with him for not having brought them to any villages. The man said that there were none in this part of the country. Chirisophus then struck him, but did not have him bound. As a result of this he ran away and escaped in the night, leaving his son behind. This affair– ill-treating the guide and then not taking adequate precautions –was the only occasion on the march when Chirisophus and Xenophon fell out. Plisthenes was devoted to the young man, took him home with him, and found him a most trusty companion.

They then marched for seven days, doing fifteen miles a day, to the river Phasis, which was a hundred feet across. Next came a two days' march of thirty miles. At the pass which led down into the plain there were Chalybes, Taochi and Phasians to bar their way, and, when Chirisophus saw that the enemy was holding the pass, he came to a halt, keeping about three miles away from them, so as not to approach them

while marching in column. He sent orders to the other officers
to bring up their companies on his flank, so that the army
should be in line. When the rearguard had got into position
he called a meeting of the generals and captains, and spoke
as follows: 'As you see, the enemy are holding the pass over
the mountain. Now is the time to decide what is the best
method of dealing with them. What I suggest is that we give
orders to the troops to have a meal, and meanwhile decide
whether it is best to cross the mountain to-day or to-morrow.'

'I think, on the other hand,' said Cleanor, 'that we should
get ready for battle and make an attack, as soon as we have
finished our meal. My reason is that, if we let this day go by,
the enemy who are now watching us will gain confidence and,
if they do, others will probably join them in greater numbers.'

Xenophon spoke next, and said: 'This is my view. If we
have to fight a battle, what we must see to is how we may
fight with the greatest efficiency. But if we want to get across
the mountain with the minimum of inconvenience, then, I
think, what we must consider is how to ensure that our
casualties in dead and wounded are as light as possible. The
mountain, so far as we can see, extends for more than six miles,
but except just for the part on our road, there is no evidence
anywhere of men on guard against us. It would be a much
better plan, then, for us to try to steal a bit of the undefended
mountain from them when they are not looking, and to
capture it from them, if we can, by taking the initiative, than
to fight an action against a strong position and against troops
who are waiting ready for us. It is much easier to march uphill without fighting than to march on the level when one
has enemies on all sides; and one can see what is in front ot
one's feet better by night, when one is not fighting, than by
day, if one is; and rough ground is easier for the feet, if one
is not fighting as one marches, than level ground is, when
there are weapons flying round one's head. I do not think

that it is impossible for us to steal this ground from them. We can go by night, so as to be out of their observation; and we can keep far enough away from them to give them no chance of hearing us. And I would suggest that, if we make a feint at attacking here, we should find the rest of the mountain even less defended, as the enemy would be likely to stay here in a greater concentration. But I am not the person who ought to be talking about stealing. I gather that you Spartans, Chirisophus,—I mean the real officer class—study how to steal from your earliest boyhood, and think that so far from it being a disgrace it is an actual distinction to steal anything that is not forbidden by law. And, so that you may become expert thieves and try to get away with what you steal, it is laid down by law that you get a beating if you are caught stealing. Here then is an excellent opportunity for you to give an exhibition of the way in which you were brought up, and to preserve us from blows, by seeing to it that we are not caught stealing our bit of mountain.'

'Well,' said Chirisophus, 'what I have gathered about you Athenians is that you are remarkably good at stealing public funds, even though it is a very risky business for whoever does so; and your best men are the greatest experts at it, that is if it is your best men who are considered the right people to be in the government. So here is a chance for you too to give an exhibition of the way in which you were brought up.'

'Then,' said Xenophon, 'I am prepared, as soon as we have had our meal, to take the rearguard and go to seize the position in the mountains. I have got guides already, as my light troops ambushed and made prisoners of a few of the natives who have been following behind to pick up what they could. I have also been informed by them that the mountains are not impassable: they provide pasture for goats and cattle. If, therefore, we once get hold of a part of the range, there will be a possible route for our baggage animals as well. I do not expect either that the enemy will stand their ground when they see that we are holding the heights and on a level with them, as they show no willingness at the moment to come down on to a level with us.'

'But why,' said Chirisophus, 'should you go and leave vacant the command of the rearguard? It would be better to send others, that is if some good soldiers do not come forward as volunteers.'

Then Aristonymus of Methydria, a commander of hoplites, and Aristeas of Chios, and Nicomachus of Oeta, commanders of light infantry, came forward, and it was agreed that they would light a number of fires as soon as they had seized the heights. When this was settled they had their meal, and afterwards Chirisophus led the army forward about a mile in the direction of the enemy, so as to give the impression that it was at this point that he intended to attack.

When they had had supper and it became dark, the troops detailed for the job set off and seized the mountain height, while the others rested where they were. As soon as the enemy realised that the heights had been occupied, they were on the look-out and kept a number of fires burning through the night. At daybreak Chirisophus offered sacrifices and then advanced on the road, while the troops who had seized the mountain ridge made an attack along the heights. Most of the enemy stood their ground at the pass, but part of them went to engage the troops on the heights. However, before the main bodies came to close quarters, the troops on the heights were in action and the Greeks were winning and driving the enemy back. At the same moment in the plain the Greek peltasts advanced at the double against the enemy's battle line, and Chirisophus with the hoplites followed at a quick march behind. However, when the enemy guarding the road saw that their troops higher up were being defeated, they took to flight. Not many of them were killed, but a very great number of shields were captured. The Greeks cut these shields up with their swords and so made them useless. When they reached the summit, they offered sacrifices and set up a trophy. Then they descended into the plain and came among villages full of plenty of good food.

Chapter 7

THE GREEKS CATCH SIGHT
OF THE SEA

NEXT came a five days' march of ninety miles into the country of the Taochi, and here provisions began to run short. The Taochi lived behind strong fortifications inside which they had all their provisions stored up. The Greeks arrived at one of these fortifications, which had no city or dwellings attached to it, but into which men and women and a lot of cattle had got together, and Chirisophus, as soon as he reached the place, launched an attack on it. When the first body of attackers became tired, another body of troops relieved them, and then another, since it was impossible to surround the place with the whole lot together, as there was precipitous ground all round it. On the arrival of Xenophon with the rearguard, both hoplites and peltasts, Chirisophus exclaimed: 'You have come where you are needed. This position must be taken. If we fail to do so, there are no supplies for the army.'

They then discussed the situation together, and, when Xenophon asked what it was that was stopping them from getting inside, Chirisophus said: 'This approach, which you see, is the only one there is. But when one tries to get in by that way, they roll down boulders from that rock which overhangs the position. Whoever gets caught by one, ends up like this.' And he pointed out some men who had had their legs and ribs broken.

'But,' said Xenophon, 'when they have used up their boulders, what is there to stop us getting inside? In front of us we see only these few men, and of these only two or three who are armed. And, as you can see yourself, the piece of ground where we are bound to be exposed to the stones, as we go over it, is about a hundred and fifty feet in length. Of this distance, about a hundred feet is covered with large pine trees spaced at intervals. If the men take shelter against their trunks, what damage could come to them either from the rolling stones or the stones flying through the air? All that is left is fifty feet, over which we must run when the stones cease coming at us.'

'But,' said Chirisophus, 'as soon as we begin to advance towards the wooded part, great numbers of stones are hurled down at us.'

'That,' said Xenophon, 'is just what we want. They will use up their stones all the quicker. Let us advance, then, to the point from which we shall not have far to run forward if we are to do so, and from which we can easily retreat if we want to.'

Then Chirisophus and Xenophon went forward, accompanied by one of the captains, Callimachus of Parrhasia, since on that day he held the position of chief officer among the captains of the rearguard. The other captains stayed behind in safety. Afterwards about seventy men reached the shelter of the trees, not in a body, but one by one, each man looking after himself as well as he could. Agasias of Stymphalus and Aristonymus of Methydria (also captains of the rearguard) with some others were standing by outside the trees, as it was not safe for more than one company to stand among them.

Callimachus had a good scheme. He kept running forward two or three paces from the tree under which he was sheltering, and, when the stones came down on him, he nimbly drew back again. Each time he ran forward more than ten waggon loads of stones were used. Agasias saw that the whole army was watching what Callimachus was doing, and feared that he would not be the first man to get into the fortification; so, without calling in the help of Aristonymus, who was next to him, or of Eurylochus of Lusia, though both of them were

friends of his, he went ahead by himself and got beyond everyone. When Callimachus saw that he was going past him he
seized hold of him by his shield. Meantime Aristonymus of
Methydria ran past them, and after him Eurylochus of Lusia.
All of these men were keen rivals of each other in doing brave
things, and so, struggling amongst themselves, they took the
place. For, once they were inside, no more stones were thrown
down from above.

Then it was certainly a terrible sight. The women threw
their children down from the rocks and then threw themselves
after them, and the men did the same. While this was going
on Aeneas of Stymphalus, a captain, saw one of them, who
was wearing a fine garment, running to throw himself down,
and he caught hold of him in order to stop him; but the man
dragged him with him and they both went hurtling down
over the rocks and were killed. Consequently very few
prisoners were taken, but there were great numbers of oxen
and asses and sheep.

Then came a seven days' march of a hundred and fifty miles
through the country of the Chalybes. These were the most
warlike of all the tribes on their way, and they fought with
the Greeks at close quarters. They had body-armour of linen,
reaching down to the groin, and instead of skirts to their
armour they wore thick twisted cords. They also wore
greaves and helmets, and carried on their belts a knife of about
the size of the Spartan dagger. With these knives they cut the
throats of those whom they managed to overpower, and then
would cut off their heads and carry them as they marched,
singing and dancing whenever their enemies were likely to see
them. They also carried a spear with one point, about twenty
feet long. They used to stay inside their settlements, and then,
when the Greeks had gone past, they would follow behind
and were always ready for a fight. They had their houses in
fortified positions, and had brought all their provisions inside

the fortifications. Consequently the Greeks could take nothing from them, but lived on the supplies which they had seized from the Taochi.

The Greeks arrived next at the river Harpasus which was four hundred feet across. Then they marched through the territory of the Scytheni, a four days' march of sixty miles over level ground until they came to some villages, where they stayed for three days and renewed their stocks of provisions. Then a four days' march of sixty miles brought them to a large, prosperous and inhabited city, which was called Gymnias. The governor of the country sent the Greeks a guide from this city, with the idea that he should lead them through country which was at war with his own people. When the guide arrived, he said that in five days he would lead them to a place from which they could see the sea; and he said he was ready to be put to death if he failed to do so. So he led the way, and, when they had crossed the border into his enemies' country, he urged them to burn and lay waste the land, thus making it clear that it was for this purpose that he had come to them, and not because of any goodwill to the Greeks.

They came to the mountain on the fifth day, the name of the mountain being Thekes. When the men in front reached the summit and caught sight of the sea there was great shouting. Xenophon and the rearguard heard it and thought that there were some more enemies attacking in the front, since there were natives of the country they had ravaged following them up behind, and the rearguard had killed some of them and made prisoners of others in an ambush, and captured about twenty raw ox-hide shields, with the hair on. However, when the shouting got louder and drew nearer, and those who were constantly going forward started running towards the men in front who kept on shouting, and the more there were of them the more shouting there was, it looked then as though this was something of considerable importance. So Xenophon mounted his horse and, taking Lycus and the cavalry with him, rode forward to give support, and, quite soon, they heard the soldiers shouting out 'The sea! The sea!' and passing the word down the column. Then certainly they all began to run, the rearguard and all, and drove on the baggage animals and the horses at full speed; and when they had all got to the top, the soldiers, with tears in their eyes, embraced each other and their generals and captains. In a moment, at somebody or other's suggestion, they collected stones and made a great pile of them. On top they put a lot of raw ox-hides and staves and the shields which they had captured. The guide himself cut the shields into pieces and urged the others to do so too. Afterwards the Greeks sent the guide back and gave him as presents from the common store a horse, and a silver cup and a Persian robe and ten darics. What he particularly wanted was the rings which the soldiers had and he got a number of these from them. He pointed out to them a village where they could camp, and showed them the road by which they had to go to the country of the Macrones. It was then evening and he went away, travelling by night.

Chapter 8

THEY ARRIVE AT TRAPEZUS

THEN the Greeks did a three days' march of thirty miles through the country of the Macrones. On the first day they came to the river which forms the boundary between the territories of the Macrones and the Scytheni. On their right there was a defensive position which looked a very awkward one, and on the left there was another river, into which flowed the river that formed the boundary and which they had to cross. The banks of this river were covered with trees which, though not large, were growing thickly together. The Greeks cut the trees down when they came up to them, being anxious to get away from the place as quickly as they could. The Macrones, armed with shields and spears, and wearing hair tunics, were drawn up in battle order facing the crossing-place. They kept shouting to each other and hurling stones which fell harmlessly into the river as they failed to reach the other side.

At this point one of the peltasts came up to Xenophon. He said that he had been a slave in Athens and that he knew the language of these people. 'Indeed,' he went on, 'I think that this is my own country. If there is no objection, I should like to speak to them.'

'There is no objection at all,' Xenophon said. 'Speak to them and find out first of all who they are.'

He asked them this, and they replied that they were Macrones.

'Now ask them,' said Xenophon, 'why they are drawn up to oppose us and why they want to be our enemies.'

Their reply to this was: 'Because it is you who are invading our country.'

The generals then told the man to say, 'We are not coming with any hostile intentions. We have been making war on the King, and now we are going back to Greece and want to get to the sea.'

The Macrones asked whether the Greeks would give pledges that they meant what they said, and they replied that they would like both to give and to receive pledges. The Macrones then gave the Greeks a native spear, and the Greeks gave them a Greek one, as they said that these were the usual pledges. Both sides called on the gods to witness the agreement.

After exchanging pledges, the Macrones immediately helped the Greeks to cut down the trees and made a path for them in order to help them across. They mixed freely with the Greeks and provided them, as well as they could, with opportunities for buying food, and led them through their country for three days, until they brought them to the Colchian frontier. There were mountains here, which, though high, were not steep, and the Colchians were drawn up in battle order on the mountains. At first the Greeks formed up opposite them in line, with the intention of advancing on the mountain in that formation; but in the end the generals decided to meet and discuss what would be the best method of making the attack. Xenophon then expressed the opinion that it would be better to break up their present formation and to advance in columns. 'The line,' he said, 'will lose its cohesion directly, since we shall find some parts of the mountain easy going and other parts difficult. It will immediately make the men lose heart, if after being drawn up in line they see the line broken. Then, if we advance in a line many ranks deep, the enemy will have men on both our flanks, and can use them however they like. On the other hand, if we go forward in a line which is only a few ranks deep, there would be nothing surprising in our line being broken through, with masses of missiles and men all falling on us together. And if this takes place at any single point, the whole line will suffer for it. No, I propose that we should form up with the companies in column, spaced out so as to cover the ground in such a way that the companies on our extreme flanks are beyond the two wings of the enemy. By adopting this plan we shall out-flank the enemy's line, and, as we are advancing in columns, our bravest men will be the first to engage the enemy, and each officer will lead his company by the easiest route. As for the gaps between the columns, it will not be easy for the enemy to infiltrate, when there are companies both on his right and left; and it will not be easy to break through a com-pany that is advancing in column. If any company is in diffi-culties, the nearest one will give support; and if at any point any one company can reach the summit, you can be sure that not a man among the enemy will stand his ground any longer.'

This plan was agreed upon, and they formed the companies into columns. Xenophon rode along from the right wing to the left and said to the soldiers: 'My friends, these people whom you see are the last obstacle which stops us from being where we have so long struggled to be. We ought, if we could, to eat them up alive.'

When everyone was in position and they had formed the companies, there were about eighty companies of hoplites, each company with roughly the strength of a hundred. They formed up the peltasts and the archers in three divisions, one beyond the left flank, one beyond the right, and one in the centre, each division being about six hundred strong. The order was then passed along for the soldiers to make their vows and to sing the paean. When this was done, they moved forward. Chirisophus and Xenophon, with the peltasts attached to them, were advancing outside the flanks of the enemy's line, and, when the enemy observed this, they ran to meet them, some to the right, some to the left, and lost cohesion, leaving a great gap in the centre of their line. The peltasts in the Arcadian division, commanded by Aeschines the Acarnanian, thinking that the enemy were running away, raised their battle-cry and advanced at the double. They were the first to get to the top of the mountain, and the Arcadian hoplites, commanded by Cleanor of Orchomenus, came after them. As soon as they charged, the enemy failed to stand their ground and ran away in a disorganised flight.

The Greeks ascended the mountain and camped in a number of villages which were well stocked with food. There was nothing remarkable about them, except that there were great numbers of bee hives in these parts, and all the soldiers who ate the honey went off their heads and suffered from vomiting and diarrhoea and were unable to stand upright. Those who had only eaten a little behaved as though they were drunk, and those who had eaten a lot were like mad people. Some actually died. So there were numbers of them lying on the ground, as though after a defeat, and there was a general state of despondency. However, they were all alive on the next day, and came to themselves at about the same hour as they had eaten the honey the day before. On the third and fourth days they were able to get up, and felt just as if they had been taking medicine.

A two days' march of twenty-one miles from here brought them to the sea at Trapezus, an inhabited Greek city on the Euxine, a colony of Sinope in Colchian territory. They stayed here, camping in the Colchian villages, for about thirty days, and, using these villages as their base, they ravaged the Colchian country. The people of Trapezus provided the Greeks with facilities for buying food, and gave them presents of oxen and barley and wine. They also negotiated with them on behalf of the Colchians in the neighbourhood, particularly those who lived in the plain, and from them too there arrived presents of oxen.

Then the Greeks prepared to offer the sacrifice which they had vowed. Enough cattle had come in for them to be able to sacrifice to Zeus the Saviour and to Heracles, for safe guidance, and to make the offerings which they had vowed to the other gods. They also held athletic sports on the mountain where they were camping. They elected as organiser and president of the sports the Spartan Dracontius, who had been an exile from his home since boyhood because he had accidentally killed another boy with a dagger.

When the sacrifice was finished, they gave the hides to Dracontius and told him to lead the way to the place where he had set out the course. He then pointed to the ground where they were actually standing, and said: 'This hill is an excellent place for running, wherever one likes.'

'But how,' they asked, 'will people be able to wrestle on ground that is so hard and rough?' To which he replied: 'All the worse for the man who gets thrown.' Boys, mostly from among the prisoners, competed in the short-distance race, and more than sixty Cretans ran in the race over a long distance. There were also wrestling and boxing events, and all-in wrestling. It was a very fine performance, as there were many entrants for the events, and, with their comrades as spectators, the rivalry was keen. There was also a horse race in which they had to gallop down a steep bit of ground, turn round in the sea, and ride back to the altar. On the way down most of them had a thorough shaking, and on the way up, when the ground got very steep, the horses could scarcely get along at walking pace. So there was a lot of noise and laughter and people shouting out encouragements.

BOOK

V

THE MARCH
TO PAPHLAGONIA

Chapter 1

CHIRISOPHUS GOES TO GET SHIPS

AFTERWARDS they held a meeting to discuss the remainder of their journey. Leon of Thurii stood up first, and spoke as follows: 'Speaking for myself, soldiers, I am already tired out with packing up baggage, and walking and running, and carrying arms, and marching in the ranks, and going on guard, and fighting. What I want is to have a rest now from all this, and since we have got to the sea, to sail for the rest of the way, and so get back to Greece stretched out at my ease on deck, like Odysseus.'

When they heard this, the soldiers shouted out in support of the speech. Another man got up and spoke to the same effect, and so did everyone there. Then Chirisophus got up and spoke as follows: 'Soldiers, Anaxibius is a friend of mine, and happens to be in command of a fleet. If, then, you authorise me to go to him, I feel confident that I shall come back with triremes and transports to carry us. Since you want to go by sea, wait here until I return. I shall come quickly.' When they heard this, the soldiers were delighted and voted that he should set sail as soon as he could.

Then Xenophon stood up and spoke as follows: 'Chirisophus is being sent to fetch ships, and we shall wait here for him. I am now going to say what I think we ought to do while we are staying here. The first point is that we have to get our provisions from enemy country, as there is not sufficient food available in the market, nor have we, except for a few of us, enough money to buy what there is. The country round us is hostile, and therefore, if you do your foraging in a slack and unorganised way, there is danger of us losing a lot of men.

I think, then, that you ought to go out in regular detachments to get provisions, and not wander about except in detachments, and that we, the officers, ought to be responsible for this.'

This   suggestion was agreed upon, and then Xenophon continued: 'Now listen, please, to these further points. Some of you will be going out on plundering expeditions. I think the best thing is for those who intend to go out to inform us beforehand and tell us in what direction they are going, so that we may know the numbers of those out of camp and those in camp, and make our dispositions accordingly; also so that, if occasion arises for sending out reinforcements, we may know where to send them, and if any soldiers who are rather lacking in experience are planning an attack in any particular direction, we may give them advice and try to find out the strength of the enemy against whom they are going.'

This proposal too was carried. 'And now,' Xenophon said, 'there is also this to consider. The enemy will have opportunities for robbing us, and it is quite natural for them to be plotting against us, as we are in possession of their property. Moreover, they are practically sitting on top of us. There should be, then, I think, guards posted round the camp. If we take turns, therefore, at going on guard and at patrolling, the enemy will not have the same chance of catching us unprepared. Then there is this point too. If we were quite certain that Chirisophus would come back with an adequate number of ships, there would be no point in saying what I am going to say. But as it is, since this is uncertain, I think we should attempt to provide ourselves with ships from here as well. If he does return with ships, we shall be all the better off on our voyage, if we have some here already; and if he fails to produce any, we can make use of what we have here. I notice that ships frequently sail past here, and if we were to ask the people of Trapezus for warships and were to bring them in to shore, remove the rudders, and keep them under guard until we had enough to bring us home, then, I imagine, we should be in no difficulty about the right sort of transport.'

This proposal too was carried. 'Next,' said Xenophon, 'consider whether it is not the right thing for us to support from our common funds the sailors whom we bring in here, for as long as they stay here for our convenience, and to come to an arrangement about passage money, so that, since they are doing us a good turn, we may do them one too.'

This was also carried. 'And now,' Xenophon went on, 'I think that, in case all our efforts to secure sufficient boats are unsuccessful, we ought to request the cities on the coast to repair the roads, which we gather are in a very bad condition. They will do what we ask, both because they are afraid of us and because they want to get rid of us.'

At this point they shouted out that there was no need to march by land, and Xenophon, realising their inability to face facts, did not put the proposal to the vote. He did, however, persuade the cities voluntarily to build roads, pointing out that they would get rid of the Greeks all the sooner if the roads were in good repair.

They got a warship of fifty oars from the people of Trapezus, and put Dexippus, a Spartan 'perioikos', in command of it. Dexippus, with no sense of his responsibility to collect ships, deserted and escaped outside the Black Sea, taking the ship with him. However, he got what he deserved later. When he was engaged in some intrigue in Thrace at the Court of King Seuthes, he was killed by the Spartan Nicander.

They got another fifty-oared ship which they put under the command of Polycrates, an Athenian, who brought in to the camp all the ships he could get hold of. What cargoes there were the Greeks removed, and put them under guard so as to keep them safe, commandeering the ships for their own transport.

While all this was going on, the Greeks went on plundering expeditions, some of which were successful and others not. Cleaenetus, who took another company as well as his own against a difficult position, was killed, as were many others of the troops with him.

Chapter 2

A PLUNDERING EXPEDITION

In the end it was no longer possible to get provisions from close at hand so as to return to camp on the same day. Xenophon therefore took some of the people of Trapezus as guides, and led half the army against the Drilae, leaving the other half behind to guard the camp–a necessary measure, since the Colchians, driven out as they had been from their own homes, had collected in large numbers and were occupying dominating positions on the heights. The people of Trapezus failed to lead the Greeks to places where it was easy to get provisions, since they were on friendly terms with the inhabitants of such places. However, they were willing enough to show them the way to the country of the Drilae, from whom they had suffered harm. It was difficult and mountainous ground, and the people were the most warlike of all the inhabitants of the Black Sea coast-line.

As the Greeks advanced into the interior, the Drilae fell back, first setting fire to all their settlements which seemed to them indefensible. Thus there was nothing for the Greeks to take except for an odd pig or ox or other animal that had escaped the fire. They had one position which was their capital, and there they all gathered together. There was a tremendously deep ravine all round the place, and the roads into the fortification were difficult to get at.

The peltasts had got about a half a mile ahead of the hoplites, and, crossing over the ravine and seeing a lot of cattle and other booty, they attacked the fortifications. A number of spearmen, who had come out for plunder, followed after them, so that there were more than two thousand who crossed over the ravine. However, they were not able to take the place by assault, which was not surprising, as there was a broad ditch round it with the earth thrown up to form a rampart, and with a palisade on top of the rampart and wooden towers erected at frequent intervals. They therefore tried to retreat, but the enemy pressed hard upon them. Being unable, then, to get back, as the way down from the fortifications to the ravine was only broad enough for people to go down it in a single file, they sent a messenger to Xenophon, who was at the head of the hoplites. The messenger said that the place was full of all kinds of supplies. 'But,' he said, 'we cannot take it, because the enemy come out and attack us, and our return route is a difficult one.'

On receiving this information Xenophon advanced to the ravine and ordered the hoplites to halt there. He himself with the captains crossed over and examined the position to see whether it would be better to withdraw the troops who had crossed already, or, on the assumption that the place could be taken, to bring the hoplites across too. It seemed that it would be impossible to withdraw without considerable loss of life: the captains were of opinion that they could take the place; and Xenophon agreed with them, relying also on the results of the sacrifices, for the soothsayers had indicated that there would be a battle, but the final result of the expedition would be successful. He therefore sent the captains back to bring the hoplites across, and stayed where he was himself. He brought all the peltasts back from the ditch and forbade any of them to engage in long-range fighting. When the hoplites arrived, he ordered each captain to form up his company in the way in which he thought his men would fight best; for the captains who were continually competing with each other in doing brave deeds, were now next to each other. They did as they were told, and Xenophon then ordered all the peltasts to advance with their javelins at the ready, and the archers to have their arrows fitted to the string, as they would both have to discharge their weapons as soon as he gave the signal. He told the light troops to have their wallets full of stones, and sent reliable people to see that these orders were obeyed.

When everything was ready, and the captains and lieutenants and other officers who considered themselves just as good men as their immediate superiors, had all taken up their positions, they were all actually in sight of each other, since, because of the nature of the ground, they were in a crescent-shaped formation. Then, after they had sung the paean and the trumpet had sounded, the hoplites raised the war-cry and charged, with the missiles all being hurled together–spears, arrows, stones from slings, and a lot also thrown by hand, together with fire-brands, which some people used in the attack. Under this weight of weapons the enemy were forced to abandon the palisade and the towers. This gave Agasias the Stymphalian an opportunity. He stripped off his armour and climbed up, only wearing his tunic. Others then helped each other up or climbed up by themselves and, to all appearance, the position was won. The peltasts and light infantry rushed inside, each man making off with what booty he could. Xenophon, however, stood by the gates and kept back as many of the hoplites as he could outside, since there were fresh enemy troops coming into sight in strong positions on the high ground. Before much time had gone by, there was a shout from inside, and people came running out, some carrying booty, with here and there a wounded man among them. There was a crush around the gates and, in reply to questions, the men who were being driven out said that there was a citadel inside and a large enemy force which kept charging down from it and falling on the Greeks who were inside.

Xenophon then ordered Tolmides the herald to proclaim that those who wanted plunder had permission to go in. A lot of men surged forward and, as the ones who were pushing their way in forced back those who were being driven out, they shut the enemy up again inside the citadel. Everything outside the citadel was plundered and the Greeks brought the booty out of the gates. The hoplites took up position, some at the palisade, and some on the path that led up to the citadel. Xenophon and the captains then considered whether it was possible to capture the citadel. If they could, it would mean that they could get away safely: otherwise it appeared that it would be a very difficult business to retire. After considering the matter, they came to the conclusion that the position was absolutely impregnable, and therefore made their dispositions for the retreat.

Each man pulled up the stakes in the palisade opposite him. They sent back those who were unfit for action or carrying booty, together with most of the hoplites; and the captains kept with them the men in whom each had special confidence. When they began their retreat, large numbers of the enemy, armed with shields, spears, greaves and Paphlagonian helmets, charged out at them from inside, and others climbed on to the roofs of the houses on each side of the way leading up to the citadel. Thus it was not safe even to drive them back by the gates leading there, since they threw down great pieces of timber and so made it awkward for them either to stay where they were or to retreat. The approach of darkness increased their alarm.

However, while they were still fighting and still doubtful what to do next, some god showed them a way of saving themselves. One of the houses on the right, through someone or other's action, suddenly caught fire. When this house collapsed, the enemy fled from the row of houses on the right. Xenophon, by a stroke of luck, saw what had happened, and gave the order to set fire to the houses on the left as well. These, being of wood, were soon blazing, and so the enemy fled from these houses too. Now the only enemy force which still caused trouble was the one in front, and it was obvious that these intended to fall upon them on their way out of the town and down into the ravine. Xenophon then ordered all those who were out of range of the missiles to carry wood into the space between them and the enemy. When enough wood had been brought, they set fire to it and also set fire to the houses next to the rampart, so that the enemy might have their attention attracted there. In this way they managed with difficulty to retreat from the place under the protection of a fire between them and the enemy. The whole city was burned to the ground–houses, towers, palisade and everything else except the citadel.

Next day the Greeks marched back, taking their supplies with them. They were apprehensive about the return journey to Trapezus, as the road was steep and narrow; and so they pretended to set an ambush. A Mysian in the army, who was called Mysus too, took ten Cretans with him and stayed behind in some wooded country, pretending that he was trying to keep out of enemy observation. The shields of the party, which were of brass, kept on flashing into sight. The enemy observed all this and were alarmed just as if it was a real ambush, and meanwhile the army carried out the descent. When Xenophon considered that they had got far enough away, he signalled to the Mysian to run back at full speed. So he and his men started up and ran for it. The Cretans (who saw that they were being overtaken in the race) jumped down from the road into a wood and, rolling over and over among the undergrowth, got away safe. The Mysian ran down the road and shouted for help. Soldiers came to his aid and picked him up wounded. Then the rescue party retreated step by step and, being shot at by the enemy, with some of the Cretan archers shooting back at the enemy. So they all got back safely to the camp.

Chapter 3

THE GREEKS LEAVE TRAPEZUS·
XENOPHON'S ESTATE IN
LATER YEARS

As Chirisophus did not come back, and there were not enough ships to transport them, and it was no longer possible to get provisions, they came to the conclusion that they would have to leave Trapezus. They put on board ship the sick, and those who were over forty years old, and the women and children, and all the baggage which it was not essential to have with them. The rest travelled by land, the roads being now in a good state of repair.

After three days' march they arrived at Cerasus, a Greek city on the coast, a colony of Sinope, in Colchian territory. They stayed here for ten days, and a review was held of the troops under arms and their numbers were taken. The number was eight thousand six hundred. They had got away safe, while the remainder had perished either in the fighting or from the snow, and a few had died of illness.

At this place also they distributed the money that had come in from the sale of their prisoners. The generals took over the tenth part, which they had set aside for Apollo and for Artemis of Ephesus, to keep for this religious purpose. Each general took a share of the tenth, and Neon of Asine took charge of Chirisophus's share. Later Xenophon had an offering made for Apollo and put it in the Athenian treasury at Delphi. He had it inscribed with his own name and with the name of Proxenus, who was killed with Clearchus, for he had been his friend. As for the part which belonged to Artemis of Ephesus, when Xenophon was returning from Asia on the march to Boeotia with Agesilaus, he left it in the keeping of Megabyzus, the warden of the temple of Artemis, as he thought that his journey would be a risky business. He asked Megabyzus to return the money to him if he got home safe, but if anything happened to him, he was to have something made which he thought would please the goddess, and dedicate it to her. When Xenophon had been banished and had already settled at Scillus on land near Olympia, which had been granted to him by the Spartans, Megabyzus came to Olympia to see the games and gave back the money which had been deposited with him.

When Xenophon received it, he bought an estate as an offering to the goddess in a place where the oracle had instructed him. There happened to be a river called the Selinus which ran through the estate, and in Ephesus there is also a river Selinus which runs past the temple of Artemis. There are fishes and shellfish in both rivers. On the estate at Scillus there is hunting also, and all kinds of game are available. Xenophon also used the sacred money for building an altar and a temple, and ever afterwards he used to take a tenth of the season's produce from the land and make a sacrifice to the goddess. All the townspeople, and the men and women of the district used to take part in the festival, and the goddess provided those who camped out there with barley, bread, wine, dainties and a share both of the animals sacrificed from the sacred herds and also of the animals caught in hunting. There were plenty of them as Xenophon's sons and the sons of other townspeople used to go hunting specially for the festival, and anybody else who liked joined them in the hunt. Pig, antelopes and stags were caught, partly from the sacred land itself and partly from Mount Pholoe. The land is on the road from Sparta to Olympia, about two miles from the temple of Zeus at Olympia. In the ground sacred to Artemis there are meadows and thickly wooded hills, good breeding country for pig and goats and horses as well, and consequently it is possible to provide fodder for the animals of those who come to the festival. Round the temple itself there has been set a plantation of fruit trees which produce fruit to eat in all the appropriate seasons. The temple is a small-scale version of the great temple at Ephesus, and the image is as like the one in Ephesus as a cypress statue can be like one of gold. A pillar stands by the temple, with the following inscription on it:

THIS GROUND IS SACRED TO ARTEMIS . HE WHO OWNS IT AND TAKES ITS PRODUCE IS TO OFFER THE TENTH PART TO ARTEMIS EVERY YEAR . FROM THE REMAINDER HE IS TO KEEP THE TEMPLE IN REPAIR . WHOSOEVER NEGLECTS TO DO THIS WILL NOT ESCAPE THE NOTICE OF THE GODDESS.

Chapter 4

THE BARBAROUS MOSSYNOICI

FROM Cerasus the same people as before continued the voyage by sea, and the others marched on by land. When they reached the frontier of the Mossynoici, they sent Timesitheus, who was a native of Trapezus and had diplomatic relations with the Mossynoici, to ask them whether they were to assume that their march was to be through friendly or hostile country. The Mossynoici, relying on the strength of their positions, replied that they would not let the Greeks through their land.

Timesitheus then told the Greeks that the Mossynoici in the country beyond were at war with these Mossynoici, and it was decided to send for some of them to see whether they were willing to make an alliance. Timesitheus was sent to them and came back bringing their chief men with him. On their arrival there was a meeting between the chiefs of the Mossynoici and the Greek generals. Xenophon, with Timesitheus as his interpreter, spoke as follows: 'My Mossynoican friends, we, since we have no ships, want to get back safe to Greece by land. These people, who, we hear, are enemies of yours, are stopping us from doing so. You can, then, if you like, have us as your allies, and pay them back for the harm they have done to you, and have them in your power for the future. If you let this opportunity slip, can you imagine how you will ever get a second chance of having such a great force as this one of ours on your side?'

The chief of the Mossynoici then replied to him and said that they welcomed the proposal and accepted the alliance.

'Very well,' said Xenophon, 'and now tell us in what way you will want to make use of us, if we become your allies, and what help you will be able to give us in getting through the country.'

'We have forces available,' they said, 'to invade the western frontier of our joint enemies, and also to send you ships here and troops to fight along with you and show you the way.'

On these terms they exchanged pledges, and then the chiefs went away. Next day they returned with three hundred dug-out canoes, each carrying three men. Two out of every three disembarked and paraded with their arms, while one stayed in the canoe. Those in the canoes then sailed back again, and those who remained fell in in the following order. They stood in lines with about a hundred in each line, facing each other like dancers. They all had shields made of the skins of white oxen and with the hair still on, shaped like an ivy leaf; and in the right hand they carried a spear about nine feet long, with a point at one end and a round knob made out of the wood of the shaft at the other end. They wore short tunics, which did not reach down to the knee, and were about as thick as a linen clothes-bag. On their heads they had leather helmets of the Paphlagonian type, with tufts of hair wound round the middle so as to produce the effect of a tiara. They also carried iron battle-axes.

The next thing was that one of them took the lead, and the rest followed him, chanting in chorus. They went through the Greek line, past the hoplites, and marched immediately against the enemy to attack a position which appeared easy to take. This was a fortification in front of the city which they called their metropolis, and which contained the highest ground in the country of the Mossynoici. This fortification had been the cause of the present war, since those who held it were supposed also to hold the sovereignty over all the Mossynoici, but, according to the Mossynoici who were allies of the Greeks, the other party had no right to hold it; it should have been shared, but they had seized it and so secured an

unfair advantage. Now some of the Greeks too followed
them, not on the instructions of their officers, but merely for
the sake of plunder.

So long as they were approaching the position the enemy
made no move, but when they got close they charged out and
forced them to retreat, killing a number of the natives and a
few of the Greeks who had joined with them in the assault.
They kept up the pursuit until they saw the Greeks coming to
the rescue; then they turned and went back. They cut off the
heads of those who had been killed, and showed them to the
Greeks and to their own enemies, dancing at the same time
and singing to a sort of tune.

The Greeks were badly upset by this. The action had increased the enemy's confidence, and the Greeks who had gone
out with their allies had run away, although they had been in
considerable numbers. This was a thing which had never
occurred before in the whole campaign. Xenophon called the
Greeks to a meeting and spoke as follows: 'Soldiers, you must
not be downhearted because of recent events. I can assure you
that there are as many advantages as disadvantages in what has
happened. First, you have the assurance that the men who are
going to act as our guides are genuine enemies of those whom
we have to fight. Then there is the fact that those Greeks
who neglected to stay with us in their positions, and considered
themselves capable of having the same success with the natives
as they have under our command, have been taught a lesson,
and will be less inclined on another occasion to leave the post
where we have put them. What you have to do is to conduct
yourselves in such a way that you will appear to the natives,
even the ones on our side, as better men than they are, and
make it plain to the enemy that they will not have to fight
now with the same sort of people as they did when you were
not properly organised.'

For that day they stayed as they were. On the next, after

they had sacrificed and found the omens favourable, they had breakfast and formed up with the companies in column, placing the native troops, drawn up in the same formation, on the left. They then marched forward, with the archers in the space between the companies, and with the front ranks of the hoplites not far behind them, since the enemy had some light troops who kept running down the hill and hurling stones. The archers and peltasts dealt with these, while the rest of the army moved steadily forward. They went first to the position from which the natives and the Greeks with them had been driven back on the previous day, since it was here that the enemy was formed up to meet them. The natives stood their ground and fought with the peltasts, but they fled as soon as the hoplites got close to them. The peltasts immediately followed them in pursuit up the hill to their city, and the hoplites came after in regular formation. They made the ascent and were at the outskirts of the metropolis, and at this point the enemy, who were now all in one body, fought back, hurling javelins and using some long thick spears, so big that a man could hardly carry one, in an attempt to hold off the Greeks in close fighting. The Greeks, however, so far from giving ground, moved forward to engage them at close quarters, and then the natives fled from this place too and entirely abandoned the position. Their king, who was in the wooden tower built on high ground, and whom they all guard while he stays there and contribute towards his upkeep, would not come outside, nor would the one in the position that they had captured previously; so they and the towers were both burnt up together. In looking for booty in these positions the Greeks found in the houses stores of loaves piled up and, according to the Mossynoici, made of last year's flour, with the new corn, stalk and all, set aside. It was mostly coarse wheat. Slices of dolphin, pickled in jars, were also found, and dolphin fat in containers. The Mossynoici used this fat just as the Greeks use olive oil. In the attics there were quantities of chestnuts–the broad kind with a continuous surface. They used these in large quantities for eating, boiling them and then baking loaves of them. Wine was found there too. When unmixed it tasted sour because of its roughness, but it smelt and tasted good if mixed with water.

The Greeks had their meal here and then marched on, handing over the position to the Mossynoici who had fought on their side. They passed a number of other towns belonging to the opposite faction, and, when they were easy to reach, the natives either abandoned them or voluntarily came over to the Greeks. Most of the towns fell into this category. The average distance between the cities was eight miles, but yet the people could hear each other shouting from one city to another, so mountainous and full of valleys is the country.

When the Greeks advanced further and reached the country of their allies, they pointed out to them some boys belonging to the wealthy class of people, who had been specially fatted up by being fed on boiled chestnuts. Their flesh was soft and very pale, and they were practically as broad as they were tall. Front and back were brightly coloured all over, tattooed with designs of flowers. These people wanted to have sexual intercourse in public with the mistresses whom the Greeks brought with them, this being actually the normal thing in their country. Both men and women were pale skinned. Those who were on the expedition used to say that these people were the most barbarous and the furthest removed from Greek ways of all those with whom they came in contact. When they were in a crowd they acted as men would act when in private, and when they were by themselves, they used to behave as they might do if they were in company; they used to talk to themselves, and laugh to themselves, and stop and dance wherever they happened to be, just as if they were giving a display to others.

Chapter 5

XENOPHON SPEAKS FOR THE ARMY

THE Greeks marched for eight days though this country, including both the friendly and hostile parts of it, and came to the country of the Chalybes. This is a small tribe, subject to the Mossynoici. Most of them get their livelihood by working in iron.

Next they reached the Tibareni, whose country was much flatter and had towns on the coast which were not so well fortified. The generals wanted to attack these towns and so do the army a good turn. They therefore refused to accept the tokens of friendship which came from the Tibareni, and, telling those who brought them to wait until they had considered the matter, they held a sacrifice. They offered a number of victims, and in the end the soothsayers unanimously declared their opinion, which was that the gods were not at all in favour of fighting. So then they accepted the gifts and marched on for two days through the country, which they treated as allied territory, until they arrived at Cotyora, a Greek city and a colony of Sinope, situated in the land of the Tibareni.

They stayed here for forty-five days, in the course of which they first of all sacrificed to the gods, and then organised processions, each according to the manner of their own people, and held athletic sports. They took their supplies partly from Paphlagonia and partly from settlements of the people of Cotyora, since they would not give the Greeks facilities for buying food and would not even take the sick men inside their walls.

While this was going on, ambassadors came from Sinope. They were anxious both about the city of Cotyora (since it

was their property and paid tribute to them) and also about
the land, because they had heard that it was being ravaged.
They came up to the camp and made their speech. Hecatonymus, who had the reputation of being a clever speaker, was
their spokesman. 'Soldiers,' he said, 'the city of Sinope has
sent us to offer you our congratulations because you are Greeks
and have conquered foreigners; also to testify to our joy that
you have arrived here safely, after going through, as we have
heard, all kinds of terrible experiences. But we, who are
Greeks ourselves, feel entitled to expect from you, who are
also Greeks, good treatment and no injuries. Certainly we
have never started by doing you any harm. These people of
Cotyora here are colonists of ours, and it was we who took
the land from the natives and handed it over to them. For
this reason they pay us a regular tribute, just as the people of
Cerasus and Trapezus do. Therefore whatever harm you do
to them, the city of Sinope will consider is done to it also. Our
present information is that some of you have made their way
into the city by force and are taking up their quarters in the
houses; that you are taking what you want from the settlements by force and not as the result of any agreement. We do
not consider this right, and if you go on acting in this way,
we shall be forced to make alliances with Corylas and the
Paphlagonians and anyone else available.'
    Xenophon then stood up to reply and spoke for the army as
follows: 'Men of Sinope, we were glad enough to get here
with whole skins and our arms in our hands. We had no
chance of bringing with us all our booty and fighting the
enemy at the same time. Now we have come among Greek
cities, and at Trapezus, where they gave us the facilities, we got
our food and paid for it. We made the right sort of return to
them for the honours they gave us and the gifts they gave to
the army. We kept our hands off any native tribe which was
allied to them, and we did all the damage we could to their

enemies, against whom they themselves led us. Ask them what sort of people they found us. You can do so, since the guides, whom the city sent with us out of friendship, are still here. But when we come to a place where we are given no opportunities to buy food, then, whether it is native country or Greek country, we take our own supplies and do this not out of wanton aggression, but from necessity. Although the Macrones are natives, we looked on them as our friends when they did their best to provide us with these opportunities, and we took by force nothing that belonged to them. As for the people of Cotyora, who you say are your subjects, if we have taken anything of theirs, it is their own fault. They did not act towards us like friends. They shut their gates to us, and neither let us inside their city nor gave us a chance of buying food outside their walls. And they said that the person responsible for this action was their governor, appointed by Sinope. As for your charge that some of us have made their way in by force and are quartered there, these are the facts. We asked them to receive our sick into their houses, and when they did not open their gates, we went inside at a place where the nature of the ground made it possible to do so. Otherwise we have committed no act of violence. Our sick are quartered in the houses at their own expense, and we are placing a guard at the gates so that our sick and wounded may not be at the mercy of your governor, but we may be in a position to withdraw them when we want. The rest of us, as you see, camp in the open air and in our formations, ready, if we are treated well, to make a good return for it, and to defend ourselves if we are treated badly. As for your threat that, if you think good, you will make an alliance with Corylas and the Paphlagonians, we, if we are forced into it, are quite prepared to fight both you and them. We have fought already against enemies many times your number. On the other hand, if we decide to make friends with the Paphlagonian king (and we hear that he has designs on your city and the settlements along the coast), we shall try to become his friends by helping him to obtain what he desires.'

Hecatonymus's fellow ambassadors were now quite obviously displeased at what he had said. One of them came forward and said that they had not come to start a war, but to make it clear that they were friends. 'If you come to Sinope', he said, 'we will welcome you there with gifts of friendship, and for the present we will tell the people here to give you what they can. We realise that all that you say is true.

After this the people of Cotyora sent gifts of friendship, and the generals of the Greeks entertained the ambassadors from Sinope. There was much friendly conversation and, among other things, each asked the other party what they wanted to know about the remainder of the journey.

Chapter 6

XENOPHON THINKS OF
FOUNDING A CITY

So that day ended. On the next the generals called a meeting of the soldiers at which it was decided to ask the men from Sinope to join in a discussion about the rest of their journey. If they had to go by land, the people of Sinope seemed likely to be useful, as they knew about the country of Paphlagonia. And if they went by sea, it appeared that they would also need their help as they were the only people who seemed capable of providing enough ships for the army. So they invited the ambassadors to the meeting and asked them for their advice, telling them that they relied in the first place on the claims of their common Greek nationality for a considerate attitude and for the best possible advice.

Then Hecatonymus stood up and, first of all, made his apology for his remarks about making friends with the Paphlagonians. What he had meant, he said, was not that they had any intention of making war on the Greeks, but that, though they were in a position to make friends with the natives, it was the Greeks whom they would choose. When they asked him to give his advice, he spoke as follows, beginning with a prayer to the gods. 'If I give you the advice which I myself consider best, I pray that much good may come to me, and if I do the opposite, then let me suffer accordingly. "Counsel is sound" says the proverb, and it is just this sort of counsel which we have here. There will be many to praise me if it appears that I have advised you well, and many to curse me if my advice turns out bad.

'Now I am aware that it will mean much more trouble for us if you travel by sea, since we shall have to provide you with ships, while, if you go by land, it will be up to you to do the fighting. Nevertheless, I must tell you what I know, and I am in a position to speak both about the geography and the resources of Paphlagonia. It is a country which has both the most beautiful plains and the most enormous mountains. Now, first, I know the part where you will have to begin your invasion. The only possible way in is where there are high mountain peaks on each side of the road, and if these were held even by a very small force, it would be strong enough. All the men in the world could not get past, once these positions are occupied. I could show them to you, if you cared to send someone with me. Next, I know, come the plains, and also a cavalry force which the natives themselves consider to be superior to all the King's cavalry. Just recently, when the King summoned them, they did not obey. Their leader was too proud for that. However, if you succeeded in stealing across the mountains or occupying the pass before the enemy, and if you won a victory in the plain, fighting not only against their cavalry but also against more than 120,000 infantry, you would then come to their rivers. First, the Thermodon, three hundred feet broad, which I should say is a difficult one to cross, especially when there are numbers of enemy troops in front and many more following you from the rear. Then the Iris, also three hundred feet broad; and the third river is the Halys, which is a quarter of a mile broad and cannot be crossed without boats. And where would you find anyone to supply you with boats? The Parthenius is equally difficult to cross, and this is the river which you would come to, if you got across the Halys. Personally, then, I do not so much consider your march difficult as absolutely impossible. If, however, you go by sea, you can sail along the coast from here to Sinope, and from Sinope to Heraclea. After Heraclea there will be no more difficulty in going either by land or sea. There are plenty of ships also in Heraclea.'

At the end of this speech some people were suspicious that he had spoken out of friendship for Corylas–with whom he had official relations; others thought that he would get paid for giving this advice; others suspected that the reason why he had spoken in this way was that they should not do any harm to the land belonging to Sinope by marching there on foot. However, the Greeks voted for making the voyage by sea.

Afterwards Xenophon spoke as follows: 'Men of Sinope, the army has chosen the method of travelling which you recommend. Now this is the position: if there are going to be enough ships so that not a single man of us will be left behind, we will go by sea; but if some of us are going to be left behind and others to sail, we will not go on board. We know that where we are in full strength we can both save our own lives and secure supplies for ourselves, but if we are caught at a disadvantage in strength over our enemies, it is plain enough that we shall be no better than slaves.'

When the ambassadors heard this, they asked the Greeks to send representatives to Sinope. They appointed Callimachus, an Arcadian, Ariston, an Athenian, and Samolas, an Achaean. These men, then, left for Sinope.

Meanwhile, when Xenophon considered the numbers of Greek hoplites that there were, and the numbers of peltasts and archers and slingers and cavalry, now, after all their experiences, in a very high state of efficiency, and when he considered that they were in the Euxine, where such a powerful force could never have been assembled without enormous expense, he thought it would be a fine thing to found a city there and so gain more territory and more power for Greece. It would be a great city, he thought, when he reckoned up the number of the Greeks themselves and of the people living round the Euxine. With a view to this plan he held a sacrifice before mentioning the idea to any of the soldiers, and he called in for the sacrifice Silanus of Ambracia who had been Cyrus's soothsayer. Silanus, fearing that the plan might come off and that the army might remain somewhere there, spread a rumour among the troops that Xenophon wanted the army to stay there and to found a city and so win a great name and power for himself. Silanus himself wanted to get back to Greece as soon as he could, as he had saved up the three thousand darics which he got from Cyrus at the time when he sacrificed for him and gave a correct prophecy about the ten days.

When the soldiers heard the story, some of them thought that the best thing was to stay there, but most did not. Timasion the Dardanian and Thorax the Boeotian got into conversation with some merchants from Heraclea and Sinope who were there, and told them that if they did not provide money for the army so that they could get their provisions on the voyage, there was a risk that this great force might stay in the Euxine. 'This,' they said, 'is what Xenophon wants, and he is urging us, as soon as the ships arrive, not to lose a moment in addressing the army. "Soldiers" (we are to say), "you see now that you have no means either of getting provisions on the return voyage or of doing any good to your people at home, assuming you get home. If, however, you care to do so, you can select some place, wherever you like, in the inhabited districts round here in the Euxine and occupy it, and allow those who want to return home to return and those who want to stay here to stay; and there are ships available for you, so that you could make a sudden descent on any port you wanted." '

On hearing this, the merchants reported it back to their cities, and Timasion the Dardanian sent Eurymachus the Dardanian and Thorax the Boeotian with them to tell the same story. When the people of Sinope and Heraclea heard it, they sent messengers to Timasion, urging him to accept a sum of money and take the lead in agitating for the army to sail away from the Euxine. He welcomed the proposal, and made the following speech in a meeting of the soldiers: 'Soldiers, we ought not to be thinking about staying here, we ought not to consider anything more important than Greece. Yet I hear that there are some people who are making sacrifices with the idea of staying, and have not even told you about it. Now I can guarantee to pay each one of you, if you sail out of the Euxine, a stater of Cyzicus a month, starting from the first of the month. And I will take you to the Troad, from which I was exiled, and my city will support you, since they will be glad to have me back. Then I will lead you myself to places where you will get plenty of money. I have had experience of Aeolia and Phrygia and the Troad and of the whole of Artabazus's province, partly because this is where I come from and partly through having done some fighting there with Clearchus and with Dercylidas.'

Thorax the Boeotian, who opposed Xenophon on the question of the command, then stood up again and said that, if they sailed out of the Euxine, they would have the Chersonese, a fine prosperous land, in front of them, so that anyone who wanted to could stay there, and those who did not could return home. It was absurd to go looking for land in foreign parts when there was enough and plenty of it in Greece. 'And until you get there,' he said, 'I, as well as Timasion, will guarantee you your pay.' He said this because he knew what the people of Heraclea and Sinope were promising on condition that they sailed away.

During these speeches Xenophon remained silent. Then Philesius and Lycon, both Achaeans, stood up and said that it was a monstrous thing for Xenophon to go to work privately persuading people to stay there and holding sacrifices for that purpose, and meanwhile saying nothing in public about all this.

Then Xenophon was forced to stand up and speak. He spoke as follows: 'As you know, soldiers, I make what sacrifices I can both on your behalf and my own; my aim is that my words and thoughts and deeds may be the ones likely to bring most good and most honour to you and to me. It was just this that was the object of my sacrifice on the present occasion—whether it would be better to make a start by speaking to you and discussing the plan, or to give up the idea altogether. The soothsayer Silanus gave me his answer on the most important point, namely, that the appearance of the victims was propitious. He had to, since he was aware that I myself, because of always being present at sacrifices, had some experience in these matters. But he said that some treachery or intrigue against me was revealed in the sacrifice—naturally enough, since he knew that he himself was plotting to make an attack on me in front of you. He did so by spreading the story that I was contemplating putting this plan into operation without getting your consent to it first. Actually, if I saw you were without means, I should be trying to think out a plan by which you might occupy a city, and then whoever wanted could sail home at once, and the others could wait till they had acquired sufficient money to do some good to their people at home. Now, however, I see that the people of Heraclea and Sinope are sending you ships for the outward voyage, and these men are promising you regular pay from the first of the month; so I think it is an excellent idea for us to get where we want to be in safety, and be paid for it into the bargain. I myself give up the plan I had formed, and I recommend all those who have come to me and said we ought to carry it out to give it up too. This is what I think: so long as you keep together in your present great force, you are sure both of respect and of finding supplies. One of the results of power is the ability to take what belongs to the weaker. But if you became dispersed, and if this force of ours was broken up into small detachments, then you would not be able to secure your food, and it would be a sad business getting away from here. My view, then, is the same as yours—that we should set out for Greece: but if anyone is discovered leaving us before the whole army is safe, I think he should be put on trial for misconduct. Will those who agree with this put up their hands?'

Everyone raised his hand. Silanus, however, shouted out and tried to make a speech to show that it would be justifiable for those people to go away who wanted to do so. But the soldiers would not put up with it, and threatened to make him pay for it if they caught him running away.

When after this the people of Heraclea heard that it had been decided to sail out of the Euxine, and that it had been Xenophon himself who had put the matter to the vote, they sent the ships, but failed to keep their word about the money which they had promised to Timasion and Thorax. Seeing that it was they who had promised the pay, they were now much upset and frightened of the army. They therefore came to Xenophon, bringing along with them the other generals with whom they had been in consultation about their previous intrigue, and these were all of them except for Neon of Asine, the deputy commander to Chirisophus, who had not yet come back. They told Xenophon that they were sorry for what they had done, and that they thought the best thing to do was to sail to the river Phasis, since there were ships available, and occupy the Phasian land. A grandson of Aietes was then king of the country.

Xenophon replied that he did not propose to mention any of this to the army. 'But,' he said, 'you can call a meeting, if you like, and make the proposal.'

Timasion the Dardanian then put forward his opinion, which was that it would be better not to call an assembly, but that each of them should first try to win over his own captains. They then went off and did this.

Chapter 7

XENOPHON DEFENDS HIMSELF

So the soldiers found out that the whole question was being stirred up again, and Neon made out that Xenophon had talked over the other generals and was thinking of deceiving the soldiers and taking them back again to the Phasis. The soldiers were angry when they heard this: meetings were held: they got together in crowds, and gave every reason to fear that they might act as they had acted in the case of the Colchian heralds and the officials of the market. Xenophon, when he became aware of how matters stood, decided to call a meeting of the army at once rather than let them get together on their own authority, and so he instructed the herald to call an assembly. As soon as they heard the herald's voice, they flocked to the meeting and were evidently eager for it. Xenophon made no accusations against the generals for having approached him on the matter. Instead he spoke as follows: 'Soldiers, I hear that someone is accusing me of wanting to deceive you and take you to the Phasis. I must beg you therefore to give me a hearing. If it is proved that I am doing you wrong, then I ought not to leave this place without suffering for it. If, on the other hand, it is proved that it is my accusers who are doing the wrong, then you must treat them just as they deserve. Now I feel sure that you know in what quarter the sun rises and where it sets, and that if one is going to go to Greece one has to travel westwards, whereas, if one wants to go towards native territory, one has to go in the opposite direction, towards the east. Now is it conceivable that anyone could deceive you into thinking that the sun rises over there and sets here, or sets here and rises there? And then you know this well enough too–that the north wind is the wind for taking us out of the Euxine towards Greece, and it is the south wind that takes us towards the Phasis. When the north wind blows, the saying goes round that it is good sailing weather for Greece. Is it, then, really possible that anyone could deceive you into going on board when the south wind is blowing? You may say that I would get you on board during a calm. But I shall be sailing in one ship, and you in at least a hundred. How then could I possibly force you to sail with me against your will, or deceive you into following me? But let us imagine that you have been deceived, or rather bewitched, by me and that we reach the Phasis. We then go ashore, and you will have a pretty clear idea that you are not in Greece. I, who have deceived you, shall be just one man and you will be nearly ten thousand, with arms in your hands. How could a man hand himself over to justice more effectively than by making this sort of arrangement for himself and for you? No, all these stories come from silly people or from people who are jealous of me, because I am treated with distinction by you. Though they can have no possible reason for being jealous. When have I stopped any of them from speaking in front of you, if he has anything valuable to say, or from fighting, if he wants to fight for you and for himself, or from staying awake at night thinking out plans for your safety? Do I stand in any-one's way when it is a question of electing officers? I am quite prepared to resign and let him take my place. Only I should like to be sure that he is the sort of man who will do you good service. But really, as far as I am concerned, I have said enough on this subject. If any one of you thinks that he could himself have been deceived in this way, or that anyone else could have deceived him in it, let him speak and tell us all about it.

'But when this is settled satisfactorily, do not break away from the meeting before listening to what I have to say about a certain tendency which I notice in the army. If this persists and becomes what it looks like being, the time has come for

us to think seriously about our own position, and see that we
are not shown up before mankind and before heaven, before
friend and enemy, as a most worthless and dishonourable
crowd of people.'

When the soldiers heard this, they wondered what he meant
and asked him to continue. He then began speaking again. 'I
am sure that you remember that there were some places in the
mountains which belonged to the natives and which were on
friendly terms with the people of Cerasus. Some of the inhabitants used to come down and sell us animals for sacrifice
and other things of theirs; and I think that some of you too
went to the nearest of these settlements and came back again
after making your purchases. Clearatus, one of the captains,
found out that this place was a small one and, because its
people assumed that we were their friends, was unguarded. So
he went against them by night with the intention of sacking
the place and without telling any of us about it. His plan was
that, if he took the place, he would not return to the army, but
would embark on a ship in which his friends were sailing along
the coast, put on board any plunder he got and sail right away
outside the Euxine. Those friends of his in the ship had made
this arrangement with him, as I now know. So he called
together those whom he had induced to go with him and led
them against the place. The sun had risen, however, before
he got there, and the inhabitants formed into a body, hurled
down missiles from their strongholds, fought back and killed
Clearatus with a number of the others, though some of them
got back to Cerasus.

'This took place on the day when we were starting on our
march here, but there were still in Cerasus some of those who
were going by sea and had not yet weighed anchor. Afterwards, according to the people of Cerasus, three of the older
men from the place arrived at Cerasus and asked for an interview with our general assembly. When they found that we

had gone, they told the people of Cerasus that they were surprised that we had thought of attacking them, and when the
people of Cerasus told them that the action had been un-
authorised, they were glad to hear it, and intended to sail here
to tell us what had happened and to give permission to those
concerned to come and recover their dead for burial. However, some of the Greeks who had escaped happened to be still
in Cerasus. When they found out where these natives were
going they committed the outrage of stoning them and of
calling on the rest to follow their example. So these men, the
three ambassadors, were stoned to death. After this had taken
place, the people of Cerasus came to us and told us of it, and,
when we generals heard their story, we were much upset by
what had happened and we discussed with the people of
Cerasus the question of how the dead bodies of the Greeks
could be given burial. We were sitting together outside the
place where the arms are kept, when we suddenly heard a
great disturbance and shouts of "Strike them down! Throw
your stones!" and the next thing we saw was numbers of men
running up with stones in their hands and others picking up
stones. The people of Cerasus, who had seen what had happened in their own city, were naturally enough frightened and
made their way to their ships. Yes, and there were some of us
too who were frightened. I, however, went up to them and
asked them what it was all about; and there were some of them
who had no idea what it was, but still had stones in their hands.
In the end I found someone who did know, and he told me
that the officials of the market were treating the army disgracefully. At this point someone caught sight of the official
Zelarchus making his way down to the sea, and raised a shout.
As soon as the others heard it, they rushed at the man, as
though it was a wild boar or stag that had appeared. The
people of Cerasus, seeing the soldiers coming in their direction,
felt sure that they were the object of their attack and ran away

fast, throwing themselves into the sea. There were actually some of us too who jumped into the sea with them, and those who did not know how to swim were drowned. Now why do you imagine they acted like this? They had done us no harm, but they feared that we had suddenly gone raving mad, like dogs. Now if this sort of thing goes on, just think what the state of our army will be like. You, the whole body of the army, will lose the power both of making war on whoever you like and of ending hostilities: anyone who cares to will go off on his own and lead a force against any objective that takes his fancy. And when ambassadors come to you to sue for peace or for any other purpose, anyone who likes can kill them and so prevent you from hearing the pleas of those who apply to you. And then those whom you, in a general assembly, elect as officers will have nowhere to stand, while any self-elected general who wants to shout out "Throw your stones at him!" will have sufficient authority to put an officer or any private soldier among you to death without trial, if he feels inclined to do so, and if there are people prepared to obey him, as there certainly were on this occasion.

'Now consider what these self-made generals have actually done for you. If the official Zelarchus has done you any injury he has sailed right away and given you no satisfaction for it. If, on the other hand, he was guiltless, he has fled from the army in terror of being unjustly put to death without a trial. Those who stoned the ambassadors to death have brought it about that you are the only Greeks for whom it is unsafe to enter Cerasus, unless you go there in force. As for the dead, though previously those who killed them gave you an opportunity of burying them, now these people have made it unsafe for you to go and recover the bodies even if you have an official herald's staff with you. Who will go as a herald if he has killed heralds himself? We have, however, requested the people of Cerasus to give them burial.

'Now if these actions are right, then give them your approval, so that we may know that things are going to go on like this in future and so that every man can watch out for himself and try to pitch his tent in some unassailable position. If, however, you think that this sort of conduct is more like that of wild beasts than of human beings, then let us consider how we can put a stop to it. Unless we do, how, in heaven's name, can we go on sacrificing to the gods with an easy conscience when we are doing wicked things? And how can we fight our enemies if we kill our own people? What city will give us a friendly welcome when it sees this state of lawlessness among us? Who will feel any confidence in giving us facilities for buying our food if we are known to be guilty of acts of such great gravity? At home, certainly, we expect to win praise from everyone; but who will praise us if this is going to be our character? I am sure that we ourselves would have no good to say of people who do such things.'

Then they all stood up and said those who had taken the lead in these goings-on should be punished, and in future there should be no chance of starting lawless behaviour, and those who did should be put to death; the generals should hold a legal enquiry into all these cases, and there should also be enquiries into any other cases where anyone had been wronged since Cyrus's death. They appointed the captains to act as jurymen.

On Xenophon's recommendation, which had the support of the soothsayers, it was decided to purify the army, and the ceremony of purification took place.

Chapter 8

XENOPHON JUSTIFIES DISCIPLINE
IN EMERGENCY

IT was decided that an enquiry should be held also into the conduct of the generals during the past. As a result of this enquiry Philesius and Xanthicles were fined twenty minae for their inefficient watch over the cargoes of the merchant ships, and Sophaenetus was fined ten minae, because he had been given a position of responsibility and had neglected it.

Some people brought charges against Xenophon, alleging that they had been beaten by him and making the basis of their accusations that he had acted in an overbearing manner. Xenophon asked the man who had spoken first to say where the incident had taken place. 'It happened,' he said, 'in the place where we were dying of cold and when there was all that snow.'

'Well,' said Xenophon, 'when the weather was like you say it was, when our food was giving out and we had not even a smell of wine, when a lot of us were sinking under all our hardships and the enemy were following us up behind, if I really acted then in an overbearing way, then I admit that I must have a more overbearing character even than the donkey has; and they say that donkeys are so overbearing that they never get tired. All the same, tell us what was the reason why you were beaten. Did I ask you for something, and then strike you because you did not give it to me? Was I getting something back from you? Was it a fight over some good-looking boy? Or did I ill-treat you when I was drunk?'

He said that it was not a case of any of these things, and Xenophon then asked him whether he was one of the hoplites. He said 'no'. Was he a peltast? He said 'no' again; he was a free man who had been given the job of driving a mule by his commander.

Xenophon then recognised him and asked: 'You're the man, then, who was carrying one of the casualties?'

'Yes, I certainly am,' he said, 'and you made me do it. And you scattered all my comrades' equipment all over the place.'

'As for scattering the equipment about,' said Xenophon, 'this was how it was. I gave it to other men to carry and I ordered them to hand it in to me. When I got it from them, I handed it all back to you safe and sound, after you had produced the man whom you were carrying. But you all ought to hear what actually happened. It is worth listening to. A man was being left behind, because he could no longer go on marching. All I knew of the man was that he was one of us. I compelled you to carry him so that his life might be saved. The enemy, I think, were following close on us.'

The man corroborated all this and Xenophon continued. 'I sent you forward,' he said, 'and did I not then come up to you again with the rearguard and find you digging a hole in order to bury the man? I stood by you, did I not, and commended you for it? Then, when we were standing by, the man drew in his leg and the people there shouted out that he was alive; but you said, "He can be as much alive as he likes, I am not going to carry him." It was at this point that I struck you, and you are quite right about that. It was because I had the impression that you looked as though you knew that the man was alive.'

'What about it?' the man replied. 'He died all the same, did he not, after I had shown him to you?'

'No doubt we shall all die,' said Xenophon. 'Is that any reason why we should all be buried alive?'

They then all shouted the man down, saying that Xenophon had not beaten him half enough.

Xenophon then asked anyone else to give the reasons why

he had been beaten; but, as no one stood up, he went on speaking himself. 'I admit, soldiers,' he said, 'that I have struck men in cases where there has been lack of discipline–the sort of people who were quite content to have their lives saved by you marching in formation and fighting when it was called for, but who left the ranks themselves and ran ahead and wanted to get more than their fair share of booty. If we had all behaved like this, we should all have been wiped out. Then, too, in cases where a man was losing his grip on himself and refused to stand up and was giving himself up to the enemy, I have both struck people and forced them to continue marching. This was because I myself on one occasion during the intense cold, while I was waiting for some men who were packing their kit, sat down for a long time and then found that I could hardly stand up and stretch my legs. So afterwards, as a result of my own personal experience, I used to drive on other people when I saw them sitting down and slacking. Moving about and being energetic kept one's body fairly warm and one's limbs fairly supple; but I saw that sitting down and doing nothing had a lot to do with the freezing of the blood and mortification of the toes, from which, as you know, a lot of people suffered. And then perhaps, when there were cases of people loitering behind because they were lazy and so prevented both you in the front and us in the rearguard from getting on with the march, I have struck a man or two with my fist, but that was to stop them being struck by an enemy's spear-blade. Yes, and now that they are in safety they have an opportunity of getting redress, if they have had any unjust treatment from me. If, on the other hand, they had fallen into the hands of the enemy, whatever their sufferings might have been, what sort of legal redress do they think they would have got? My case is really quite simple. If I have punished any-one for his own good, then I think I should answer for it in just the same way as parents in the case of their children and schoolmasters in the case of their pupils. Doctors too use knives and hot irons for the good of their patients. But if you think that my actions are the result of an overbearing character, then please reflect that at the present moment I am, thank God, more confident than I was then, and I am now bolder than I was then, and drink more wine too, and yet, in spite of this, I never strike anybody. That is because I see that you are now enjoying fine weather. But as soon as a storm gets up and the sea runs high, you must have noticed how the officer in the prow gets angry with his men merely for a movement of the head, and so does the steersman with those under him. This is because even small mistakes at such a time are capable of upsetting everything. And you yourselves have admitted that I was right in striking these men. You were standing by me at the time, and you had swords in your hands, not voting pebbles; you could have come to their help if you had wanted. In point of fact you did not come to their help, nor did you join with me in punishing people who were behaving in a disorderly way. The result is that, by turning a blind eye to them, you have given the worst elements among them a chance of becoming insufferable. My opinion is that, if you care to look around you, you will find that the men whose behaviour was worst then are at this moment the most insufferable char-acters. Take the case of Boiscus, the Thessalian boxer. In those days he made a great song about being too ill to carry his shield; and now, I hear, he has already robbed many of the people of Coytora. If you are sensible, you will treat him quite differently from the way people treat dogs. They keep bad-tempered dogs on the chain during the day, and let them loose at night; but, if you are sensible, you will chain him up at night, and let him loose during the day.

'All the same,' Xenophon added, 'I am surprised at the fact that, in cases where I offended any of you, you remember it and talk about it, but as for the times when I helped you during

the cold weather, or kept off the enemy, or made my contribu-
tion to relieving anybody who was ill or in want–no one
remembers any of this; nor do you remember any of the
occasions when I have praised a man for some good bit of
work, or given all the honour I could to a soldier who behaved
gallantly. Yet it is an honourable thing, and a just and upright
thing, and more pleasant too to remember what is good rather
than what is bad.'

People then got up and gave examples of some of these
things, and the final result was that it all ended satisfactorily.

BOOK

VI

THE MARCH TO THE
BOSPORUS

Chapter 1

XENOPHON REFUSES THE OFFER
OF THE SUPREME COMMAND

AFTERWARDS, throughout the time that they spent here,
they lived partly by buying food and partly by plunder from
the country of Paphlagonia. The Paphlagonians, too, were
extremely clever at making away with stragglers, and during
the night tried to do damage among those who were camping
in advanced positions. As a result there was very bitter feeling
on both sides.

Corylas, who was governor of Paphlagonia at this time,
sent ambassadors to the Greeks. They had horses with them
and fine garments, and said that Corylas was prepared to make
an agreement by which neither side was to do harm to the
other. The generals answered that they would have to discuss
this proposal with the army; but in the meantime they gave
the ambassadors a hospitable reception, and also invited people
out of the rest of the army who, they thought, deserved the
distinction.

After sacrificing some of the oxen which they had captured
and other animals too, they provided a feast which was quite
a good one, though they ate reclining on low couches and
drank out of horn cups which they had come across in the
country. When they had poured the libations and sung the
paean, first of all two Thracians stood up and performed a
dance to the flute, wearing full armour. They leapt high into
the air with great agility and brandished their swords. In the
end one of them, as everybody thought, struck the other one,
who fell to the ground, acting all the time. The Paphlagonians
cried out at this, and the other man stripped him of his arms
and went out, singing the ballad of Sitalces. Then some more

Thracians carried the man out, as though he was dead, though actually he had not been hurt in the slightest.

After this some Aenianes and Magnesians stood up and, wearing full armour, danced what they call 'the Sower's Dance'. The way the dance is done is that one man lays down his arms and begins to sow. He is driving a yoke of oxen and keeps on looking round as though he is afraid. Then a robber appears, and as soon as the sower sees him, he snatches up his arms and goes to meet him and fights for the yoke of oxen. (They acted all this to the music of the flute.) Finally the robber ties the other man up and carries him off with the oxen; though sometimes it is the ploughman who binds the robber, and then he ties him to the oxen and drives him off with his hands bound behind his back.

After this a Mysian came forward with a light shield in each hand and danced. He made himself look sometimes as though there were two people attacking him, and sometimes he used the shields as though he was fighting against one other person; and sometimes he would whirl round and go head over heels, still holding the shields, and giving a very fine show. Finally he danced the Persian dance, clashing the shields together and bending his knees and then leaping up again; and he did all this keeping time to the flute.

After him some Mantineans and other Arcadians stood up, wearing the best-looking armour they could find, and marched forward to a flute accompaniment, keeping time to the rhythm used for war dances. They sang the paean and danced as is done in religious processions.

The Paphlagonian spectators thought that it was a marvellous thing to perform all these dances in armour, and when the Mysian saw how impressed they were with the performance he obtained the permission of one of the Arcadians who owned a dancing girl, and brought her in, after he had got her the best dress he could and given her a light shield. She then

danced the Pyrrhic dance with great agility, and there was a
lot of applause. The Paphlagonians asked whether the women
too fought alongside the men, and the Greeks said that it was
the women who had driven the King out of the camp. And
so the evening's entertainment came to an end.

On the next day they brought the ambassadors before the
army. The soldiers decided to agree to the proposal that
neither side should do harm to the other, and then the ambassadors went away.

As there seemed to be sufficient ships, the Greeks went on
board and sailed for a day and a night with a fair wind, keeping
Paphlagonia on the left. On the next day they reached Sinope
and came to anchor at Harmene, the port of Sinope. The
people of Sinope live in Paphlagonian territory and are
colonists of Miletus. They sent the Greeks gifts of friendship
consisting of four thousand bushels of barley-meal and fifteen
hundred jars of wine.

Chirisophus came here too with a trireme. The soldiers
thought that he was coming with something for them, but he
brought nothing at all except a message to say that Anaxibius
the Spartan admiral and the other Spartans sent their congratulations to the army, and that Anaxibius promised that
they would have pay once they got outside the Euxine.

The soldiers stayed five days in this anchorage at Harmene.
As they thought that they were now not far from Greece, the
desire not to return home empty-handed became even stronger
with them than before. They thought that, if they appointed
one man as commander-in-chief, this one man would be able
to make better use of the army, both by night and by day,
than was possible under the present system when the command
was divided: it would be easier to hide what they were doing
if there should be occasion for secrecy, and, if they had to act
quickly, there would be less risk of striking too late, as there
would be no need for conferences among several people;

instead the decisions of the supreme commander would be acted upon, whereas previously the generals had done everything in accordance with a majority vote.

As they were thinking along these lines their choice fell on Xenophon. The captains came to him and told him that this was the feeling of the army; each of them expressed his personal good feeling towards him and tried to persuade him to accept the command. In some ways Xenophon was willing to do so. He reflected that, if he did, his own fame would be greater among his friends and his name would become better known at Athens, and it might well be that he might be the cause of doing some good to the army. Considerations of this kind certainly made him inclined to desire the position of commander-in-chief. When, however, he reflected that no man can tell what the future will bring, and that for this reason there was a risk of losing even the reputation which he had won already, then he became uncertain what to do. Hesitating, as he was, over his decision, he decided that the best thing to do was to put the matter before the gods; so he brought two victims to the altar and made a sacrifice to Zeus the King, who had been declared by the oracle at Delphi to be the god whom he ought to consult. He thought, too, that it was this god who had sent the dream which he had had at the time when he was first put in the position of sharing in the responsibility for the army. Then he remembered also that when he was setting out from Ephesus to be introduced to Cyrus, an eagle had called to him from the right. The bird, however, had been sitting, and the soothsayer who was escorting him had said that the omen meant something great, out of the ordinary and glorious, yet it also foretold hardship, since other birds are particularly apt to attack the eagle when sitting. He said, too, that the omen did not indicate a great fortune, since the eagle mostly got its food when on the wing.

When Xenophon sacrificed the god made it plain to him

that he was not to seek an additional command and not to accept it if they elected him. This, then, was the end of the matter. The army, however, met and everyone spoke in favour of electing one commander. When this was decided upon, they put forward Xenophon's name, and, as it was clear that they would elect him if anyone put the matter to the vote, Xenophon got up and spoke as follows: 'I am much pleased, soldiers, as any man in my position would be, by the honour which you are doing me. I thank you for it, and I pray the gods that they may make me the means of doing you some good. But I do not think it is either in your interests or mine that I should be put forward by you as commander when there is a Spartan available for the post. You would be all the less likely to get help from them, if you needed it, and I think, too, that the position would not be a very safe one for me. I know well that the Spartans did not stop making war on my own country until they had made the whole city admit that the Spartans had power over them as over the rest of Greece. Once they had admitted this, they stopped making war and did not blockade the city any more. If, then, knowing this, I should get the reputation of undermining their prestige when I have the power to do so, what I fancy is that I shall very quickly be brought to my senses. As for your view that there is less chance of trouble with one commander than with several, let me assure you that, if you appoint someone else to the command, you will not find *me* causing trouble. I think that anyone who makes trouble for his commander when there is a war on is making trouble for himself. On the other hand, if you elect me, I should not be surprised if you found people resentful both of your action and my position.'

After he had made this speech, many more of them rose to their feet and said that he ought to accept the command. Agasias the Stymphalian said that if this was how it was it would be an absurd state of affairs. 'Would the Spartans be angry,' he asked, 'if, even when people met for a dinner-party, they did not appoint a Spartan as master of the ceremonies? If this is how things stand,' he went on, 'we, it seems, as Arcadians, cannot even command a company.' At this they all shouted out in approval of what Agasias had said.

Xenophon realised that he would have to add something to what he had said, and so he came forward and spoke again. 'My friends,' he said, 'so that you may be quite sure of the facts, I swear to you by all the gods and goddesses that, as soon as I found out how you were thinking, I made a sacrifice to find out whether it would be better or not for you to entrust me with this command and for me to undertake it. The gods made it clear to me by the appearance of the victims (and so clear that even a person with no experience would have understood) that I ought not to accept the undivided command.'

So they elected Chirisophus. After he was elected he came forward and spoke as follows: 'I can assure you of this, my friends,—that if you had elected someone else, I should not have worked against him. All the same, you have done Xenophon a good turn by not electing him. As it is, Dexippus was going as far as he could to do him harm in the eyes of Anaxibius, though I was doing my best to keep him quiet. Dexippus said that he thought that Xenophon would prefer to share the command of Clearchus's army with Timasion, who was a Dardanian, than with himself, who was a Spartan. However,' he continued, 'since you have elected me, I too shall try my best to do you good service. Get ready, then, to sail tomorrow, if the weather is right for sailing. Our course will be for Heraclea, and you must all try to get there. We will discuss all other matters once we have arrived at Heraclea.'

Chapter 2

THE ARMY SPLITS INTO THREE

THEY set sail from here next day, and sailed along the coast for two days with a fair wind. As they sailed along they saw Jason's Beach, where the *Argo* is said to have been moored, and the mouths of various rivers: the Thermodon, the Iris, the Halys and then the Parthenius. After sailing past the Parthenius they arrived at Heraclea, a Greek city and colony of Megara, in the country of the Maryandyni. They anchored near the Acherusian Peninsula, where Heracles is said to have descended into the lower world to fetch Cerberus and where they still show evidence of his descent for a quarter of a mile down into the earth. The people of Heraclea sent the Greeks gifts of friendship consisting of four thousand bushels of barley-meal, two thousand jars of wine, twenty oxen and a hundred sheep. In this place a river called the Lycus, about two hundred feet broad, runs through the plain.

The soldiers held an assembly here and discussed the question of whether they should travel the rest of the way out of the area of the Euxine by land or by sea. An Achaean called Lycon stood up and spoke as follows: 'I am surprised, my friends, at the generals for not making any attempt to provide us with money to buy food. The presents we have had cannot conceivably last us for as much as three days, and we have nowhere to go to get food for ourselves. My view, therefore, is that we should ask the people of Heraclea for at least three thousand staters of Cyzicus.'

Someone else said: 'At least ten thousand,' and proposed the immediate election of delegates who should be sent to the city while the assembly was still in session, so that they should know what the answer was and take measures accordingly.

They then proposed the names of delegates, first of all Chirisophus, because he had been appointed commander, and then
some people put forward Xenophon's name. Chirisophus and
Xenophon were strongly opposed to the suggestion, since they
both felt the same thing–that it was wrong to bring force
to bear on a Greek city which was in friendly relations with
them to secure anything which the people of the city would
not give them of their own accord. As they were evidently
against the plan, the soldiers sent Lycon the Achaean, Callimachus of Parrhasia and Agasias the Stymphalian, who went
to Heraclea and told the people what the army had decided.
Lycon was said to have added threats of what would happen
to them if they did not act as they were requested. The people
of Heraclea listened to the delegates and said they would discuss the matter. They then immediately collected their property from outside the city, and brought inside the walls all
the provisions which they had had outside for sale. The gates
were shut and men under arms appeared on the fortifications.

As a result of this the people who had caused the trouble
accused the generals of spoiling their plans. The Arcadians and
Achaeans held meetings of their own, their chief leaders being
Callimachus of Parrhasia and Lycon the Achaean. Their arguments were to the effect that it was a disgraceful thing for an
Athenian and a Spartan, who had brought no troops into the
army, to be in command of Peloponnesians; that they did the
hard work and other people got the rewards for it, though it
was they who had been responsible for the fact that they were
still alive; the rest of the army hardly counted (and, in actual
fact, more than half the army were Arcadians and Achaeans);
so, they said, if they had any sense, they should all come
together, elect their own generals, and, by marching on independently of the rest, try to do themselves some good.

This was the course they decided upon. The Arcadians and
Achaeans who were in Chirisophus's or Xenophon's com-

mand left them and joined up with the rest. They elected ten
generals out of their own body and voted that these generals
should carry out whatever was approved by a decision of the
majority. Thus Chirisophus's supreme command came to an
end six or seven days after he had been appointed to it.

Xenophon's intention now was to make the journey in their
company, as he thought that this would be a safer thing to do
than for each person to go on his way separately. Neon, however, persuaded him to go by himself. He had heard from
Chirisophus that Cleander, the governor of Byzantium, had
said that he would come with some triremes to Port Calpe,
and so he gave Xenophon this advice with the idea that no one
else should share the information but that just they and their
soldiers should make the voyage out of the Euxine on these
triremes. Chirisophus, who was discouraged by recent events
and at the same time had, as a result of them, turned against
the army, told Xenophon that he could do as he liked. Xenophon still aimed at leaving the army altogether and sailing
away; but when he made a sacrifice to Heracles the Guider
with a view to enquiring whether it would be a better and a
wiser thing to march with the soldiers who remained there or
to leave them altogether, the god made it clear by the appearance of the victims that he should march with them. Thus the
army was split into three. The Arcadians and Achaeans, more
than four thousand of them and all hoplites, constituted one
body. Then there were about fourteen hundred hoplites with
Chirisophus and about seven hundred peltasts, the Thracians
that Clearchus had; and with Xenophon there were about
seventeen hundred hoplites and about three hundred peltasts.
Xenophon was the only one who had cavalry, a force of about
forty horsemen.

The Arcadians got ships from the people of Heraclea and
sailed first, with the idea of falling suddenly upon the
Bythinians and getting as much booty as possible. They

landed at Port Calpe somewhere about the middle of Thrace. Chirisophus started right away from the city of Heraclea and proceeded on foot through the Heraclean country. When he crossed the border into Thrace he marched along the coast, as he was by that time in bad health. Xenophon secured some ships and landed on the frontier between Thrace and the country belonging to Heraclea. He then marched by an inland route.

Chapter 3

XENOPHON RESCUES
THE ARCADIANS

THE fortunes of each division were as follows. The Arcadians landed by night at Port Calpe and marched on the first villages, which were about three miles from the sea. When it was light, each commander led his own force against a village. In cases where a village looked to be of a considerable size, the commanders joined forces and led two together against it. They also fixed on a hill on which they were all to reassemble. As a result of making their attack unexpectedly, they seized a number of slaves and surrounded large flocks of cattle. The Thracians, however, who got away, formed themselves into a body, and as they were light troops, there were numbers of them who got away right out of the hands of the hoplites. When they had formed up, they first attacked the company commanded by Smicres, who was one of the Arcadian generals. This company was already on its way back to the appointed rendezvous with a lot of booty. For some time the Greeks marched and fought back at the same time, but at a place where they had to cross a watercourse the Thracians routed them and killed the whole lot, including Smicres. In the case of another company commanded by one of the ten generals, Hegesander, they only left eight survivors, Hegesander himself being one who escaped. The other companies joined up again, some without difficulty and others after hard fighting.

After winning this success, the Thracians shouted round to each other and mustered their forces during the night in a very confident frame of mind. At dawn all round the hill where the Greeks were camped there were drawn up great numbers of cavalry and peltasts, with more coming up all the time. In attacking the Greeks they were safe themselves, since, while the Greeks did not have even a single archer or javelin-thrower or horseman, they ran or rode forward to discharge their weapons, and, when the Greeks charged, easily fell back again, while others attacked from a different direction. On the one side there were a number of people wounded, and on the other side no one at all, and the result was that the Greeks could not move from their position and finally the Thracians cut them off even from their water supply. In this very difficult situation they began to negotiate for a truce. Some conditions were agreed upon, but, when the Greeks asked for hostages, the Thracians refused to give them, and on this point the negotiations broke down. This, then, was what happened to the Arcadians.

Meanwhile Chirisophus had marched safely along the coast and arrived at Port Calpe. Xenophon was making his way by the inland route, and some of his horsemen, who were ranging over the country, fell in with some old men who were travelling somewhere or other. When they were brought to him, Xenophon asked them whether they had heard anywhere of another Greek army. They told him the whole story and said that the Greeks were now being blockaded on a hill and the Thracians in full force had surrounded them. Xenophon then had these men carefully guarded so that they might act as guides when needed. He sent out pickets and, after assembling the soldiers, spoke to them as follows: 'Soldiers, some of the Arcadians have been killed, and the rest are being blockaded on a hill. My own view is that if they are wiped out, there will be no safety for us either, with the enemy in such numbers and at the same time so full of confidence. The best thing, therefore, for us to do is to come to these people's help as quickly as we can, so that, if they still survive, we may join with them in the fighting and not be left alone to meet the danger by ourselves. We have no chance of getting away safe in any direction from here. It is a long road back again to Heraclea, and a long road across country to Chrysopolis. And the enemy are close. The shortest road is the one to Port Calpe, where we imagine that Chirisophus is, if he has got there safely. You may say that there are no ships there for us to sail away in, and, if we stay there, not even a day's food supply. But suppose the men who are being blockaded are killed, it will be a harder job for us to face the future just by ourselves with Chirisophus's men than it would be if we had these Arcadians safe, and if we all joined together and made a united effort to save ourselves. No, we must go ahead with our minds made up; either we must die with honour, or else perform a most gallant action in saving so many Greek lives. Perhaps it is the will of heaven which guides us, that will which intends to bring low those who boasted that they knew best, and to give us, who began our enterprise by asking the advice of heaven, a more honourable place than theirs. Now you must follow me and be on the alert so that you can carry out the orders which you receive. For the moment let us go forward until we decide it is time for supper and then camp. While we are marching, Timasion is to ride ahead with the cavalry, keeping his eye on us and also investigating what lies ahead, so that nothing can take us by surprise.'

After this speech he led them forward. He also sent out to the flanks and to the high ground some of the most active of the peltasts, so that they could give warning if they saw any movement anywhere. He ordered them to set fire to anything they found which would burn. The cavalry spread out as far as it was safe to do so and started fires. The peltasts marching along the heights on the flanks set fire to everything nflammable which they saw, and the main body did likewise if they came across anything left by the others, so that it looked as though the whole country was on fire and that the Greek army was in great strength.

When the time came, they climbed a hill and pitched camp. They could see the enemy's camp fires (they were about four miles away) and they lit as many fires as they could themselves. As soon as they had had dinner the order was given to put out all fires. For the night they posted sentries and had their sleep, and at dawn, after prayers to the gods, they drew up in battle formation and marched forward as fast as possible. Timasion and the cavalry, who rode ahead with the guides, were on the hill where the Greeks had been blockaded before they realised where they were. There were no troops in sight, friend or foe, and they reported this back to Xenophon and the main body. All that they saw were some old men and women and a few sheep and oxen that had been left behind. At first they wondered what could have happened, but afterwards they found out from the people left there that the Thracians had gone off at nightfall and that the Greeks, according to them, had gone away too. In what directions they did not know.

When Xenophon's men heard this, they had their meal, packed up their kit, and marched on, wanting to join forces with the others at Port Calpe as soon as possible. On this march they saw the tracks made by the Arcadians and Achaeans on the road to Calpe. When the two bodies met they were glad to see each other and greeted each other like brothers. The Arcadians asked Xenophon's men why they had put out the fires. 'When we saw the fires out,' they said, 'we thought that you were going to attack the enemy during the night. And the enemy, as far as we could make out, feared this too, and retreated. It was just about this time that they went off. However, when you did not appear and the time went on, we thought that you had heard what was happening to us and been alarmed at it and had gone off in flight to the sea. We decided not to be left behind you, so we also marched in this direction.'

Chapter 4

THE ARMY REUNITED
DIFFICULTIES ABOUT PROVISIONS

FOR that day they camped there on the shore near the harbour. This place called Port Calpe is in Asiatic Thrace, and Asiatic Thrace begins from the mouth of the Euxine and comprises the country on one's right as one sails into the Euxine as far as Heraclea. For a trireme using oars it is a long day's voyage from Byzantium to Heraclea, and between these two cities there is no other Greek or allied city, only Thracians and Bithynians, who are said to treat disgracefully any Greeks whom they get hold of after being shipwrecked or from any other mishap. Port Calpe lies half-way along the route between Heraclea and Byzantium. There is a promontory jutting out in the sea, and the part that faces the sea itself is a steep cliff of not less than twenty fathoms at its lowest point; the neck of the headland which connects it with the land is about four hundred feet across, and the area of the neck is large enough to accommodate ten thousand men. The harbour is right underneath the cliff, with the beach facing west. Just by the sea and within the limits of the headland there is a spring of fresh water which flows plentifully. There is a lot of timber and particularly a lot of very good timber for ship-building growing right down to the sea. The mountains extend about two miles inland and in that direction the soil is earthy and free from stones; the part along the coast, for more than two miles, is covered with a lot of big trees of all kinds. There is a lot of other good country round about containing a number of villages with people in them. The land produces barley, wheat, all kinds of vegetables, millet, sesame, plenty of figs, a lot of vines from which good wine is made, and everything else except olives.

This is what the country was like. They settled down on the beach close to the sea and did not want to camp in the part that might have been made into a fortified position: indeed they thought that even going near the place implied some ulterior motive and suggested that some people were wanting to found a city there. Most of the soldiers had joined up for this service because they had heard accounts of Cyrus's generosity and not because they had been hard up; some had brought men with them, some had gone to additional expense in equipping themselves; others had left fathers and mothers or children behind at home with the idea of coming back again with money to give them, since they had heard that the other Greeks with Cyrus were doing very well for themselves. This was how they felt, and so they longed to get back safe to Greece.

At dawn on the day after the two divisions had joined up Xenophon made a sacrifice to enquire about leading a force out of camp. It was a matter of necessity to do this to get provisions, and he was also thinking of burying the dead. As the appearance of the victims was favourable the Arcadians too went with him, and they buried most of the bodies at the spot where each had fallen. As they had now lain there for five days it was no longer possible to bring them away; but they collected some of the bodies from the roads and gave them the best burial they could from the means at their disposal. They made a great cenotaph and put garlands on it for those whom they could not find, and, when they had done this, they went back to the camp, had their meal and slept for the night.

Next day, largely on the initiative of the captains, Agasias the Stymphalian, Hieronymus the Elean and other senior people among the Arcadians, all the soldiers held a meeting. They passed a resolution that if anyone in future proposed splitting the army up, the penalty for this should be death that the army should return to its original formation and that the original generals should be in command. Chirisophus by this time was dead as a result of taking a drug while he was in a fever, and Neon of Asine took over his command.

After this resolution had been passed, Xenophon stood up and spoke as follows: 'Soldiers, it appears that we shall have to make our journey on foot, as we have no ships; and we shall have to start now, as there are no supplies for us if we stay here. We will therefore make a sacrifice, and, as for you, you must get ready to fight as hard as you ever have fought, since the enemy have got back their confidence.'

Afterwards, the generals made a sacrifice and had the services of Arexion the Arcadian as soothsayer. Silanus of Ambracia had already hired a boat from Heraclea and made off home. They made the sacrifice with a view to leaving, but the appearance of the victims was unfavourable, and so they rested for that day. Some people had the face to say that Xenophon, wishing to found a city in the place, had persuaded the soothsayer to say that the omens were not right for leaving. Xenophon thereupon had it given out that anyone who liked could be present at the sacrifice on the next day, and invited anyone who was a soothsayer to come and join in the inspection of the victims. The sacrifice was held and there were many people at it, but, though they sacrificed three times with a view to leaving, the omens were still against it. The soldiers were upset at this, since the provisions which they had brought with them were running short and there was no possibility of buying any food in the neighbourhood.

Afterwards they held another meeting and Xenophon again addressed them. 'My friends,' he said, 'as you see, we have still no favourable omens for our marching and I see that you are going short of provisions. I think, therefore, that we shall have to make a sacrifice just on this very point.'

Someone then got to his feet and said: 'There is a perfectly good reason why the omens are not favourable to us. I got some accidental information yesterday from someone on a ship which put in here, to the effect that Cleander, the governor of Byzantium, is on the point of coming here with triremes and other vessels.'

Everyone then was in favour of staying, but it was a matter of necessity to set out in search of provisions. They then sacrificed three times again with a view to making the expedition, but the omens were against it. Now the soldiers came right up to Xenophon's tent complaining that they had no provisions, but he refused to lead them out as long as the omens were unfavourable.

Next day there was another sacrifice held and, since the business concerned everyone, practically the whole army gathered round the sacrifice. The victims did not give the desired results and the generals did not lead a party out. They called a meeting, however, at which Xenophon said: 'Perhaps the enemy have got together in a body and we shall be forced to fight. If, therefore, we leave our equipment behind in the strong defensive position here and march out in battle order, it may be that the victims will turn out favourable to us.'

When the soldiers heard this, they shouted out that there was no point in taking them to the fortified position; instead the sacrifice ought to be held at once. There were no sheep left, but they bought some draught-oxen and used them for the sacrifice. Xenophon urged Cleanor the Arcadian to be ready for action if anything came of it, but not even then were the omens favourable.

Neon had taken over Chirisophus's command, and when he saw the state in which his men were because of the lack of food, he wanted to do them a good turn. He found a man from Heraclea who said that he knew of some villages near by from which it was possible to seize supplies, and he had it given out that anyone who liked could set out after them and there would be a guide to show them the way. Then about two thousand men went out, armed with small spears and carrying leather bags and various kinds of sacks; but when they had arrived at the villages and were scattered about for collecting the provisions, the first thing that happened was that Pharnabazus's cavalry fell on them. They had come to reinforce the Bithynians, with the intention of joining with them and preventing the Greeks, if possible, from entering Phrygia. This cavalry force killed at least five hundred of the Greeks, and the rest fled to the mountains.

Afterwards one of the fugitives got back to camp and reported what had happened. As the sacrifices had not been favourable that day, Xenophon took an ox from a waggon (there were no other victims available), and, after sacrificing it, went to the rescue with all the other soldiers who were below thirty years old. They picked up the survivors and came back to camp with them.

By this time it was about sunset, and the Greeks, in a state of deep despondency, were getting their evening meal ready. Suddenly, under cover of the thickets, some of the Bithynians made an attack on the outposts, killed some men and drove the rest right back to the camp. There was a lot of shouting and all the Greeks ran to their arms; but, as the country was thickly wooded, it did not seem safe to start a pursuit or move camp during the night. So they spent the night under arms, with enough sentries posted to keep them safe.

Chapter 5

A GREEK VICTORY

IN this way they passed the night. At dawn the generals led the way to the strong defensive position, and the soldiers collected their arms and equipment and followed them. Before it was time for their meal they had dug a trench across the way into the position, and built a palisade all along it, leaving three gates in it. A ship also arrived from Heraclea, bringing barley, cattle and wine.

Xenophon got up early and made a sacrifice with a view to ea ving their position. The omens taken in the case of the first animal were favourable, and, just as the sacrifice was over, the soothsayer Arexion of Parhasia saw an eagle, indicating good luck, and he told Xenophon to lead the army out. They then crossed the ditch and formed up in order. They had it proclaimed that, after their meal, the soldiers were to march out ready for action, leaving the general crowd and the slaves where they were. All the others, then, with the exception of Neon, marched out. It was considered best to leave him behind in charge of the people in the camp. However, when the captains and soldiers had left him there, the others felt ashamed at not following when all the rest had gone, and so they left behind just those who were over forty-five. These stayed in the camp, while the others marched out.

They were already coming across dead bodies before they had gone a mile and a half, and so they brought up the rear of their column to the first bodies they saw and buried all who were covered by the column. When they had buried this lot, they marched on and again brought up the rear to the first of the next unburied bodies and in the same way buried all who were uncovered by the troops. When they arrived at the road leading out of the villages, where the bodies were lying about in great numbers, they collected them all together and buried them.

It was now afternoon, and they had led the army right through the villages. The soldiers were taking all the supplies which they could see within the cover of their line, when suddenly they saw the enemy coming over some hills in front of them, numbers of cavalry and foot in battle formation. It was Spithridates and Rhathines who had come from Pharnabazus with a strong force.

When the enemy saw the Greeks, they came to a halt about a mile and a half away from them. Arexion the Greek sooth-sayer immediately sacrificed and the omens were favourable in the case of the first sacrifice. Then Xenophon spoke to the officers and said: 'My opinion is that we should hold some companies in reserve behind the battle-line, so that we can have troops to come to the relief of the line if they are wanted, and so that, when the enemy have lost their cohesion, they may come up against troops who are fresh and in good order.'

They all agreed with this suggestion and Xenophon said: 'You march on, then, towards the enemy. We do not want to stand still now that we have seen and been seen by them. I shall be there, after I have put the rear companies in the order which you agreed upon.'

The others then marched on, and Xenophon took the three rear formations of two hundred men each. He instructed one of them to follow behind on the right, leaving about a hundred feet between them and the main body. Samolas the Achaean was in command of this detachment. He posted another detachment to follow up in the centre, with Pyrrhius the Arcadian in command of it; and the third detachment on the left under the command of Phasias the Athenian.

So they marched forward, and the men in front came to a large wooded gulley where the going was difficult. Here they halted, not knowing whether this gulley was to be crossed or not, and they passed the word back for the generals and captains to come to the front. Xenophon wondered what it could be that was holding up the march and, as soon he heard the word being passed back, he rode up as fast as he could. When the officers were assembled Sophaenetus, the oldest of the generals, said that the question whether a gulley like this could be crossed or not was hardly worth considering. Xenophon joined in eagerly and said: 'You know quite well, my friends, that I have never at any time gone out of my way to introduce you to any danger. This is because I am aware that what you want is rather to keep alive than to gain a reputation for courage. But this is how things stand at present. We cannot get away from here without fighting, since, if we do not advance on the enemy, they will follow after us and fall upon us when we retreat. You must consider, then, which is the better course to follow–to advance on them with your arms at the ready, or to turn about and then see the enemy coming after us from the rear. You know well, however, that retreat in the face of the enemy does not look like any sort of gallant action, while a pursuit gives even cowards confidence. As far as I am concerned, I should certainly be happier with half the number of men if I were engaged in a pursuit than I should be with twice the numbers on a retreat. As for these enemies here, if we attack them, I know that you yourselves do not expect that they will stand up to us; but, if we retreat, we all know that they will have the courage to come after us. As for the argument that by crossing over we are putting a difficult ravine in our rear just when we are going to fight, is not this really something that we ought to jump at? I should like the enemy to think it easy going in every direction for him to retreat; but we ought to learn from the very position in which we are placed that there is no safety for us except in victory. Personally, too, I am surprised at anyone thinking that this gulley is more formidable than the rest of the ground over which we have marched. How can we cross the plain if we do not defeat their cavalry? How can we get back over the mountains which we have crossed if all these peltasts are on our heels? And if we manage to get safely to the sea, we shall find the Euxine a good-sized gulley! There are no ships there to take us away, and no food to supply us while we stay there, and the quicker we get back there, the quicker we shall have to set out again after supplies. It is better then to fight now that we have had a meal, than to fight to-morrow on an empty stomach. Fellow soldiers, the sacrifices are favourable to us, the omens are on our side, the appearance of the victims as good as could be desired. Let us set about these people. There is no doubt that they have seen us, and we don't want to give them a chance of having dinner at their ease or camping where they like.'

After this the captains told Xenophon to lead on, and no one raised any objections. He therefore took the lead, and gave the order that everyone was to cross over the gulley at the point where each happened to be. In this way he thought that the army would reach the other side in a more compact body than if they defiled over the bridge which lay across the gulley. When they had crossed over, he went along the line and addressed the troops. 'Soldiers,' he said, 'remember all the battles in which, with the help of the gods and by coming to close quarters, you have been victorious, and remember what happens to those who run away from the enemy. Think of this too—that we are now on the threshold of Greece. Go forward, then, with Heracles the Guider to lead you, and call out to your comrades by name as you go. It's good to think that whoever says or does something brave and gallant now is making himself remembered among the people whom he would want to remember him.'

So he spoke as he rode along the front, and at the same time he began to lead them forward in line of battle, and, with the peltasts on each flank, they advanced against the enemy. The order had been given for spears to be kept at the slope until the signal was given by the trumpet: they were then to bring their spears down to the position for attack, and go forward at a steady pace: no one was to advance at the double. After this the word was passed along–'Zeus the Saviour, Heracles the Guider'.

The enemy stayed where they were, thinking that they had a good position. When the two armies were close together the Greek peltasts raised a shout and ran towards the enemy before anyone had given them the order. The enemy charged to meet them, both the cavalry and the Bithynians in close order, and they drove the peltasts back. But when the line of hoplites came up, moving at a quick pace, and at the same time the trumpet sounded and they sang the paean and then raised a shout as they brought their spears down for the attack, then the enemy stood their ground no longer, and took to flight. Timasion and the cavalry went after them and they killed as many as they could, considering their small numbers. The enemy's left wing, where the cavalry were in pursuit, broke up at once, but their right wing, since the pursuit was not being pressed very hard against it, re-formed on a hill. When the Greeks saw that the right wing was making a stand, the easiest and safest thing to do seemed to be to charge them at once. So they sang the paean and attacked immediately, and the enemy failed to stand their ground. Then the peltasts set off in pursuit until the right wing was broken up. Not many were killed, as the enemy's cavalry, which was in great strength, imposed caution on the Greeks.

The Greeks saw that Pharnabazus's cavalry was still standing in formation, and the Bithynian cavalry were gathering together to join it, and looking down from a hill-top on what was happening. They were tired out, but all the same decided that they should attack the cavalry too with all the strength at their command, to prevent them getting back their breath and regaining confidence. So they formed up and advanced; and then the enemy cavalry fled down the hill just as though it was cavalry that was pursuing them. A gulley, of which the Greeks were not aware, gave them shelter. As for the Greeks, they broke off the pursuit, as it was late. They then returned to the place where they had made the first charge, set up a trophy and got back to the sea about sunset. The distance to their camp was about six miles.

Chapter 6

SOME TROUBLE WITH
THE SPARTANS

AFTER this the enemy kept themselves to themselves and moved their families and their property as far off as they could. Meanwhile the Greeks waited for Cleander and the triremes and transports that were supposed to be coming. Every day they went out of camp with their baggage animals and slaves, and brought in, with no fear of being attacked, wheat, barley, wine, vegetables, millet and figs. The country produced everything one could want, except olives.

When the army was resting in camp, permission was given to individuals to go out after plunder, and those who did so kept their plunder; but when the whole army was out on an expedition, whatever anyone got hold of, if he went off on his own, was counted as public property.

There was now plenty of everything. And in addition food was brought for sale from the Greek cities on all sides, and people sailing along the coast were glad to put in here, as they had heard that a city was being founded, and that there was a harbour available. Enemy tribes, too, who lived in the vicinity, now began to send messengers to Xenophon, since they had heard that he was in charge of the arrangements for founding the city, and asked him what they had to do in order to be on friendly terms. Xenophon let the soldiers see these envoys.

In the middle of all this Cleander arrived with two triremes but no transports. When he arrived the army happened to be out of camp, but some stragglers had gone off into the mountains after plunder and had seized a number of sheep. Fearing that the sheep would be taken away from them, they told Dexippus (the man who ran away from Trapezus with the

ship of fifty oars) about it, and urged him to look after the
sheep for them, taking a share for himself and giving them
back the rest. Dexippus immediately pushed out of the way
the soldiers who were standing round and were pointing out
that the sheep were public property, and then went to
Cleander and said that they were trying to make off with the
sheep themselves. Cleander gave orders that whoever did so
should be brought to him, and Dexippus arrested one of the
soldiers and started to take him along. Agasias, however, met
the party and rescued the man, who was a soldier in his own
company. The other soldiers who were there started throwing
stones at Dexippus, and kept on shouting out 'Traitor!' At
this many of the men from the triremes were frightened too,
and fled to the sea, Cleander among them. Xenophon and the
other generals tried to stop them, and told Cleander that there
was nothing to be afraid of, pointing out that the reason for
the trouble was the decision passed by the army.

Cleander, however, had been put into a state of excitement
by Dexippus and was himself ashamed at having shown that
he was frightened. He said that he proposed to sail away from
them and would give the order that they were to be treated
as public enemies, and no city was to receive them. At this
time the Spartans were supreme over all Greece.

It now looked a bad business for the Greeks, and they
begged him not to carry out his threats. He, however, refused
to make any change in his plans unless the man who had
rescued the prisoner was handed over to him. The man whom
he was looking for was Agasias, who had always been a friend
of Xenophon's, which, indeed, was the reason why Dexippus
was accusing him.

At this point, since no one knew what to do, the officers
called a meeting of the army. Some of the soldiers thought
very little of Cleander, but Xenophon regarded the matter as
by no means unimportant. He got up and spoke as follows:

Soldiers, in my view, it is a serious business if Cleander goes away, as he says he will, feeling about us as he does at present. The Greek cities are not far away, and the Spartans are the masters of Greece. They have the power, yes, each individual Spartan in the cities has the power, to do what they like there. If, then, Cleander first of all shuts us out of Byzantium, and then gives orders to the other Spartan governors in the various cities not to admit us, on the ground that we are disobeying the Spartans and are outlaws, and then if the same report of us comes to the admiral Anaxibius, it will be a difficult thing for us either to stay here or to sail away. At the present time the Spartans have supreme power both on land and sea. It is not right, then, that, for the sake of one or two men, all the rest of us should be shut off from Greece. No, we ought to do what they tell us. Speaking for myself (and I hear that Dexippus is telling Cleander that Agasias would not have done what he did if I had not ordered him to do so),–speaking for myself, I am ready to clear both you and Agasias from blame if Agasias says himself that I had any responsibility for what happened, and I am ready to condemn myself to the severest punishment, and I will undergo that punishment, if I was the instigator of stone-throwing or any other act of violence. I suggest, too, that if Dexippus is accusing anyone else, that person ought to give himself up to Cleander for trial. In this way you would be freed from all responsibility in the affair. As things are at present it will be hard if, instead of all our expectations of getting honour and glory in Greece, we are not even looked upon as on a level with our fellow country-men, and are shut out of their cities.'

After this speech Agasias rose up and spoke as follows: 'I swear to you, soldiers, by all the gods and goddesses that Xenophon never ordered me to rescue the man, and nor did anyone else among you. But when I saw a good soldier, a man from my own company, being led away by Dexippus, who you know was a traitor to you, it seemed to me insufferable, and I rescued the man; I admit it. And there is no need for you to hand me over. I shall, as Xenophon suggests, give myself up to Cleander to try me and do what he pleases with me. Don't, for the sake of this, make enemies of the Spartans. I want you to get safely home where each man wants to be. But I should like you to choose some people and send them with me to Cleander, so that they can speak on my behalf and do what they can if I leave anything out.'

The army then gave him the opportunity to choose whom he liked to go with him, and he chose the generals.

After this Agasias and the generals and the man who had been rescued went to Cleander. The generals spoke as follows: 'The army has sent us to you, Cleander, and it requests that, if you are accusing all of us, you will try the case yourself and treat us as you think fit: if you are accusing one or two or more, they think that the right thing is for them to give themselves up to you for judgment. So, if you are accusing any of us, we are here before you. If anyone else, you have only to tell us his name. No one who is willing to obey our orders will refuse to attend.'

Next Agasias stepped forward and spoke as follows: 'I, Cleander, am the man who rescued this soldier when Dexippus was carrying him off, and I gave the order to throw stones at Dexippus. This was because I knew that this soldier was a good man, and I knew Dexippus too. I knew that he had been chosen by the army to command the ship of fifty oars which we persuaded the people of Trapezus to give us so that we could collect transports for bringing us home safe, and I knew that Dexippus ran away and played the traitor to the soldiers in whose company his life had been saved. So we were left, having taken the ship away from the people of Trapezus, and consequently with a bad reputation there, and, so far as Dexippus had a share in the business, we were lost men ourselves. He had heard, just as we had, of how impossible it was to cross the rivers and get safely to Greece by going on foot. This was the sort of man from whom I rescued this soldier. If it had been you who was leading him off, or any of your people, and not one of our deserters, you can be sure that I would never have acted as I did. And if you kill me now, remember that you will be killing a good man because of a wretched coward.'

After listening to this Cleander said that if Dexippus had acted as had been stated, it was impossible to approve of his conduct. On the other hand, he considered that, not even if Dexippus was an utter scoundrel, ought he to suffer by violent action. Instead he should have a trial and then get what he deserved. 'Just,' said Cleander, 'as you yourselves are now claiming a trial. Now,' he continued, 'go away and leave Agasias with me.. Come back when I tell you, to be present at his trial. I make no accusation either against the army or against anyone else, since this man admits himself that he rescued the prisoner.'

The man who had been rescued then spoke. 'As for me, Cleander,' he said, 'if you think that I was being led away because I had done anything wrong, I never struck anybody or threw stones. I merely said that the sheep were public property, as it was a decision passed by the soldiers that if anyone got any plunder by himself when the army was out on an expedition, what he got was to be considered public property. This was what I said, and the next thing was that Dexippus seized hold of me and was leading me off, so that no one could say a word about it, while he himself could take his own share and keep the rest of the plunder for the robbers, against the resolution of the army.'

Cleander replied to this as follows: 'Since you are involved in this, stay behind, so that we can decide what to do about you too.'

After this Cleander's party had dinner. Xenophon called a meeting of the army and advised sending delegates to Cleander to ask him to treat the men leniently. They decided to send the generals and captains and Dracontius the Spartan and any of the others who seemed likely to be useful and instruct them to beg Cleander most earnestly to release the men. Xenophon therefore went to Cleander and spoke as follows: 'You have the men in your power, Cleander, and the army has given you the authority to act as you please both as concerns the two men and also as concerns all the soldiers. They now most earnestly beg you to give them back these men and not to put them to death. In times past the two of them have done a lot for the army. If the soldiers gain their request, they promise you, as a return for this, that, if you are willing to be their commander, and if the gods are kind, they will give you a demonstration of their good discipline and will show you that, in obedience to their commander and with the help of heaven, they do not know the meaning of fear in the face of the enemy. They have another request to make too. It is that, when you have come and taken over the command, you will give to Dexippus and to the rest of them a chance of showing what each is good for, and that you will reward each according to his merits.'

Cleander listened to this, and then said: 'By the twin brethren, I shall give you a quick answer. I give you back the two men and I shall come and join you myself. And, if the gods give me the power, I shall lead you from here to Greece. Your own words are very different from the reports which I had about some of you, and which suggested that you were alienating the army from the Spartans.'

Then the delegates thanked Cleander and went away, taking the two men with them. Cleander offered a sacrifice with a view to making the journey and associated with Xenophon on very friendly terms. Indeed they made an agreement for mutual hospitality. When he saw how the soldiers carried out their orders in a smart disciplined way, he became even more anxious to be their commander. However, although he sacrificed on three separate days, the omens did not turn out favourable, and so he called the generals together and spoke as follows: 'The omens have not turned out right for me to lead you away from here: but you must not be discouraged on that account. You are the people, it seems, to whom has been given the task of bringing the army home. Lead on, then, and when you get to Byzantium, we shall give you the best reception we can.'

After this the soldiers decided to make him a present of the sheep which were public property. He accepted the gift, and then gave it back to them again. Then he set sail.

The army, after disposing of the corn which they had collected and the rest of their booty, marched on through the country of the Bithynians. Marching along the direct road, they fell in with no opportunities of securing any booty to take with them into the friendly country where they were going, and so they decided to march back on their tracks for a day and a night. By doing this they secured large numbers both of slaves and cattle. After six days they arrived at Chrysopolis in Chalcedonia where they stayed for seven days to sell their booty.

BOOK
VII
BYZANTIUM, THRACE
AND ASIA MINOR

Chapter 1

TROUBLE AT BYZANTIUM

PHARNABAZUS now became alarmed at the possibility of the army marching into his province, and so he sent to the admiral Anaxibius, who was at Byzantium, begging him to transport the army across from Asia, and promising to give him all the necessary help in doing so. Anaxibius summoned the generals and captains to Byzantium and promised that, if they crossed the straits, the soldiers would have a chance of earning money. The rest of the officers said that they would discuss the proposal and then report back, but Xenophon told him that he was going to leave the army at once and that he wanted to sail away. Anaxibius, however, urged him to cross over with the others and then leave, and Xenophon agreed to do this.

Meanwhile Seuthes, the Thracian, sent Medosades to Xenophon with a message asking him to join with him in trying to get the army to cross the straits. He said that if Xenophon helped him in this, he would not be sorry for it. Xenophon's reply was: 'The army will cross the straits in any case. As far as this is concerned there is no need to pay anything to me or anybody else. Once it has crossed, I am going to leave it; so Seuthes should get in touch with those who are staying and whom he thinks to be reliable people to help him.'

After this the whole army crossed to Byzantium. Anaxibius, however, failed to produce any pay for them. Instead he had it proclaimed that the soldiers were to take their arms and baggage and march out of the city: he was going to send them home and at the same time count their numbers. The soldiers were angry at this announcement, because they had no money to buy themselves provisions for their journey, and they did their packing in an unwilling way.

Xenophon had become a friend of Cleander, the Spartan governor, and, as he intended to sail away at once, he went to say goodbye to him. Cleander, however, said to him: 'Don't go away. If you do, you will be under suspicion. Even now some people are saying that it is your fault that the army is not moving out of here fast.'

Xenophon replied: 'I am not responsible for that. It is the soldiers themselves, who are short of provisions and for that reason are not keen on marching out.'

'All the same,' said Cleander, 'I advise you to go out of the city as though you are going to accompany the army. Once the army is outside, then you can leave them.'

'Very well,' Xenophon said, 'we will go to Anaxibius and get this settled.'

So they went to him and told him of their conversation. Anaxibius said that Xenophon should act as had been suggested and that the army were to pack up their equipment and march out as quickly as possible. He also gave notice that whoever was not on the parade for taking the numbers would be laying himself open to blame.

After this they marched out of the city, the generals first and the rest after. They had all marched right outside, except for a few, and Eteonicus had taken up his position by the gates, so that, when they were all outside, he could shut the gates and put the bar across. At this point Anaxibius called for the generals and captains and spoke to them as follows: 'You can get your supplies from the Thracian villages. There is a lot of barley and wheat and other food to be found there. When you have got your supplies, march on to the Chersonese, where Cyniscus will give you your pay.'

Some of the soldiers heard this, or else one of the captains told the army about it. Meanwhile the generals were discussing the question whether Seuthes was going to be a friend or a foe, and whether they would have to march over the

Holy Mountain or make a detour through central Thrace. While these conversations were going on, the soldiers seized hold of their arms and ran back to the gates, so as to get back inside the wall. When Eteonicus and his men saw the hoplites charging down, they shut the gates and put the bar across. The soldiers hammered at the gates, saying that they were being treated extremely unfairly, and were being pushed outside into enemy country, and they threatened to break the gates down unless the people inside opened them voluntarily. Some ran down to the sea and got into the city over the breakwater running out from the wall; some of the soldiers, who were still inside, when they saw what was happening at the gates hacked through the bar with axes and threw the gates open; and then they all rushed in.

When Xenophon saw what was going on, fearing that the army might start looting and that irreparable damage might be done both to the city and to the interests of himself and the soldiers, he ran forward and rushed inside the gates with the crowd. The people of Byzantium, seeing the army forcing its way in, fled out of the market-place. Some took refuge in their ships and some in their houses; those who happened to be indoors ran out into the streets; some dragged down the triremes into the water with the idea of getting away safe on them; and they all thought they were lost men, as though the city had been captured by the enemy. Eteonicus fled to the citadel. Anaxibius ran down to the sea and sailed round to the citadel too in a fishing boat. He then immediately sent for troops from the garrison of Chalcedon, as those he had in the citadel did not seem to be capable of holding out against the Greeks.

As soon as the soldiers saw Xenophon, a lot of them rushed up to him and said: 'Now is your chance, Xenophon, to become a great man. You have a city, you have triremes, you have money, you have an army in us. Now, if you wanted to, you could do good to us and we could make you great.'

Xenophon replied: 'You are speaking sense, and that is what I shall do. If this is what you want, fall in at once in your proper formations.' He said this with the intention of calming them down, and not only gave the order himself but told the others to pass on the command to fall in. They then began to arrange themselves in their detachments, and soon the hoplites were standing in eight ranks and the peltasts had run round to their positions on the two wings. The place where they were was called the Thracian Square and was as good a place as one could want for a parade, since it was clear of houses and the ground was level.

When the men had grounded arms and had calmed down a little, Xenophon called the army together and spoke as follows: 'I am not surprised, soldiers, at your being angry and at your thinking that you have been deceived and treated outrageously. If, however, we give way to our feelings, and make the Spartans who are here pay for their deception, and sack the city which is in no way responsible, then we must consider what comes next. We shall be at war, declared by ourselves, with the Spartans and their allies. And from what we have seen or can recall of recent history we can imagine what sort of a war that would be. When we Athenians went to war with Sparta and her allies, we had at least three hundred triremes, either at sea or in the docks; we had a large reserve of money in the Acropolis, and a yearly revenue from taxation at home and abroad amounting to at least a thousand talents. We were masters of all the islands, and we held many cities both in Asia and Europe, including this city of Byzantium where we are at present; and yet we were worn down by the war to the fate which you all know about. What do you think, then, our fate would be now, when the Spartans not only have all their original allies still available, but have been joined by the Athenians and all who then used to be allies of

Athens, when Tissaphernes and all the other natives on the
coast are our enemies, and our bitterest enemy of all is the
King of Persia against whom we marched with the intention
of depriving him of his empire and killing him, if we could?
With all this together on one side, can anyone be so mad
as to think that we should have a chance of winning? For
heaven's sake let us not go off our heads and die in dishonour,
fighting against our own native cities and our own friends and
kinsmen, all of whom are in the cities that would be making
war on us. And they would be quite right in making war on
us if, although with all the power in our hands we never
wanted to get control of a foreign city, now we plunder the
first Greek city to which we have come. I pray heaven that I
may be buried ten thousand fathoms underground before I see
such a thing done by you. My advice to you is that, since you
are Greeks yourselves, you should try to get justice by obeying
the leaders of the Greeks. If you are unsuccessful in this, we
must put up with the injustice and at least not cut ourselves off
from Greece. What we should do now, I think, is to send
envoys to Anaxibius with this message: "We have entered the
city with no intention of taking violent action. What we want
is to obtain some practical help from you. If we receive none,
we shall at least make it clear that we are leaving the city because we obey your orders, and not because of a trick." '

This proposal was carried and they sent Hieronymus of Elis
to deliver the message, with Eurylochus the Arcadian and
Philesius the Achaean to accompany him. These men then
went away to carry out their instructions.

But while the soldiers were still sitting down a Theban
called Coiratidas came up to them. He was not an exile from
Greece, but travelled about on the look-out for a job as a
general, and advertising his abilities in that capacity if any city
or nation needed one. On this occasion he came forward and
said he was prepared to lead the army into the part of Thrace

known as the Delta, where they would get a lot of booty; and he would supply them with food and drink to their heart's content while they were on their way there. While the soldiers were listening to this proposal the reply from Anaxibius was brought back. He said that, if they obeyed his orders, they would not be sorry for it; he would send in a report of the whole affair to his home government, and would like personally to do them what service he could.

After this the soldiers took Coiratidas as their general and marched out of the city walls. Coiratidas arranged that he would come back to the army on the following day with victims for sacrifice and a soothsayer, and also food and drink for the troops. As soon as they had left the city Anaxibius had the gates shut and issued a proclamation that any soldier found inside the walls would be sold as a slave. The next day Coiratidas arrived with the animals for a sacrifice and the soothsayer. In his company there were twenty men carrying barley meal, twenty more carrying wine and three carrying olives. One man had as big a load of garlic as could be carried, and another man an equal weight of onions. Coiratidas had these set out ready for distribution, and then made his sacrifice.

Xenophon asked Cleander to come and see him, and to arrange for him to come inside the city and take ship from Byzantium. When Cleander arrived he said: 'Here I am, after having had a lot of trouble in arranging matters. Anaxibius says that he does not like the idea of the soldiers being outside the wall and Xenophon inside. The Byzantines too, he says, are split up into a number of hostile camps. All the same he said you could come in, if you are prepared to sail in his company.'

Xenophon then said goodbye to the soldiers and went inside the city with Cleander.

Meanwhile Coiratidas failed to secure favourable omens at his sacrifice on the first day, and did not distribute any food to the army. On the second day the victims were put in position by the altar and Coiratidas had put a garland on his head all ready for the sacrifice, when Timasion the Dardanian and Neon of Asine and Cleanor of Orchomenus came up to him and told him not to sacrifice, as he was not going to lead the army unless he produced supplies. Coriatidas then ordered the food to be distributed, but what he had was nothing like enough to provide one day's rations for each man. He therefore went off, taking the animals for sacrifice with him and giving up the idea of holding the command.

Chapter 2

XENOPHON NEGOTIATES
WITH SEUTHES

NEON of Asine, the Achaeans Phryniscus, Philesius and
Xanthicles, and Timasion the Dardanian remained to command the army. They marched forward to some Thracian
villages in the neighbourhood of Byzantium and camped
there. Here there was a difference of opinion among the
generals. Cleanor and Phryniscus wanted to take the army to
Seuthes, who had won these two over by giving one of them
a horse and one of them a woman. Neon wanted to go to the
Chersonese, his idea being that, once they were under Spartan
control, he would be put in command of the whole army.
Timasion was in favour of crossing the straits back again into
Asia, as he thought that he could then secure his recall to his
city. The soldiers supported his plan, but, as time was being
wasted in discussions, many of them sold their arms in the
country and sailed away on their own, and others drifted into
the cities. Anaxibius welcomed the news of the army breaking
up, as he thought that, while this was what was happening,
he was acting in the most obliging manner towards Pharnabazus.

On his voyage from Byzantium Anaxibius was met at
Cyzicus by Aristarchus, who had come to replace Cleander as
governor of Byzantium. It was reported, too, that Polus, who
was to replace Anaxibius as admiral, was now on the point of
entering the Hellespont. Anaxibius instructed Aristarchus to
sell as slaves all the soldiers of Cyrus whom he found left
behind in Byzantium. Cleander had not sold any of them;
indeed he had taken pity on the sick and wounded, and looked
after them, making the people of the town put them up in

billets. Aristarchus, however, as soon as he arrived, sold at least four hundred as slaves.

Anaxibius sailed along the coast to Parion and from there, as had been arranged, sent a message to Pharnabazus. Pharnabazus, however, when he discovered that Aristarchus had arrived to take over the governorship of Byzantium and that Anaxibius no longer held his command as admiral, ceased to bother about Anaxibius and instead began to enter with Aristarchus into the same sort of negotiations about Cyrus's army as he had previously been having with Anaxibius.

After this Anaxibius called for Xenophon and urged him to sail back to the army as quickly as possible, using every means to that end which were available. He told him to keep the army together and to bring back into it as many of the deserters as possible: he was then to lead the army to Perinthus and transport it from there to Asia as quickly as he could. At the same time he gave Xenophon a ship of thirty oars and a letter of introduction, and sent with him a man to tell the people of Perinthus to supply him with mounts so as to reach the army as soon as possible. Xenophon then sailed across and came to the army. The soldiers gave him a good reception, and were glad to follow him immediately with the idea of crossing from Thrace into Asia.

When Seuthes heard that Xenophon had come back again, he sent Medosades to him by sea and begged him to bring the army to him, promising at the same time anything which he thought likely to win him over. Xenophon, however, replied that the whole thing was impossible, and, after receiving this answer, Medosades went away. When the Greeks reached Perinthus, Neon, with about eight hundred men, separated from the rest and camped apart. The rest of the army was all together in camp by the walls of Perinthus.

Xenophon now busied himself in collecting ships, so as to cross over as soon as possible. At this point Aristarchus, the

Spartan governor of Byzantium, arrived with two triremes, and, since he had been won over to the interest of Pharnabazus, forbade the captains of the ships to transport the Greeks. He then went to the army and told the soldiers not to cross into Asia. Xenophon informed him that Anaxibius had given the order, 'and,' he said, 'he sent me here for this very reason.'

Aristarchus then spoke again. 'Anaxibius,' he said, 'is no longer admiral. I, on the other hand, am governor here, and, if I catch any of you sailing, I shall sink your ships.' And with these words he went off into the city.

Next day he sent for the generals and captains of the army, but when they were already near the wall someone gave Xenophon the information that if he went inside he would be arrested and either be dealt with on the spot or else actually be handed over to Pharnabazus. On receiving this information Xenophon sent the others on ahead and said that he himself wanted to make a sacrifice. He then went back and sacrificed with a view to enquiring whether the gods would allow him to make the attempt to bring the army over to Seuthes. He did this because he saw that it was not safe to make the crossing, since those who wanted to prevent it had triremes; nor did he want to go to the Chersonese and be shut up there, with the army short of everything and in a position where it would be necessary to obey the orders of the governor on the spot and where the army would be unlikely to get any supplies.

While Xenophon was thinking along these lines, the generals and captains came back from Aristarchus and reported that he had told them to go away for the time being, but to come back to-morrow. This made his treachery even more obvious. The sacrifices had turned out favourable for Xenophon and the army to march in safety to Seuthes, and so Xenophon, taking Polycrates the Athenian captain with him, and also one man in whom the generals concerned had confidence from each of the generals except Neon, set out by night on a ride of six miles to Seuthes's army. When they were nearly there, he came across fires with no one guarding them. His first thought was that Seuthes had moved off somewhere else, but, after hearing some shouting and the noise of Seuthes's men exchanging passwords, he realised that the reason why Seuthes had had the fires lit in front of his sentries was that both the numbers and the position of the sentries might be concealed in the darkness, while those who approached would not do so without being seen, since they would be shown up in the light.

Realising what the position was, Xenophon sent ahead the interpreter whom he had with him, and told him to inform Seuthes that Xenophon was there and wanted to speak with him. The Thracians enquired whether it was Xenophon the Athenian, from the army, and when the interpreter replied that it was, they leaped on the horses and hurried away. A little later about two hundred peltasts appeared and escorted Xenophon and his party to Seuthes.

Seuthes was in a tower and was very carefully guarded. There were horses, all ready bridled, standing round the tower. From fear of danger he used to let the horses graze during the day, and at night had them ready bridled as a precaution. This was because in former times his ancestor, Teres, with a large army, was said to have lost a lot of men in this part of the country and to have had his baggage train taken from him by the natives, who are called Thyni and are supposed to be the most dangerous of all the tribes, especially at night fighting.

When they got close to the tower, Seuthes gave orders that Xenophon with any two men he chose might enter. They went in, and then they first of all greeted each other and drank to each other according to the Thracian custom, in horns full of wine. With Seuthes was Medosades who acted as his ambassador on all occasions.

Xenophon then spoke. 'The first time, Seuthes,' he said,

'you sent Medosades here to me in Chalcedon you asked me to join with you in trying to get the army across from Asia, and you promised that, if I succeeded in doing so, you would repay me for it; or that was what Medosades here said.'

He then asked Medosades whether he had reported the conversation correctly, and Medosades agreed that he had.

'Then,' continued Xenophon, 'Medosades came to me again, after I had crossed over once more to the army from Parion. He promised me that, if I brought the army to you, you would treat me as a friend and a brother, and, in addition to this, you would make me a gift of the towns along the coast which belong to you.'

He then again asked Medosades whether this was what he had said, and Medosades agreed again.

'Now then,' said Xenophon, 'tell Seuthes first what answer I gave you at Chalcedon.'

'You said,' said Medosades, 'that the army would cross to Byzantium and that there was no need to pay out anything either to you or anyone else as far as that was concerned. And you said that, when you had crossed the straits, you were leaving the army. Everything happened as you said it would.'

'And what did I say,' Xenophon asked him, 'when you came to me at Selymbria?'

'You said that it was impossible, that the army was going to Perinthus and then across into Asia.'

'And now,' said Xenophon, 'here I am, and here is Phryniscus, one of our generals, and here is Polycrates, one of our captains. Outside are men particularly trusted by each of our generals, except for Neon the Spartan. If you want our negotiations to be even more binding, call them inside too. And you, Polycrates, go and tell them that my orders are for them to leave their arms outside. Leave your own sword outside too before you come back.'

When he heard this, Seuthes said that he could never distrust any Athenian: he knew that there was a bond of kinship between him and them, and he regarded them as his true friends. Then, after the men who were wanted had come in, Xenophon first of all asked Seuthes what he wanted to use the army for.

Seuthes made the following speech: 'My father was Maesades, and he ruled over the Melanditae, the Thyni and the Tranipsae. Owing to the decline of the power of the Odryssae my father was driven out of this country. He fell ill and died, and I was brought up as an orphan at the court of the present king, Medocus. But as soon as I became a young man I could not face the idea of living as a dependent at another man's table. I sat down before him as a suppliant and begged him to give me as many men as he could, so that I might do all the damage I could to those who had driven us out, and live in future without being a dependent on his hospitality. He thereupon gave me all the men and the horses which you will see when it is day. And now I live with them by laying waste my own native kingdom. If you were to join me, I think that, with the help of heaven, I should easily regain power. This is what I want you for.'

'Suppose we joined you,' said Xenophon, 'what could you give to the army and to the generals and to the captains? Tell us, so that these men can report back to the army.'

Seuthes promised to give each soldier a stater of Cyzicus every month, with double pay for the captains and four times as much for the generals: also as much land as they wanted, yokes of oxen and a fortified town on the coast.

'If,' said Xenophon, 'we attempt to do what you want but are unsuccessful in it, and we are in danger from the Spartans, will you receive in your own country anyone who wants to take refuge with you?'

'Yes,' said Seuthes, 'I will; and I will make you my brothers and table companions and give you a share of all our gains. To you, Xenophon, I will give my daughter, and, if you have a daughter, I will, according to the Thracian custom, buy her from you; and I will give you Bisanthe as a place to live in, which is the best of all my towns on the coast.'

Chapter 3

THE GREEKS MARCH
WITH SEUTHES

WHEN the Greeks had heard what he had to say, they shook
hands with the Thracians as a sign of friendship and rode back.
They reached camp before dawn and gave in their separate
reports to those who had sent them. At daybreak Aristarchus
once more summoned the generals to him, but they decided
to call together the army and not bother about going to
Aristarchus. All the troops came to the assembly except those
under Neon's command, who were in camp about a mile
away. When they were all together, Xenophon stood up and
spoke as follows: 'My friends, Aristarchus with his triremes is
preventing us from sailing across to where we want to be, and
it is therefore not safe to embark in our transports. This same
Aristarchus tells us to make our way by force over the Holy
Mountain to the Chersonese. If we manage to force our way
through and get to our objective, he says that he will not sell
any more of you as slaves, as he did in Byzantium, and he
will not practise any more deception on you: instead you will
receive a wage, and he will not allow you to go on living short
of supplies as you are at present. This is what Aristarchus
says. Seuthes, on the other hand, says that, if you join him,
he will be a benefactor to you. Now you must consider
whether you will stay here to discuss what to do, or whether
you will first go back for supplies. My own view is that, as
we have no money to buy food, and as they will not let us
take it without paying for it, we should go back to the
villages where the inhabitants are weaker than we are and will
let us take what we want: then, when we have our supplies,
we can listen there to what offers are made to us and choose

what seems to us the best. Will those who agree with this proposal put up their hands?'

They all put their hands up, and Xenophon went on: 'Go back, then,' he said, 'and pack your kit. Follow your own officers when the order to march is given.'

After this Xenophon took the lead and the rest followed. Neon and some people sent by Aristarchus tried to make them turn back, but they paid no attention to them. When they had marched about three miles, Seuthes met them, and, when Xenophon saw him, he asked him to ride up to them, so that he could say what he thought was in the general interest with as large a number of people as possible listening. When he came close to them, Xenophon spoke as follows: 'We are marching to a district where the army is likely to get food. When we are there, we shall listen to what you and what the Spartans have to offer, and we shall choose what seems to us best. We shall consider that you are treating us hospitably if you lead us to a place where supplies are most plentiful.'

'Very well,' said Seuthes. 'I know of a number of villages close together and full of all sorts of supplies. They are so near that you could get over to them comfortably in time for a meal.'

'Lead the way, then,' said Xenophon.

They reached the villages in the afternoon, and then the soldiers assembled and Seuthes spoke to them as follows: 'I want you, my friends, to serve with me and I promise to give the soldiers a Cyzicene every month, with the usual extra pay to the captains and generals. Apart from this I will give promotion to those who deserve it. You will take your food and drink from the country, as you are doing now, but I shall claim to keep myself all the booty which we get, so that I can dispose of it and so be able to provide your pay. When our enemies take refuge in flight, we shall be able to go after them and track them down: if they stand up to us, we shall try with your help to overcome them.'

Xenophon then asked him: 'How far from the sea will you want the army to follow you?'

He replied: 'Never more than seven days' march, and usually less than that.'

Afterwards anyone who wished was given opportunity to speak, and a number of people made speeches to the same effect, saying that the proposition of Seuthes was an extraordinarily good one. They pointed out that it was winter and therefore, even if one wanted to sail home, it was impossible to do so; nor could they exist in a friendly country if they had to pay money for their food; and as for living in and getting their supplies from enemy territory, this was a safer thing to do when they were with Seuthes than if they were by themselves: and to get pay in addition seemed a real stroke of luck.

On the strength of this Xenophon said: 'If anyone has anything to say against the proposal, let him speak. If not, I shall put the matter to the vote.'

As no one had anything to say in opposition, he put it to the vote, and the proposal was carried. Xenophon at once told Seuthes that they would join him in his campaign.

After this, while the rest of the army camped in their formations, Seuthes, who was occupying a village near by, invited the captains and generals to dinner. When they were at the entrance to Seuthes' quarters and were waiting to go in to dinner, a man from Maronea, called Heraclides, put in an appearance. This man made advances to everyone who, he thought, had anything to give to Seuthes. First of all he approached some people from Parion, who were there with the idea of concluding an alliance with Medocus, the king of the Odrysae, and who had brought presents for the king and his wife. Heraclides told them that Medocus was up country, a twelve days' march from the sea; Seuthes, on the other hand, now that he had got this army, would be the master of the coastal districts. 'He is going to be your neighbour there,' he said, 'and will be best placed both for doing you good or harm. If you are wise, it is to him that you will give what you have with you. That will be a better bargain for you than if you give it to Medocus, who lives a long way away.'

In this way he talked them over. Then he approached Timasion the Dardanian, having heard that he had some goblets and Persian carpets. He told Timasion that, when Seuthes invited people to dinner, the custom was that the guests gave presents to their host. 'And,' he said, 'if Seuthes becomes a great man in these parts, he will be in a position either to send you back home or to make you a rich man, if you stay here.'

In the same way he went up to each of the guests, trying to get something for Seuthes. He approached Xenophon too and said to him: 'You come from the greatest city in Greece, and your name stands highest with Seuthes. Perhaps you will think it a good thing to hold some fortified place and some land in this country, as others of your countrymen have done. It is worth your while, then, to show your appreciation of Seuthes on the most generous scale. I give you this advice, because I am a friend of yours, and I know that the more you give Seuthes, the greater will be the services that he will give you.'

Xenophon was embarrassed at hearing this, as all he had brought across from Parion was one slave and just enough money to live on.

They then went in to dinner. The company consisted of the chief Thracians who were there, the generals and captains of the Greeks, and ambassadors who had come from various states. They sat down in a circle for dinner, and then three-legged tables were brought in for everyone. The tables were loaded with slices of meat piled up, with large leavened loaves attached to the meat by skewers. The tables were always placed nearest to the guests. This was a custom of theirs and

Seuthes had started it. Seuthes also took the loaves which were put by him, broke them up into pieces and threw the bits to anyone whom he chose. He did the same thing with the meat, only leaving just enough to taste for himself. The others who had the tables by them followed his example. An Arcadian, however, called Arystas, who was a tremendous eater, gave up any idea of handing the food round, grabbed hold of a colossal loaf, put the meat on his knees and settled down to his meal. Meanwhile they were bringing round horns of wine and everyone took some. However, when the wine-bearer came to Arystas with the horn, Arystas looked across at Xenophon, who had not yet started eating, and said: 'Give some to him. He has some time to spare. I haven't yet.'

Seuthes heard the remark and asked the wine-bearer what he had said. The wine-bearer, who knew Greek, told him and this produced a lot of laughter.

As the wine was going round, a Thracian came in, leading a white horse. He took hold of a horn full of wine and said: 'Seuthes, I drink your health and I make you a present of this horse. On his back you will pursue and overtake your foes, and, when you are in retreat, you will never fear an enemy from behind.'

Another man brought in a boy and presented him to Seuthes in the same way, after drinking his health; and another man brought clothes for Seuthes's wife. Timasion too drank his health and presented him with a silver cup and a carpet worth ten minae. An Athenian called Gnesippus stood up and said that it was a good old custom that those who had anything should give a present to the King so as to show their respect, and that the King should give presents to those who had nothing. 'I too,' he said, 'would like to have something to give you to show my respect.'

Xenophon had no idea what to do, and he was also in the place of honour, sitting on the chair next to Seuthes, and

Heraclides now ordered the wine-bearer to hand him the horn. However, as he was slightly drunk, he stood up confidently, grasped the cup and spoke as follows: 'Seuthes, I make you a present of myself and of my comrades here to be your trusty friends, and none of them hanging back, indeed all of them wanting your friendship even more than I do. Here they are then, with no other demands to make on you, but longing to incur hardships and dangers for you of their own free will. With their help, if the gods so will it, you will win much land–some will be your own inheritance which you will recover, some will be the result of new conquests. You will win numbers of horses, numbers of men and beautiful women; and these you will not have to take by force. They will come to you with gifts in their hands.'

Seuthes then stood up and joined him in drinking up the wine and then in sprinkling the dregs over their garments. Afterwards people came in and played on horns like the ones they use for signalling orders in war: others had trumpets made of raw ox-hides with which they performed regular tunes of the sort played on the magadis. Seuthes himself stood up and shouting out a war-cry, leapt about with great agility, giving an imitation of a man getting out of the way of a weapon. Some professional buffoons also appeared.

When the sun was on the point of setting, the Greeks stood up and said that the time had come for posting the sentries and giving the password. They asked Seuthes to give the order that no Thracian was to come into the Greek camp by night. 'This,' they said, 'is because our enemies are Thracians and you, our allies, are also Thracians.'

As they were going out Seuthes stood up, not appearing in the least drunk, and went outside and called the Greek generals together separately. 'My friends,' he said, 'our enemies do not know yet of our alliance. If, therefore, we march against them before they have taken precautions against a surprise or made their dispositions for defence, we should have a very good chance of seizing both prisoners and booty.'

The generals approved of this suggestion and told him to lead the way. 'You get ready then,' he said, 'and wait for me. When the time comes, I will come to you, and then, with the peltasts and you with me, I will, with the help of the gods, lead you on.'

'If we are going to march by night,' said Xenophon, 'I should like you to consider whether the Greek practice is not a better one. In our daylight marches the part of the army which leads the way is the one which is, at the moment, best adapted to the nature of the country; it might be the hoplites, or the peltasts or the cavalry. But by night the Greek practice is for the slowest part of the army to be in front. In this way the army is least likely to lose cohesion, and men are least likely to stray off from each other without knowing where they are When a force loses cohesion, it often happens that detachments fall foul of each other and, through mutual ignorance, damage is done on both sides.'

Seuthes then said: 'That is a very good suggestion. I shall follow your practice. I shall also give you as guides some of the older men who have the fullest knowledge of the country, and I shall bring up the rear myself with the cavalry. If necessary, I can soon get to the front.'

They fixed upon 'Athene' for the password, because of his family relationship with Athens, and, after this conversation was over, they went to have a rest.

About midnight Seuthes appeared with his cavalry, wearing their breastplates, and with his peltasts all ready for action. He assigned them their guides, and then the hoplites led the way, with the peltasts coming next and the cavalry forming the rearguard. At daybreak Seuthes rode up to the front, and expressed his satisfaction with the Greek marching order. He said that, when marching by night, even with only a few followers, he himself with the cavalry had often lost contact with the infantry. 'Now, however,' he went on, 'we all appear in one body at dawn, as we ought to be. What I want you to do now is to stay here and have a rest. I shall have a look round, and then come back to you.'

After saying this, he rode away, going by a road over the mountains. When he came to a part where there was a lot of snow, he examined the ground to see whether there were any footprints leading in one way or the other. After finding that there were no tracks on the road he came back again quickly and said: 'My friends, all will be well, if the gods are on our side. We shall be upon these people before they know anything about it. I shall now lead the way with the cavalry, so that, if we see anyone, he will not get the chance of running away to give information to the enemy. You follow after, and if you get left behind, follow in the horses' tracks. Once we have crossed the mountains we shall arrive among a number of villages, which are well stocked.'

He had reached the top of the mountains by midday, and, when he had had a look at the villages, he rode back to the hoplites and said: 'I am now going to order the cavalry to charge down into the plain and send the peltasts into the villages. I want you to follow as quickly as possible, so that you can give support if there is any resistance.'

When he had received these instructions, Xenophon dismounted, and Seuthes asked him: 'Why do you get off your horse when what we want is to go fast?'

'Because I feel sure,' said Xenophon, 'that you don't want only me by myself. You will find that the hoplites will run faster and will be more keen on doing so if I lead the way on foot too.'

Seuthes then went off, and Timasion, with about forty Greek horsemen, went with him. Xenophon called out the most active men under thirty from the companies and hurried ahead with them under his own command, while Cleanor led the rest. When they got to the villages, Seuthes rode up to him with about thirty horsemen. 'Xenophon,' he said, 'things have gone just as you said. These people are in our power. But my cavalry have got out of control and have ridden off in different directions on the pursuit; and I am afraid that the enemy may form up again somewhere in a body and do us some damage. Some of us, too, ought to stay in the villages, as they are full of people.'

'Then I,' said Xenophon, 'with my men will occupy the heights. You order Cleanor to extend his line across the plain so as to cover the villages.'

They carried out these manoeuvres, and, as a result, about a thousand slaves, two thousand oxen and ten thousand other cattle were taken.

Chapter 4

SUCCESSFUL FIGHTING
WITH SEUTHES

NEXT day Seuthes burned the villages to the ground, not leaving a single house standing, so as to strike terror into the other tribes and show them what would happen to them if they did not give in. He then marched back again, sending Heraclides to Perinthus to dispose of the booty, so as to raise funds to pay the army. He himself camped with the Greeks on the plain inhabited by the Thynians, who abandoned their homes and fled to the hills.

There was a lot of snow here, and it was so cold that the water which they brought in for their dinner, and the wine in the jars, froze, and a number of Greeks lost noses and ears through frostbite. It was then easy to see why the Thracians wear fox-skins round their heads and ears, and why they have tunics that cover their legs and not only the upper part of the body, and why, when they are on horseback, they wear long cloaks reaching down to their feet instead of our short coats.

Seuthes sent some of the prisoners into the hills and told them to say that if the inhabitants did not come down and settle in their houses and submit to him, he would burn up their villages too and destroy their crops, and they would die of hunger. As a result of this the women and children and older men came down into the plain, but the younger men camped in the villages at the foot of the mountains. When Seuthes found this out, he asked Xenophon to take the youngest men among the hoplites and follow him. They started by night and reached the villages at dawn. Most of the inhabitants ran away, as the mountains were near, but all those whom Seuthes captured he put to death by the spear without mercy.

Xenophon had with him an Olynthian called Episthenes, who was very fond of boys. On this occasion he saw a good-looking boy, just at the most beautiful age, with a shield in his hand, on the point of being put to death; so he ran up to Xenophon and begged him to do what he could for the beautiful boy. Xenophon went up to Seuthes and asked him not to kill the boy, telling him at the same time what sort of person Episthenes was, and that in the past he had raised a company and fought very gallantly with them, and that the only qualification he had looked for in his company had been physical beauty. Seuthes then said: 'And would you, Episthenes, be willing to die for the boy?'

Episthenes stretched out his neck and said: 'Strike the blow if the boy tells you to and if he will feel grateful to me afterwards.'

Seuthes then asked the boy whether he should kill Episthenes instead of him, but the boy said 'no' and begged him not to kill either of them. At this Episthenes put his arms round the boy and said: 'Now, Seuthes, you will have to fight me for him. I shall never give the boy up.'

Seuthes laughed, and did nothing more about it. He decided to camp where they were, so that the people in the mountains should not be able to get food even from their villages. He went down into the plain himself and camped there, while Xenophon with his picked men camped in the village highest up among the mountains, and the rest of the Greeks camped close by among the tribes which were called 'the mountain Thracians'.

Before many days had gone by the Thracians came down from the mountains and began to negotiate with Seuthes about peace terms and the handing over of hostages. Xenophon at the same time went to Seuthes and told him that they were living in miserable quarters with the enemy on top of them. He said that he would rather camp in a strong position in the

open than in a sheltered position where they might be cut off.
Seuthes told him to keep his spirits up and showed him the
hostages which he had with him; and some of the Thracians
from the mountains came down and begged Xenophon himself to give them help in negotiating peace terms. He agreed
to do so, and told them to keep their spirits up and guaranteed
that, if they submitted to Seuthes, they would come to no
harm. But in point of fact their enquiries had only been made
so that they could do some spying.

All this took place during the day. In the following night
the Thracians came down from the mountain and launched an
attack. The master of each house acted as a guide for them,
and indeed in the darkness it was difficult without a guide to
find where the houses were in the villages, as they were surrounded by high fences to keep in the cattle. When they were
at the doors of the houses, some hurled javelins at them and
others beat at them with the clubs with which they were
armed, so they said, in order to knock off the heads of the
spears. Others set fire to the houses, and kept calling out for
Xenophon by name, telling him to come outside and be
killed, or else he would be burnt alive where he was. Fire was
already beginning to show through the roof, and Xenophon's
men were inside the house, with their armour on, holding
their shields and swords and helmets in their hands. Then
Silanus, a Macistian about eighteen years old, blew the trumpet
call, and immediately they and the Greeks from the other
houses drew their swords and rushed out. The Thracians ran
away, slinging their shields, as their way is, behind their
shoulders. Some of them, as they were getting over the fence,
were caught suspended there, with their shields entangled in
the stakes. Others were killed because they failed to find the
ways out. The Greeks chased them outside the village, and a
few Thynians turned back in the dark and, throwing their
weapons from the cover of darkness into the light, shot at a

party of Greeks who were running past a house which was on fire. They wounded the captain Hieronymus, a Euodian, and Theogenes, a Locrian, but no one was killed. Some people, however, had their clothing and equipment burnt.

Seuthes came up to relieve them with seven horsemen at first and bringing the Thracian trumpeter with him. When he saw what was happening, he had the trumpet sounded all the time that he was on his way to their relief, with the result that this also helped to terrify the enemy. He congratulated the Greeks when he reached them, and said that he had expected to find a number of them killed.

After this Xenophon asked Seuthes to give him the hostages and, if he liked, to join him in making an attack on the mountain; if not, to let him go by himself. Next day, then, Seuthes handed over the hostages, who were elderly people and, so they said, the most important persons among the mountaineers, and he and his force marched with Xenophon. By this time Seuthes's army was three times its original size, as numbers of the Odryssae, hearing of Seuthes's successes, had come down to join with him.

When the Thyni looked down from the mountain and saw the enormous force of hoplites and peltasts and cavalry, they came down and begged for peace, promising to carry out all Seuthes's orders, and asking him to accept guarantees from them. Seuthes then summoned Xenophon and told him of their offers. He said that he would not make peace if Xenophon wanted to revenge himself on them for the attack which they had made.

Xenophon replied: 'As far as I am concerned, I think I am sufficiently revenged already if they are going to exchange their freedom for slavery.' However, he advised Seuthes in future to take as hostages the people who were most capable of doing him harm, and to let the old men stay at home.

Everyone, then, in this part of Thrace submitted to Seuthes.

Chapter 5

TROUBLE ABOUT THE PAY

THEY then crossed over to the Thracians above Byzantium, in the part called 'the Delta'. This was no longer the territory of Maesades, but had belonged to Teres, the son of Odryses. Here Heraclides arrived with what he had got from selling the booty. Seuthes produced three pairs of mules (which were all there were) and some yokes of oxen, and then sent for Xenophon. He asked him to accept these and portion out the rest among the generals and captains. Xenophon's answer was, 'Speaking for myself, I shall be quite satisfied to take something next time. I advise you to give these to the generals and captains who have served with me.'

So Timasion the Dardanian got one of the pairs of mules, and Cleanor of Orchomenus and Phryniscus the Achaean got the other two pairs. The yokes of oxen were shared out among the captains. The month had now expired, but Seuthes only gave the soldiers twenty days' pay, as Heraclides said that this was all he had been able to sell of the booty. Xenophon was angry at this and spoke seriously about it to Heraclides. 'In my opinion,' he said, 'you are not looking after Seuthes as you should. If you were doing so, you would have come back with the full pay, even if you had had to borrow the money, and, if you couldn't do it any other way, you would have sold the shirt off your back.'

This made Heraclides angry and at the same time afraid that he might lose the confidence of Seuthes, and so, from that day onward, he did all he could to produce ill feeling on the part of Seuthes towards Xenophon. The soldiers blamed Xenophon for not getting their pay, and Seuthes became unfriendly to him because he was constantly demanding the soldiers' pay from him. Up till then he had been always telling him that, when they got to the sea, he would give him Bisanthe and Ganus and the New Fort, but now he no longer referred to these places. This was the result of some more insinuations from Heraclides, who said that it was not safe to give fortified positions to a man with an army behind him.

Xenophon therefore began to wonder what he ought to do with regard to the projected march even further into the interior. Heraclides kept on bringing the other generals before Seuthes and telling them to say that they could lead the army just as well as Xenophon. He promised that in a few days they should have two months' full pay, and urged them on to join in the march with Seuthes. Timasion said: 'As far as I am concerned, I would not serve without Xenophon, even if I was going to get five months' pay,' and Phryniscus and Cleanor agreed with him.

Seuthes then reproached Heraclides for not calling in Xenophon at the same time, and the next thing was that they summoned Xenophon by himself. Xenophon, however, saw what Heraclides's game was, namely, that he wanted to make him unpopular with the other generals, and so he took with him to the interview all the other generals and the captains as well. The whole lot of them were persuaded by what Seuthes said, and they marched out with him to Salmydessus, keeping the Euxine on their right, and going through the country of the Thracians who are called the 'Melinophagi'. In this part great numbers of ships sailing into the Euxine get stranded and wrecked since there are sand-banks stretching far out to sea. The Thracians who live here put up pillars to mark their own sectors of the coast, and each takes the plunder from the wrecks on his own bit of ground. They used to say that in the past, before they put up the boundary marks, great numbers of them killed each other fighting for the plunder. Round here were found numbers of couches, boxes, written books and a lot of other things of the sort that sailors carry in their wooden chests.

They subdued the people in this district and then marched back again. By this time Seuthes had an army of his own bigger than the Greek army, as still more of the Odrysae had come down to him in great numbers, and other tribes kept joining his army directly they submitted to him. They camped about three miles from the sea in a plain above Selymbria. There was still no sign of pay, and the soldiers were extremely angry with Xenophon about it. Seuthes, too, was no longer on friendly terms with him, and whenever he went to him with the intention of speaking with him, there were now always various excuses that he was busy.

Chapter 6

XENOPHON IS ATTACKED
AND DEFENDS HIMSELF

AT this time, when nearly two months had gone by, the Spartan Charminus and Polynicus arrived from Thibron with the news that the Spartans had decided to fight Tissaphernes, and that Thibron had set sail with the intention of opening hostilities; he now wanted the services of the Greek army and offered as pay a daric a month to each man, with twice as much for the captains and four times as much for the generals.

When these Spartans arrived, Heraclides, as soon as he found out that they had come to enlist the services of the army, told Seuthes that this was an excellent thing to happen. 'The Spartans,' he said, 'need the army, while you have no further use for it. If you hand it over, you will be doing a good turn to the Spartans, and the soldiers will no longer keep asking you for their pay, since they will be leaving the country.'

On hearing this, Seuthes told him to bring the Spartans to him, and when they said that they had come to engage the services of the army, he replied that he would hand it over to them, and that he wanted to be their friend and ally. He invited them to a banquet and gave them a magnificent entertainment; but he did not invite either Xenophon or any other of the Greek generals. At the banquet when the Spartans asked what sort of person Xenophon was, Seuthes said that he was not a bad man, except that he was too much a friend of the ordinary soldiers, 'and,' he went on, 'for that reason he is not so well off as he might be.'

'He tries to make himself popular with the men, does he?'

said the Spartans, and Heraclides replied: 'Yes, that is exactly it.'

'Then won't he oppose us,' they asked, 'over the question of taking the army away?'

'No doubt,' said Heraclides; 'but if you call an assembly of the army and promise them their pay, they will give very little thought to Xenophon and will be only too pleased to go off with you.'

'How can we call an assembly, then?' they asked.

'Early to-morrow morning,' said Heraclides, 'we shall take you to the army. And I am sure,' he added, 'that, when they see you, they will come together for a meeting willingly enough.' So ended that day.

Next day Seuthes and Heraclides brought the Spartans to the army and the soldiers gathered round them. The two Spartans spoke as follows: 'Our government has decided to make war on Tissaphernes, the man who has treated you so badly. If, then, you join us, you will get your revenge on your enemy, and each of you will be paid a daric a month, with twice as much for the captains and four times as much for the generals.'

The soldiers were delighted to hear this proposal, and one of the Arcadians stood up immediately to make an attack on Xenophon. Seuthes was there too, as he wanted to know how things would end. He stood where he could hear the speeches and had an interpreter with him, though he had a fairly adequate knowledge of Greek himself.

The Arcadian then started his speech. 'Spartans,' he said, 'we should have been with you long ago, if Xenophon had not lured us into coming here, where we have been fighting all through this terrible winter, and kept on the move day and night. Meanwhile Xenophon gets all the profit from our labours. Seuthes has made him privately into a rich man, while he keeps back our pay. Speaking for myself, if I could see him being stoned to death and so made to pay for the way in which he has been dragging us around, I should think that I had been paid well enough and would have nothing to complain about over all I have suffered.'

After this several others got up and spoke to the same effect. Then Xenophon spoke as follows: 'I suppose that no man should be surprised at anything happening to him, since I am now being faced with your accusations at a time when I am conscious in my own mind of having done my very utmost to help you. I turned back, when I had already started for home, and I most certainly did not do this because I had heard that you were doing well for yourselves. It was because I knew that you were in a difficult position and I wanted to help you, if I could. When I returned to you, Seuthes here sent a number of messengers to me and made me all kinds of promises, if I would persuade you to join him. As you know yourselves, I made no attempt to do so. I led you in the direction where I thought you would most easily be able to cross over to Asia, since I thought this was the best thing for you to do, and I knew that this was what you wanted yourselves. Then Aristarchus came with his triremes and prevented us sailing, and it was after this, as was reasonable enough, I think, that I called you together to discuss what we should do next. You then heard Aristarchus's demand that you should march to the Chersonese, and you heard Seuthes urging you to join him. You all said that you would go with Seuthes, and you all voted in favour of doing so. May I ask what injury I did you on that occasion by leading you in the direction which you had all decided to take?

'The next thing was that Seuthes began to deceive us about the pay. You would be right in accusing me and hating me if I now show any approval of his actions. As it is, though I used to be his greatest friend, I am on worse terms with him now than anybody. I chose to be on your side rather than on his, and therefore how can it be right for you to blame me for just those things which resulted in my losing his friendship?

'You may say, perhaps, that I may have received your pay from Seuthes and am now trying to deceive you about it. On that assumption, this, anyway, is something one can be certain about: Seuthes, if he gave me anything, did not, I feel sure, give it to me with the idea of both losing what he gave me and paying out more still to you. No, if he did give me anything, he would, I imagine, have given it to me on the understanding that he was giving me a smaller sum so as to avoid paying a greater sum to you. So, if you think that this is what happened, you are now in a position to make the whole scheme worthless for both of us, simply by demanding your pay from him. If I have any of his money, it is obvious that Seuthes will ask for it back again, and he will be quite right in doing so if I have not done the job which I was bribed to do.

'In point of fact, I know that I am very far indeed from having your pay. I swear to you by all the gods and goddesses that I have not even got what Seuthes promised me for myself. He is present here and listening, and he knows whether I am perjuring myself or not. And I swear to you also–to make you even more surprised–that I have not had as much as the other generals have had, and indeed not even as much as some of the captains. Why, you may ask, have I not? This is why: because, my friends, I thought that by sharing in his original poverty I should make him all the more my friend when he was in a position to show his friendship. Now, of course, I see that he is doing well for himself, and I have also learned what his real character is. You may easily say to me, "Are you not ashamed of yourself for being so stupidly taken in?" I should certainly be ashamed if I had been taken in by someone who was an enemy: but in the case of a friend I think it is more shameful to practise deception than to suffer from it. In any case, if one has to take precautions with regard to one's friends,

I am sure that we have taken every precaution possible to avoid giving Seuthes any reasonable excuse for withholding from us what he promised. We have done him no harm: we have not neglected his interests: we have never fought shy of any enterprise to which he called us.

'You may say that I ought to have got guarantees from him at the start, so that he could not have deceived us, even if he wanted to do so.

'Listen, then, to what I have to say on this point. I should never have said this in his presence if it were not for the fact that you appear to be either completely out of touch with what I have been doing, or else extraordinarily lacking in a sense of gratitude. I should like you to recall to your minds the sort of situation you were in and from which I rescued you by bringing you to Seuthes. You remember approaching Perinthus, where the Spartan Aristarchus had the gates shut and refused to allow you inside? Then you camped outside in the open air, and it was mid-winter. You had to buy your provisions, and you found there was not much available for sale, nor had you much money for buying what there was. You were forced to stay in Thrace, because the triremes were anchored there and stopped you sailing across to Asia. Staying in Thrace meant that one was in enemy country, where you were up against large forces of cavalry and peltasts. We had hoplites certainly, and, by going out against the villages in full force we might perhaps have secured supplies of a sort; but we had no troops that could be used in a pursuit or for capturing slaves or cattle. I found that neither cavalry nor peltasts any longer existed as organised bodies in your army. Now, in a desperate position like this which I have described, would you have thought that I had done a bad piece of work for you if I had, without asking for any pay at all, merely secured for you the alliance of Seuthes, who had all the cavalry and peltasts which you needed? You know that, acting in co-operation with them, you came across more food in the villages, because the Thracians were compelled to get out quicker, and you also captured a bigger proportion of slaves and cattle. Enemy forces completely disappeared, once we had cavalry attached to us, whereas, before then, they came after us confidently enough with their horsemen and peltasts, and prevented us from splitting up into small detachments and so bringing in greater quantities of supplies. Now, supposing that the person who helped to provide you with this security did not at the same time pay you much money for it, is this such a terrible thing to have happened to you? Is this the reason why you think that I should on no account be allowed to remain alive?

'Consider next what your position is now that you are going away. You have had plenty of food all through the winter, with whatever you have got from Seuthes thrown into the bargain. Everything which you have consumed has been enemy property, and, while you have been living in plenty, you have seen none of your own men killed and have lost none of them alive. You preserve intact the reputation you won by fighting against the natives in Asia, and in addition you have won more glory by conquering the Thracians against whom you have fought in Europe. What I should say is that you ought to thank the gods for just these things which make you angry against me, and that you ought to look upon them as blessings.

'So much for your fortunes. Now, in the name of heaven, consider what mine are like. When I first started home, I went away greatly honoured by you, and famous because of you in the eyes of the other Greeks. I was trusted by the Spartans. Otherwise they would not have sent me back to you again. But when I go away now, I find myself prejudiced in the eyes of the Spartans because of your attacks: by acting in your interests I am on bad terms with Seuthes, who, I hoped, after the services which you and I had given him, would provide me and my children, if I had any, with both security and honour. And as for you, for whose sake I have incurred all this hatred, and from people who are much stronger than I am, you, for whom I have never yet stopped busying myself in order to do all the good I could for you, this is the opinion you have of me. Well, you have me in your hands. You did not catch me trying to escape or running away. If you do what you say you will do, remember that you will be putting to death a man who has spent long hours awake for your safety, who has borne many toils and dangers in your company, doing his fair share and more besides; one who, with the gods on our side, has together with you raised many trophies to celebrate our victories over foreigners, and who has exerted himself to the utmost in opposing your folly and seeing to it that you did not make enemies of any Greek state. As it is, you can now go freely wherever you like by land or sea.

'And now, when you are well off in every way, when you are setting sail to the homes you have so long wished for, when the most powerful state in Greece is asking for your services and pay is being offered, when Spartans, who are supposed to be the best commanders, have come to lead you, does this seem to you the proper moment to put me to death as quickly as you can? You have remarkable memories. This was not how you felt when we were in difficulties. Then you used to call me your father, and promised that you would always remember me as one who had done good to you. However, these men here who have now come to ask for your services are quite capable of forming their own opinion. In my view, they too will not think the better of you for behaving like this towards me.'

So he ended his speech, and the Spartan Charminus got up and spoke as follows: 'By the twin brethren, you don't seem to me to have any reason for being angry with this man. I myself have some evidence to put forward in his favour. When Polynicus and I asked Seuthes what sort of a person Xenophon was, the only fault he could find with him was that he was, as Seuthes said, too much of a friend to the ordinary soldiers; and, because of this, he was not as well off as he might have been, both in his relations to us Spartans and to Seuthes.'

Eurylochus, an Arcadian from Lusia, got up next and said: 'My view is, Spartans, that your first act in taking over the command ought to be to get our pay for us from Seuthes, whether he likes it or not, and that you should not take us with you until you have done this.'

Polycrates the Athenian, on Xenophon's instructions, then spoke. 'My friends,' he said, 'I see that Heraclides is here too. He is the man who took the booty which we won by fighting for it, and who sold it and then failed to give what he got for it either to Seuthes or to us. Instead he made off with it himself and still has it. If we have any sense, we shall get hold of him. He is no Thracian, but a Greek who is cheating his own countrymen.'

When Heraclides heard this he was extremely embarrassed and, going up to Seuthes, said: 'The sensible thing for us to do is to get out of the reach of these men's power.'

He and Seuthes then mounted their horses and rode away to their own camp. When they got there Seuthes sent his personal interpreter, Abrozelmes, to Xenophon, and asked him to stay in his service with a thousand hoplites, promising at the same time to give him the fortified places on the coast and everything else which he had promised him previously. He also told him in confidence that he had heard from Polynicus that he would certainly be put to death by Thibron if he fell into the hands of the Spartans. A number of other people too sent messages to Xenophon, all saying that he was under suspicion and ought to be on his guard. Xenophon, as a result of these warnings, took two animals and sacrificed them to Zeus the King, enquiring whether it would be a better thing for him to stay with Seuthes on the terms offered, or to leave with the rest of the army. The reply of Zeus was that he should leave with the rest.

Chapter 7

XENOPHON SPEAKS TO SEUTHES

AFTER this Seuthes camped some way away, and the Greeks went to take up their quarters in some villages where they intended to collect all the supplies they could before marching to the sea. These villages had been given by Seuthes to Medosades, and Medosades was far from pleased when he saw his own property in these villages being taken by the Greeks. He therefore took with him one of the most important people among the Odrysae who had come down from the north and, with about thirty horsemen as well, came and called for Xenophon from the Greek army. Xenophon went to meet him, taking some of the captains and other responsible people along with him. Medosades then spoke as follows: 'You are doing wrong, Xenophon, in laying our villages waste. We are now giving you fair notice–I on the part of Seuthes, and this man on the part of Medocus, the king of the interior–to leave this part of the country. If you fail to do so, we shall not let you have your own way, but shall treat you as enemies and defend ourselves if you do harm to our country.'

Xenophon listened to him and then replied as follows: 'Really, when you talk like this, it is difficult to give you any answer at all. What I shall say is for the benefit of this young man here, so that he may know what sort of people you are and what sort of people we are. Before we became your allies, we used to march through this country wherever we liked to go, laying it waste and destroying it by fire at our pleasure, and when you came to us as an ambassador, you used to camp with us and have no fear of any enemies. But you of Seuthes's party never came into this part of the country at all, or, if you did, you camped there with your horses all ready bridled, showing that you were in territory where your enemies were stronger than you were. Then you became our allies, and, owing to us and the help of the gods, you now control the country. At this point you attempt to drive us out of this country which we held by our own arms and which you took over from us. You know perfectly well that the enemy had not the strength to drive us out. Then, so far from offering us presents before asking us to set off home, or making any kind of return for the good service you have had from us, you are actually doing your best to stop us even camping here when we are already on our way back. In making requests of this nature you show no proper feeling either for the gods or for this man here, who sees you prosperous to-day, but, as you admitted yourself, used to know you, before you became our ally, as a person who lived on the proceeds of plundering expeditions.'

Here Xenophon broke off and then continued: 'Why is it to me that you come with these requests? I no longer hold the command. The Spartans hold it, and you handed the army over to them for them to lead it away, and you were not generous enough to invite me to take any part in the proceedings, so that, just as I became unpopular with them when I brought the army over to you, I might now do them a good turn by giving it back to them.'

The Odrysian chief, when he had listened to this, said: 'As far as I am concerned, Medosades, I feel like sinking into the earth with shame when I hear what he says. I should never have come with you if I had known this beforehand. As it is, I shall now go away. Medocus, my king, would not countenance the idea of my driving out of the country people who have done him good service.'

After making this speech, he mounted his horse and rode away, as did all the other horsemen with the exception of four or five of them. Medosades, however, who was upset by the way the country was being devastated, asked Xenophon to call in the two Spartan generals.

Xenophon then took with him the people who seemed most likely to be useful and went to see Charminus and Polynicus. He told them that Medosades wanted to see them with the intention of making the same request as he had made to him – namely, that they should leave the country. 'I think, therefore,' Xenophon said, 'that you could get hold of the pay owing to the army if you told Medosades that the soldiers have begged you to give them your help in securing their pay from Seuthes, whether he likes it or not; that they say that, once they get their pay, they will willingly follow you; that you consider that their demands are justified; and that you guarantee to leave once the soldiers have been given their rights.'

The Spartans listened to this, and replied that they would say all this and anything else they could to make it as effective as possible. They then set off immediately, taking all the senior officers with them. On their arrival Charminus spoke as follows: 'If you have anything to say to us, Medosades, then say it. If not, we have something to say to you.'

Medosades then put on a very submissive air and said: 'All I have to say is this, and Seuthes says just the same: we ask that those who have become our friends should not be ill-treated by you. When you do them any harm, you are actually doing the harm to us, since they belong to us.'

'Then,' said the Spartans, 'once those who have won you your new subjects have received their pay, we shall be quite prepared to go away. If this is not done, we are here now to give them our support and to make those who have deceived our soldiers and broken their oaths suffer for it. And if you fall into that category, we shall make a start by seeing that we get justice from you.'

Xenophon then spoke. 'Would you care, Medosades,' he

said, 'to give these people in whose country we are and who you said were your friends an opportunity of voting whether it would be more desirable for you to leave the country or us?'

Medosades was against this proposal, but he recommended, as the best course of action, that the two Spartans should go to Seuthes about the pay, and said that he thought they would be successful. If they could not go, then he suggested sending Xenophon along with him, and he promised to give him his support. Meanwhile he begged them not to burn the villages.

Later they sent Xenophon and others with him who seemed the most likely people to be useful. When he came to Seuthes he made the following speech. 'I have not come here, Seuthes, with the intention of asking you for anything, but to do my best to make it clear to you that you were wrong in being angry with me for speaking on behalf of the soldiers and keeping on asking you to pay them what you promised. Actually I considered that it was just as much your interest to pay them as it was theirs to be paid. In the first place, I know that it is they, after the gods, who have been responsible for bringing you into prominence, since they have made you king over great territories and over great numbers of people, so that whatever you do, whether it is something honourable or something dishonourable, people are sure to hear of it. That is your position now, and I thought that it was an important thing that you should not get the reputation for failing to show gratitude to those who had helped you when you sent them home. I thought it an important thing, too, that you should have a good name among our six thousand men, but most important of all that you should never put yourself in a position where people do not trust your word. When people are not trusted, their words, I notice, merely drift about without force in themselves and without inspiring confidence in others. But when people are known to have a respect for the truth, their words are just as powerful as other people's force in securing any object at which they aim. If they want to bring anyone to a proper sense of his position, I know that threats from them have just as much of a sobering effect as actual punishment inflicted by others. And if people of this sort make promises, they gain their ends just as successfully as others who pay out money on the spot. Think of your own case. How much did you pay us before you gained our alliance? You know that you paid nothing at all. No, we trusted you and believed you would be true to your word, and so you raised a great army to march with you and gain you an empire worth not only the thirty talents, which our men think they should be paid, but many times as much. First of all, then, it is this feeling that you can be trusted – the thing which won you your kingdom – which is being bartered away for this sum of money.

'I should like you to think next what a great achievement you thought it was in the past to gain all that you have now conquered and now hold. I am perfectly sure that you would have prayed for the achievement of all that has been accomplished for you rather than for many times the amount of money. Now in my view it is a more painful and a more dishonourable thing to fail to hold all these conquests than it would be never to have won them; just as it is harder to sink into poverty from riches than never to have been rich in the first place, and more painful to appear as an ordinary person after having been a king than never to have been a king at all. You realise, too, that the people who have now become your subjects were not induced to accept your government by any personal affection for you, but did so out of compulsion; and that they would try to win back their freedom if there were no feeling of fear to act as a check on them. Now suppose, first, that they see that your relations with our soldiers are so good that the soldiers would stay here if you asked them, or come back again quickly, when required, and that others, after having heard all kinds of good reports about you from our men, would quickly come and join you whenever you wished: or suppose that they get this unfavourable impression of you – that no more Greek troops are likely to come to you, because of their lack of confidence in you caused by the present state of affairs, and that even the ones here now are better disposed towards your subjects than to you yourself. Which of these two alternatives, do you think, is better calculated to make your subjects fear you and look upon your government with a proper feeling of respect? It is a matter of fact, too, that your present subjects gave in to you, not because they were inferior to us in numbers, but simply for lack of good leadership. There is now, consequently, a risk that they may take as leaders for themselves either some of our men, who think they have been badly treated by you, or even the Spartans, who are still more powerful. This is all the more likely to happen when you find our soldiers promising to serve with the Spartans all the more readily, on the condition the Spartans get their money for them now from you, and the Spartans, because of the need they have of our army, agreeing to this condition. It is perfectly clear that the Thracians, who are now your subjects, would be much more ready to march against you than with you; if you keep your power, all they get out of it is slavery, whereas, if you are defeated, they regain their freedom.

'On the assumption that you should now be looking after this country as your own property, which of these two alternatives do you think is the one calculated to keep the country most free from harm – for our soldiers to receive what they claim and go away leaving a state of peace behind them, or for them to stay on here, living as though they were in enemy territory, and for you to get hold of more troops in superior numbers, who will need their own supplies, and to initiate counter-measures against our men? Which way will you have to spend most money, by paying our men what is owed to them, or by having to hire another more powerful force and still be leaving the original debt unpaid?

'In the opinion of Heraclides, which he expressed.to me personally, the amount of money claimed is excessive. I can assure you that it is a much easier thing for you now both to receive and to pay out this amount than it would have been for you to have received or paid the tenth part of it before we came. What gives meaning to "a lot" or "a little" is not figures so much as the resources of the person who is paying it or receiving it. And at the moment your annual revenue will amount to more than the whole of your previous possessions.

'In what I have been saying, Seuthes, I have been considering your interests as those of a friend. I want you to be regarded as worthy of the good fortune which the gods have given you, and I want to avoid the complete loss of my own reputation in the army. I can assure you that at the moment, and with the army in their present mood, I could not harm my enemies, even if I wanted to, and if I wanted to bring troops to your aid again, I should not have the power to do so: that is the way the army feels about me now. Yet, before the gods, who know the truth, I can call you as a witness to the fact that I have never had anything from you for the soldiers and kept it: I have never for my own personal profit asked you for what was theirs: I have never even demanded from you what you promised me. And I swear that I would never have taken it, even if you had offered it to me, unless the soldiers were going to get what was due to them at the same time. It would have been a dishonourable action to get my own affairs straight and allow theirs to remain in a bad way, especially when I was held in honour by them.

'Heraclides, no doubt, thinks that there is nothing serious in life compared with acquiring money by every means possible. I, Seuthes, on the other hand, consider that there are no nobler and more brilliant possessions that a man, and particularly a man who holds power, can have than honour and fair dealing and generosity. A man who has these is rich in the possession of many friends and rich in the fact that many others want to become friends of his. If he is successful, he has other people who will share in his happiness; and if things go wrong with him, he is in no lack of people to come and help him.

'If you have failed to discover from my actions that I am your sincere friend, and if you are still unable to grasp the fact as a result of what I have been saying, then think of all the things the soldiers were saying. You were there yourself and heard the speeches of those who were trying to find fault with me. They accused me in front of the Spartans of favouring your interests more than the Spartan interests, and they attacked me themselves for taking more trouble to see that your affairs went well than that theirs did. They asserted that I had received bribes from you. Do you imagine that they accused me of taking these bribes from you because they had noticed that I felt any ill will towards you, or because they had actually observed that I was extremely anxious to further your interests? Everyone, I should say, thinks that goodwill ought to be shown to the man from whom someone has taken a bribe. You, before I did you any service, gave me an excellent reception, looking and speaking kindly, entertaining me, and were never tired of promising me all kinds of things in the future. Now you have won what you wanted and have become as great a man as I could make you, and how can you bear to let me be dishonoured as I am among the soldiers? I am perfectly sure that you will decide to pay the money, that time will teach you, and you yourself will not be able to endure the sight of those who freely gave you their services crying out against you. What I ask you to do, when you pay the money, is to do your best to leave me with the same reputation in the army as you found me with.'

When Seuthes had listened to this speech, he cursed the man who was responsible for the money not having been paid long ago. Everyone assumed that by this person he meant Heraclides. 'As for me,' Seuthes said, 'I never meant to deprive your men of their pay and I shall give it to them now.'

Xenophon then spoke again. 'Now that you intend to pay them, I beg you to pay the money through me, and not to allow me, because of my service to you, to go on having a different reputation in the army from the one I had when we first came to you.'

Seuthes replied: 'You will certainly not suffer any loss of reputation in the army on my account, and, if you stay with me, keeping just a thousand hoplites under your command, I will give you the fortified places and everything else which I promised.'

Xenophon spoke again. 'As for that,' he said, 'it is impossible. Let us go back now.'

'All the same,' said Seuthes, 'it would be safer anyway for you, I know, to stay with me than to go away.'

'I am much obliged to you,' said Xenophon, 'for your consideration for me, but it is not possible for me to stay. If, however, I reach a more distinguished position in any place, you must consider that that will be something to your advantage as well.'

Seuthes then spoke again: 'I have not much money', he said, 'but what I have, which is a talent, I give you. I also give you six hundred oxen, about four thousand sheep and a hundred and twenty slaves. Take them when you go away, and take also hostages from the people who behaved badly to you.'

At this Xenophon laughed and said: 'Supposing all this is not enough to make up the pay, whose talent shall I say that I have? Wouldn't it be better for me, in my dangerous position, to go home and keep out of the way of being stoned? You heard their threats.'

For that day he stayed there, and on the next day Seuthes gave them the cattle which he had promised and sent men to drive the cattle along. Up to then the soldiers were saying that Xenophon had gone off to live with Seuthes and to get what Seuthes had promised him. However, when they saw him coming back, they were delighted and ran out to meet him. As soon as Xenophon saw Charminus and Polynicus, he said: 'Owing to your influence, this has been saved for the army. I now hand it over to you, and ask you to dispose of it and divide it out to the soldiers.' Consequently they took over the cattle, appointed people to deal with it and sold it, incurring a lot of unpopularity in the process. Xenophon had nothing to do with the business, and made it clear that he was getting ready to return home. (The vote of exile against him had not yet been passed at Athens.) However, his friends in the camp came to him and begged him not to leave until he had led the army out of Thrace and handed it over to Thibron.

Chapter 8

XENOPHON LEAVES THE ARMY

THEY sailed across from here to Lampsacus, where the sooth-sayer Euclides of Phlius, the son of the Cleagoras who painted the frescoes in the Lyceum, came to meet Xenophon. He congratulated Xenophon on his safe return and asked him how much gold he had. Xenophon swore to him solemnly that he would not even have enough to support himself on his return journey unless he sold his horse and his personal possessions. Euclides did not believe him. However, when the people of Lampsacus sent presents to Xenophon and he was making a sacrifice to Apollo, he got Euclides to stand by him, and, when Euclides had inspected the victims he said that he now believed that he had no money. 'And I know,' he said, 'that even if money is likely to be coming your way, there will be some handicap or other, and, if nothing else, you will be a handicap to yourself.'

Xenophon admitted the truth of this, and Euclides went on: 'Yes, and Zeus of Propitiation is another handicap.' He then asked him if he had already sacrificed to that god, 'as I used to do for you at home,' he added, 'making sacrifices to him and offering holocausts.'

Xenophon replied that he had not sacrificed to Zeus of Propitiation ever since he had left home, and Euclides advised him to make a sacrifice just as he used to do in the past, and said that it would turn out a good thing for him.

Next day Xenophon went on to Ophrynion and made a sacrifice, burning whole pigs, according to the practice of his own country, and the omens were favourable. On the same day Bion and Nausiclides arrived to give their pay to the army. They entered into friendly relations with Xenophon, and they brought back and returned to him his horse, which he had sold in Lampsacus for fifty darics. They had heard that he was fond of the horse, and so suspected that he had sold it from necessity, and they refused to let him pay them back the price of it.

They then marched through the Troad, and, after crossing Mount Ida, came first to Antandrus, and then, going along the coast, to the plain of Thebe. They travelled from here by way of Adramyttion and Certonon to the plain of Caecus, and so reached Pergamon in Mysia.

Here Xenophon was given a good reception by Hellas, the wife of Gongylus of Eretrea, and mother of Gorgion and Gongylus. She told him that there was a Persian called Asidates, living in the plain, and that if he went by night with three hundred men he could capture this Persian together with his wife and children and property, which was considerable. She sent with him to show them the way her own cousin and a man called Daphnagoras, of whom she was extremely fond. Taking these men with him, Xenophon offered a sacrifice, and Basias, a soothsayer from Elis who was there, said that the omens were exceedingly favourable for him and that the man would certainly be made prisoner. After dinner, then, Xenophon set out and took with him, with the idea of doing them a good turn, the captains who had been his particular friends and faithful to him through everything. About six hundred others too came up to him, trying to force their services upon him, but the captains turned them away, so as not to have to give them a share of the booty, which they regarded as being theirs already.

They arrived at the place about midnight, and the slaves outside the castle, together with most of the cattle there, got away safely from them, since they were leaving all this aside in order to capture Asidates himself and his own personal belongings. They failed in their attempt to storm the tower, which was high and strong, with battlements, and manned by large numbers of good soldiers, and so they attempted to make a breach in it. The wall was eight earthen bricks thick, but by daybreak a breach was made. The moment it appeared, some-one from inside with a large spit for roasting oxen ran it right through the thigh of the man nearest to the opening. Then, by letting off volleys of arrows, they made it unsafe even to get near. The defenders shouted out too, and made signals by waving torches, and so Itamenes with his force came out to their relief, and from Comania there came some Assyrian hoplites and about eighty Hyrcanian cavalrymen, also in the King's pay, and then about eight hundred peltasts, with cavalry as well, some from Parthenion, and some from Apol-lonia, and the country near by.

The moment had certainly come for the Greeks to think how they could get away. They seized all the oxen and sheep that there were and drove them off, with the slaves too, inside a hollow square, adopting this formation not so much because they were interested in the booty, as with the idea of pre-venting their retreat from turning into a rout, as it might do, if they went away and left their booty behind, and if the enemy therefore gained confidence while their own men lost theirs. As it was, they were retreating in a way that showed that they were prepared to fight for their booty.

When Gongylus saw that the Greeks were in small numbers and that their assailants were in great strength, he came out, against his mother's will, with his own force, wanting to have his share in the action. Procles also, and Teuthranias the descendant of Damaratus, came out from Halisarne to give their support as well. Meanwhile Xenophon's men, under very heavy attack from arrows and sling stones, marched on, forming a circle so as to keep their shields in the way of the missiles, and with great difficulty got across the river Carcasus, nearly half of them being wounded. On this occasion the captain Agasias the Stymphalian, who had been fighting back against the enemy the whole time, was wounded. In the end they got back in safety with about two hundred slaves and enough sheep for sacrifices.

Next day Xenophon offered a sacrifice and led the whole army out by night, with the idea of marching as far as possible into Lydia, so that Asidates might be no longer frightened by his being close, and might relax his precautions. Asidates, however, had been informed that Xenophon had made another sacrifice with a view to attacking him and would be arriving with the whole army. He therefore went out to camp in some villages lying under the town of Parthenion. Xenophon's men found him here and captured him together with his wife and children and horses and all his possessions. In this way the omens at the first sacrifice were proved correct.

They then returned to Pergamon, and now Xenophon had good reason to be grateful to the god. The Spartans and the captains and the other generals and the soldiers all united in offering him the pick of the booty – horses, oxen and every-thing. So he was now at last in a position to do someone else a good turn.

Then Thibron came and took over the army. He attached it to the rest of his Greek army and made war against Tissa-phernes and Pharnabazus.

GLOSSARY
OF
NAMES

GLOSSARY OF NAMES

ABROCOMAS: One of the commanders of the King's army.

ABROZELMES: Interpreter of King Seuthes.

AENEAS OF STYMPHALUS: A captain in the Greek army.

AESCHINES: An Acarnanian captain of peltasts in the Greek army.

AGASIAS OF STYMPHALUS: A distinguished captain of hoplites in the Greek army.

AGESILAUS: A king of Sparta with whom Xenophon served later in a campaign against Persia.

AGIAS: An Arcadian. One of the generals of Cyrus's Greek mercenaries.

AMPHICRATES: An Athenian soldier in the Greek army.

ANAXIBIUS: Spartan admiral at Byzantium.

APOLLONIDES: A Lydian with a Boeotian accent.

ARBACES: Governor of Media and one of the commanders of the King's army.

ARCHAGORAS: An exile from Argos and captain in the Greek army.

AREXION: An Arcadian soothsayer in the Greek army.

ARIAEUS: A Persian. Second in command to Cyrus.

ARISTARCHUS: Spartan governor of Byzantium.

ARISTEAS OF CHIOS: A captain of peltasts in the Greek army.

ARISTIPPUS: A Thessalian general who raised troops for Cyrus.

ARISTON: An Athenian sent as representative of the army to Sinope.

ARISTONYMUS THE METHYDRIAN: A captain of hoplites in the Greek army.

ARTAGERSES: Persian commander of the King's bodyguard.

ARTAOZUS: A Persian commander in Cyrus's army.

ARTAPATAS: One of Cyrus's most trusted officers.

ARTAXERXES: King of Persia and elder brother of Cyrus.

ARTUCHAS: A Persian commander in Armenia.

ARYSTAS: An Arcadian officer in the Greek army.

ASIDATES: A Persian nobleman in Asia Minor.

BASIAS: An Arcadian in the Greek army.

BELESYS: A Persian governor of Syria.

BION: An officer in Thibron's army.

BOISCUS: A Thessalian boxer in the Greek army.

CALLIMACHUS OF PARRHASIA: A captain of hoplites in the Greek army.

CEPHISODORUS: An Athenian captain in the Greek army.

CHARMINUS: A Spartan officer in Thibron's army.

CHIRISOPHUS: A Spartan mercenary captain serving under Cyrus.

CLEAENETUS: A captain in the Greek army.

CLEANDER: Spartan governor of Byzantium.

CLEANOR: An Arcadian. The oldest of the Greek generals.

CLEARATUS: A captain in the Greek army.

CLEARCHUS: A Spartan exile. The most prominent of the generals serving under Cyrus.

COIRATIDAS: A Theban mercenary captain.

CORYLAS: King of the Paphlagonians.

CTESIAS: A Greek doctor in the service of the King of Persia.

CYNISCUS: A Spartan officer in the area of Byzantium.

CYRUS: Younger brother or Artaxerxes and pretender to the throne.

DAMARATUS: A Spartan king who had been exiled and taken refuge with the King of Persia.

DAPHNAGORAS: A friend or Hellas.

DARIUS II: King of Persia and father of Artaxerxes and Cyrus.

DEMOCRATES OF TEMENUS: An officer in the Greek army.

DERCYLIDAS: A Spartan commander who fought in Asia Minor.

DEXIPPUS: A Spartan officer who deserted the Greek Army.

DRACONTIUS: A Spartan exile serving in the Greek army.

EPISTHENES OF AMPHIPOLIS: Commander of the Greek peltasts at the battle of Cunaxa.

EPYAXA: Wife of the King of Cilicia.

ETEONICUS: An officer in the garrison of Byzantium.

EUCLIDES: A soothsayer in Lampsacus.

EURYLOCHUS OF LUSIA: A hoplite in the Greek army.

EURYMACHUS: A Dardanian in the Greek army.

GAULITES: An exile from Samos, serving with Cyrus.

GLOUS: One of Cyrus's interpreters.

GNESIPPUS: An Athenian officer in the Greek army.

GOBRYAS: One of the commanders of the King's army.

GONGYLUS: (1) A Greek chieftain in Asia Minor. (2) His son.

GORGIAS OF LEONTINI: A famous Sophist.

GORGION: Son of Hellas and Gongylus.

HECATONYMUS: An orator from Sinope.

HEGESANDER: A general of the Arcadians in the Greek army.

HELLAS: Wife of Gongylus.

HERACLIDES: Confidential agent of King Seuthes.

HIERONYMUS OF ELIS: A captain in the Greek army.

ITAMENES: A Persian commander in Asia Minor.

JASON: The leader of the Argonauts.

LEON OF THURII: A soldier in the Greek army.

LEONYMUS: A Spartan soldier in the Greek army.

LYCIUS: (1) A Syracusan in the Greek army. (2) An Athenian. Commander of the Greek cavalry during the retreat.

LYCON: An Achaean in the Greek army.

MAESADES: Father of King Seuthes.

MARSYAS: A mythical character who attempted with his flute to surpass Apollo in music.

MEDEA: Queen of the Medes at the time of the Persian conquest.

MEDOCUS: King of the Odrysae.

MEDOSADES: Diplomatic agent of King Seuthes.

MEGABYZUS: Warden of the temple of Artemis at Ephesus.

MEGAPHERNES: A Persian notable, executed by Cyrus.

MENON THE THESSALIAN: One of the leading Greek generals serving under Cyrus.

MILTOCUTHES: A Thracian captain with Cyrus's Greek troops.

MITHRADATES: A Persian commander in Cyrus's army.

MYSUS: A Mysian in the Greek army.

NAUSICLIDES: An officer in Thibron's army.

NEON OF ASINE: A general in the Greek army.

NICANDER: A Spartan who killed Dexippus.

NICARCHUS: An Arcadian in the Greek army.

NICOMACHUS OF OETA: A commander of peltasts in the Greek army.

ORONTAS: (1) A Persian nobleman in Cyrus's army, executed as a traitor. (2) A Persian army commander and the King's son-in-law. Governor of Armenia.

PARYSATIS: Wife of Darius II and mother of Artaxerxes and Cyrus.

PASION OF MEGARA: A mercenary captain who served under Cyrus.

PHALINUS: A Greek officer in the service of Tissaphernes.

PHARNABAZUS: Persian governor of the Hellespontine seaboard.

PHILESIUS: An Achaean general in the Greek army.

PHRASIAS: An Athenian officer in the Greek army.

PHRYNISCUS: An Achaean general in the Greek army.

PIGRES: One of Cyrus's interpreters.

PLEISTHENES OF AMPHIPOLIS: A soldier in the Greek army.

POLUS: Spartan admiral at Byzantium.

POLYCRATES: An Athenian captain in the Greek army.

POLYNICUS: A Spartan delegate from Thibron's army.

PROCLES: Governor of Teuthrania. An officer in Cyrus's army.

PROXENUS: A Theban mercenary captain and one of the Greek generals serving under Cyrus.

PYRRHIAS: An Arcadian officer in the Greek army.

PYTHAGORAS: A Spartan naval commander serving with Cyrus.

RHATHINES: A Persian commander under Pharnabazus.

SAMOLAS: An Achaean officer in the Greek army.

SEUTHES: King of Thrace.

SILANUS: (1) A Greek soothsayer in Cyrus's army. (2) A young soldier in the Greek army.

SMICRES: A general of the Arcadians in the Greek army.

SOCRATES THE ACHAEAN: A mercenary captain who served under Cyrus.

SOCRATES THE ATHENIAN: The Philosopher, and a friend of Xenophon.

SOPHAENETUS OF STYMPHALUS: A mercenary captain who served under Cyrus.

SOSIS: A mercenary captain from Syracuse who served under Cyrus.

SOTERIDAS· A soldier from Sicyon in the Greek army.

SPITHRIDATES: A Persian commander under Pharnabazus.

STRATOCLES: A Cretan. Commander of the Cretans in the Greek army.

SYENNESIS: The King of Cilicia.

TAMOS: The Egyptian admiral of Cyrus's fleet.

TERES: An ancestor of Seuthes, King of Thrace.

THEOGENES: A Locrian in the Greek army.

THEOPOMPUS: An Athenian in the Greek army.

THIBRON: Spartan commander of a force operating against Persia.

THORAX: A Boeotian serving in the Greek army.

TIMASION: A Dardanian general in the Greek army.

TIMESITHEUS: A native of Trapezus.

TIRIBAZUS: Persian governor of Western Armenia.

TISSAPHERNES: One of the commanders of the King's army and governor of the Aegean coast of Asia Minor.

TOLMIDES THE ELEAN: Herald in the Greek army.

XANTHICLES: An Achaean general in the Greek army.

XENIAS OF PARRHASIA: A Greek mercenary captain.

XENOPHON: An Athenian. General in the Greek army and author of this book.

XERXES: The Persian King who led the unsuccessful invasion of Greece in 480 B.C.

ZELARCHUS: An official of Cerasus.